Fasciculus Mervinensis, Notes Historical, Genealogical, and Heraldic of the Family of Mervyn

Fasciculus Mervinensis;

BEING

NOTES

HISTORICAL, GENEALOGICAL, AND HERALDIC

OF THE FAMILY OF

MERVYN.

BY

Sir WILLIAM RICHARD DRAKE, F.S.A.

PRIVATELY PRINTED.

LONDON, 1873.

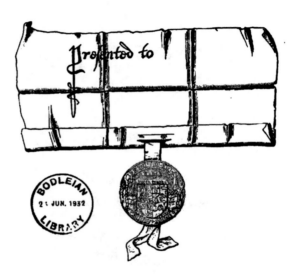

INTRODUCTORY NOTE.

IT is upwards of twenty-five years since I commenced collecting information relative to the Mervyns. My object at that time was limited to the compilation of the Pedigree of the Branch which, in the first half of the XVII. century, settled in Devonshire, and to the investigation of the precise connection between it and the family of the same name that had flourished in Wiltshire. The task I had undertaken was prosecuted at broken and lengthened intervals, and it was not until last year that I commenced a systematic arrangement of the materials I had gathered together. I then found that the information I possessed, extended far beyond the scope of my original intention, and it appeared to me, that with some little additional trouble, it could be sufficiently augmented, to enable me to write the history of the Family generally.

If, however, I had then been aware of the additional labour which the enlarged scheme involved, I should not have entered upon it; but, "having put my hand to the plough," it was not in my nature to turn back, and I resolved to proceed. My determination would however have been of small avail, and my project in all probability have remained unaccomplished, had it not been for the aid, courteously and liberally afforded by Sir Albert Woods, F.S.A., *Garter*. Not only were the Archives of the College of Arms thrown open to me, but on every point on which I sought information, Sir Albert's ready and valuable assistance was at hand.

I am the more desirous to record this circumstance, because a somewhat general impression prevails that, except upon payment of heavy fees, no information can be obtained from the College of Arms. Those (and they are many) who entertain this opinion, appear to overlook the distinction between *literary* enquiries, and *business* investigations, a distinction which according to my experience, is never lost sight of by the Officers of the College, who are always ready to acknowledge the claim of the former to facilities, which it would be idle to suppose could be accorded to the latter.

The College of Arms is a Corporation, (incorporated by Letters Patent I Ric. III.,) not maintained as is often supposed at the expense of the State; but supported by fees paid by those who seek the professional assistance of its Members.   Its Archives consist of :—

1st. The returns made by the Heralds of the results of their Visitations.

2nd. Pedigrees from time to time registered, after due investigation, in the College, at the instance of individuals who desire to have their genealogies recorded.

3rd. Official documents connected with the grant of Titles and Honours, including Coats of Arms, Funeral Certificates, Royal Licenses for change of name, &c., &c.

4th. Numerous and valuable Manuscript Collections made from time to time by Members of the College, and either bequeathed to, or purchased by the Corporation.

Of the above, the Heralds' Visitations are acknowledged as Public Records, inasmuch, as having been taken by virtue of Commissions issued under the authority of the Crown, they are admitted as evidence in courts of Law.   They would not however be so recognised, unless produced by those having the rightful legal custody of them; for example, they would not be admitted if they formed part of a miscellaneous collection of Mss. such as are to be found in the British Museum.   Hence it follows, that if they were (as some contend they ought to be) handed over to the National Library, they would lose much of their practical value.   It should however be noted that the British Museum and other public libraries contain copies of many of the earlier Visitations, and in some few instances the original note books of the Heralds, signed by the parties from whom their information was derived ; so that in those cases genealogical enquirers need be at no loss, if they merely seek information as to their contents, without resorting to the actual documents that can be adduced as *legal* evidence.

As regards the remainder of the Manuscripts in the College, there is no more reason that they should be made accessible without payment of fees, than there would be for requiring that the records of any other Corporation or the Collections of any Individual, should be thrown open to all, who from motives of curiosity or actuated by more weighty reasons, might desire to inspect them.

I will not now enter upon the consideration of the question,—How many of the enquirers at the College of Arms could, if its archives were gratuitously open to the public, avail themselves for any practical purpose of its contents, without professional aid ?   Pedigree Makers there are by hundreds, who will undertake to " find " a man's Arms and produce his genealogy (*more suorum*).

But how many, including professed genealogists, are there who are competent to deduce an involved and intricate pedigree, so as to bear the test of legal examination? It would be invidious to mention names, but I believe their number might readily be counted on one's fingers.

Do not let it be supposed that in making this remark I intend to point to the following pages as an instance of the elucidation of an intricate pedigree. All the merit I claim for my work is, that it has been carefully and conscientiously done. I have taken nothing for granted, where the means of verification were accessible; I have examined and sifted the evidence upon which my statements are founded; and I have, as far as practicable, given my authorities, with such references as will readily admit of their accuracy being tested. As regards the more recent portions of the Pedigree, they are based either on my own personal knowledge, or on information supplied to me by the present representatives of the several branches of the family:—The Earl of Verulam, Sir Henry Mervin Vavasour, Bart., Sir William Coles Medlycott, Bart., and Major John Elton Mervin Prower have each been good enough to revise those portions of it, with which they are respectively immediately connected.

That I have entirely succeeded in avoiding errors, I do not pretend; but I feel very confident that in the main, the following pages may be accepted as an accurate and reliable record of the facts they purport to chronicle. Where errors exist, they will, I think, be found limited to details of comparatively small moment.

My thanks are due to the Revd. Canon Jackson, of Leigh Delamere, for his suggestions as to the early descent of the Fountel Estate, which will be found incorporated in the account of that Branch of the Mervyn Family who became its possessors: nor must I omit to acknowledge my obligations to Mr. John Gough Nichols,* F.S.A., for the trouble he has taken in reading the proof sheets of the early part of my notes as they passed through the press, and to Mr. Alfred

---

* Since the above lines were penned, this able Author and Antiquary has died, to the sorrow of a large circle of private friends, and to the great loss of that branch of literature with which his name has for so many years been connected. Mr. J. G. Nichols was not only a valuable and conscientious contributor to the literature which appertains specially to history, biography, and heraldic research; but his extensive knowledge on those subjects was always at the disposal of those who sought it. One striking feature in Mr. Nichols's works was his love of truthful statements. He was a determined opponent of "cooked-up" pedigrees; and he rendered good service in exposing, in an unsparing manner, several of the many attempts which have been made to foist false genealogies upon the public.

Kingston for his courtesy in facilitating my inspection of documents at the Record Office.

    To Sir Bernard Burke, L.L.D., C.B., *Ulster*, I am indebted for much valuable information relative to the Irish Branch of the Mervyns. The rules imposed by "my Lords" of the Treasury, consequent upon a Government salary in lieu of fees, having lately been attached to his Office, have prevented Sir Bernard from affording me that gratuitous *official* assistance which he would have desired; but his ready aid as an old genealogical friend, has supplied the defect under which that portion of my work would necessarily have laboured from my want of opportunity of personally examining the evidences in Ireland on which the pedigree of Sir Audley Mervyn's descendants is, to a great extent, based.

OATLANDS LODGE, SURREY,
December, 1873.

CONTENTS.

———◆———

SKETCH PEDIGREE.

SHOWING THE CONNEXION BETWEEN THE SEVERAL BRANCHES

OF THE

𝕸𝖊𝖗𝖛𝖞𝖓 𝕱𝖆𝖒𝖎𝖑𝖞.

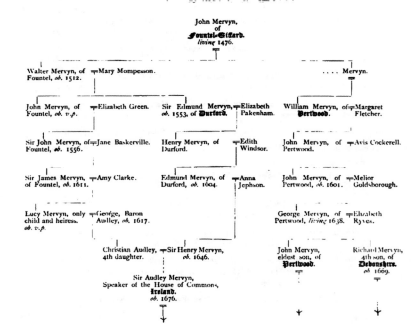

John Mervyn,
of
𝕱𝖔𝖚𝖓𝖙𝖊𝖑-𝕲𝖎𝖋𝖋𝖆𝖗𝖉.
living 1476.

Walter Mervyn, of ╤Mary Mompesson.
Fountel, *ob.* 1512.

.... Mervyn.

John Mervyn, of ╤Elizabeth Green.
Fountel, *ob. v.p.*

Sir Edmund Mervyn, ╤Elizabeth
ob. 1553, of 𝕯𝖚𝖗𝖋𝖔𝖗𝖉. | Pakenham.

William Mervyn, of╤Margaret
𝕻𝖊𝖗𝖙𝖜𝖔𝖔𝖉. | Fletcher.

Sir John Mervyn, of╤Jane Baskerville.
Fountel, *ob.* 1556.

Henry Mervyn, of ╤Edith
Durford. | Windsor.

John Mervyn, of ╤Avis Cockerell.
Pertwood.

Sir James Mervyn, ╤Amy Clarke.
of Fountel, *ob.* 1611.

Edmund Mervyn, of ╤Anna
Durford, *ob.* 1604. | Jephson.

John Mervyn, of ╤Melior
Pertwood, *ob.* 1601. | Goldsborough.

Lucy Mervyn, only ╤George, Baron
child and heiress. Audley, *ob.* 1617.
ob. v.p.

George Mervyn, of ╤Elizabeth
Pertwood, *living* 1638. | Ryves.

Christian Audley, ╤Sir Henry Mervyn,
4th daughter. | *ob.* 1646.

John Mervyn,
eldest son, of
𝕻𝖊𝖗𝖙𝖜𝖔𝖔𝖉.

Richard Mervyn,
4th son, of
𝕯𝖊𝖛𝖔𝖓𝖘𝖍𝖎𝖗𝖊.
ob. 1669.

Sir Audley Mervyn,
Speaker of the House of Commons,
𝕴𝖗𝖊𝖑𝖆𝖓𝖉.
ob. 1676.

The "chiefe house" of Fountel,
in the time of the Mervyns.

The Original Picture is in the possession of Alfred Morrison Esq of Fonthill.

THE

FOUNTEL-GIFFARD BRANCH

OF THE

Mervyn Family.

THE first of the MERVYN* family in Wiltshire, of whom I have met with any notice, was
RICHARD MERVYN of Fountayne *alias* Fountel. About the time that the Mervyn family

---

* The name is written indifferently "MERVYN, MARVYN, MARVIN, and MERVIN," either with or
without a final "e." For the sake of uniformity, I have adopted throughout the *first* spelling, except in
quoting original documents, where I have retained the orthography used in them.
  The first mention of the name "MERVYN" that I have met with occurs in the Calendar "*Placitorum
abbreviatio, p. 198,*" in which the following entry occurs :—"Pasche, anno octavo (Edw. I. 1279—80) majus
"Record. WILL'US MERVIN est nativus abb'is sci Albani per placitum prius captum, et etiam per judicium
"redditum in parliamento tento per quo est nativus, rot. 28, Hertf." On referring to the original roll
(*Coram Rege roll*, 8 *Ed. I., Easter, Majus Recordum, memb.* 28), it appears that the King, wishing to be
certified respecting the record and process of a plea before John de Reygate and his associates, Justices in
Eyre, in the county of Surrey, in their Eyre at Hertford, between WILLIAM MERVYN and the ABBOT OF
ST. ALBAN's, concerning certain trespasses done to the same William by the said Abbot, commanded the
said Justices to send him the said Record and process, which are of the following tenour :—William Mervyn
complains that the Abbot of St. Alban's, in 54 Henry III., caused four men to take three oxen and four
horses, belonging to Mervyn, value 11 marks, and to drive them to the Manor of Sandrygge (Sandridge,
about three miles from St. Alban's), where he detained them, until he (Mervyn) caused them to be
replevined by the King's writ; notwithstanding which, the Abbot made several captures subsequently of
the plaintiff's cattle, to his damage of £40. Mervyn further complains that he, being in the said town of
Sandrygge, in 55 Henry III., at his own house, the Abbot caused the said men to break his doors and
windows, and to carry away his goods there found, and also to take Mervyn, and imprisoned him at the
Abbot's Manor of Sandrygge, until he was delivered by the King's writ; upon sufficient bail to appear before the
King, to his damage of £100. THE ABBOT appears, and avows the said captures, which he made because
Mervyn is his *villan* (i. e., held his lands subject to the absolute will of the Lord, and bound to do all
services that the Lord commanded), and his tenement is the *villenage* of the said Abbot, and all Mervyn's
ancestors were villans of the Abbot and his predecessors, and did all villan customs to them, as in tallage,
at his (the Abbot's) will, and in doing "*merchet*" (i. e., paying fine or composition to the Lord on
marriage, &c.) of his own body and the bodies of his sons and daughters. But the said William contemned
and refused to do such services and customs; wherefore, the Abbot at first admonished him, when he again
refused, and the Abbot caused his cattle to be taken. As to the imprisonment, the Abbot says it was not
done by him, as at the time he was in foreign parts, and disavows the breaking into Mervyn's house; and
that the said men took him because he refused as above, and they placed him in the villenage of the said
Abbot ("et in villenag' ipsius Abbis inceperunt"). The Abbot prays that the matter may be tried by jury.
MERVYN replies that he is a free man, and of free condition; and that before Richard de Stanes, Justice
for hearing pleas, appointed by the King's writ, which the Abbot obtained, in 56 Henry III., he was
prepared to prove his freedom; but the Abbot failed to appear, so that he left Court as a free man, and to
hold his land freely and quit from all secular service, rendering yearly to the Abbot 5*s.* 3*d.* ; and he refers
to the record on the rolls. Both parties then agreed that if the said record proved that William left the
Court a free man he should continue so, and be quit from the villenage and servitude of the Abbot; if not,

appear to have settled in Wiltshire,* in the person of JOHN MERVYN of Church Lawford, who was living in 1492, and at that time a great-grandfather. He would have been contemporary with Richard Mervyn of Fountel. In

---

he should be of servile condition, and be the Abbot's villan with all his "*sequela*." A day was then appointed on which the litigants were to appear; but Mervyn failed to do so, and judgment was given for the Abbot, with power to claim Mervyn as his villan whenever he pleased. The above proceedings were sent to the King. Afterwards, in Easter term, at the next Parliament, the parties appeared. William prayed an adjournment, which was granted, on condition that if he failed to appear, final judgment should be given against him. He made default, and it not being found on the rolls of 56 Henry III. that he departed from Court a free man, it was adjudged that the land was villenage of the Abbot, and the chattels were the Abbot's also, as villan chattels. And a day of judgment was appointed with respect to William's body, in Michaelmas Term.

I have not thought it necessary to follow the proceedings further to trace what became of William Mervyn, who, although a *villan*, must have been a man of means and daring to try his rights against so powerful an individual as the Abbot of St. Alban's was in those days. I may here remark, that holding land by villenage, which was the origin of copyhold tenure, was abolished by the Statute 12 Ch. II., cap. 24; but long before that time it was found to be a system wholly unworkable—as a man might be a *pure* villan (i. e., paying merchet), tenant of one Manor or Lord, and a free tenant of other lands—conditions inconsistent with each other.

* As regards the Warwickshire family of Mervyn, my information is limited to that which is afforded by Dugdale's Warwickshire, and the wills of John Mervyn of Church Lawford (dated 22nd October, and proved 20th November, 1492), and of Margaret Mervyn, his widow (dated 23rd July, 1494, and proved 24th November, 1496). (APPENDIX I., p. v.) The pedigree, as disclosed by those wills, is as under:—

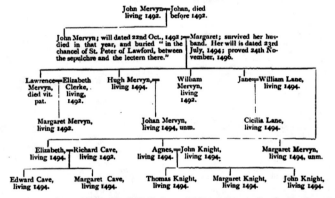

"HUGH MERVYN, Esquire" (probably Hugh, son of John and Margaret above-mentioned) was, in 13 Hen. VIII. (1521-2), returned on the Commission for taking account of the estates of Edward, Duke of Buckingham, as holding the office of Keeper of Maxstoke Park, under appointment from the Duke. *Dugd., Warwickshire, vol. ii., p. 995.*

In the time of Hen. VIII., THOMAS MERVYN was the Bailiff of Walvey or Wolvey, in Warwickshire, held under the Abbot of Combe, in that county, and is returned in the "*Valor Ecclesiasticus,*" vol. iii., p. 55, as one of the officers of that monastery, in the receipt of an annual stipend of xxvjs. viijd.

I find a will of THOMAS MARVYN, apparently of the same family, dated 16 Feb., 1620, proved in London 6 Mar., 1621, which contains a bequest of £10 "to poor of Wolvey, co. Warwick, where I was born" (*Regr. 22 Dale*). This, probably, was the Sr Thomas Marvine who was knighted at Whitehall, 23 July, 1603 (See Cott. Ms., *Claud.* C. iii, fo. 243h Harl. Ms., 6062, fo. 56).

Kent I meet with ROBERT MIRFYN* holding lands in that county, who would also be contemporary with Richard Mervyn of Wiltshire, and John Mervyn of Warwickshire. My theory is, that the above three men were brothers, or at all events, members of the same family; which in its origin was probably Welsh, possibly having for its remote ancestor, Merfyn, Lord of Powis land.

RICHARD MERVYN, of " Fountayne *alias* Fountel in Com. Wilts," married DOROTHY, the younger of the two daughters of THOMAS SQUERIE,† and

---

* In 1444-5, an Inquisition was made, to ascertain whether it would be to the King's damage, if he licensed ROBERT MIRFYN, Esquire, to grant certain messuages, lands, and tenements in Woolwich, to the Prior and Convent of St. Mary, Southwark (*Inq.* 19-23 *Hen. VI.—No.* 94), and about the same time he purchased the Manor of Wynvale, in Northflete, in that county, from John Burghwasch, and some meadow land in Newenton, co. Surrey (*Calend., Chancery proceedings, vol. ii. p. xxii.*) This purchase gave rise to a family litigation; for on the death of Robert Mirfyn some of the feoffees, including his brother George Mirfyn, refused to convey the manor and land to Robert Mirfyn, "Squyer," the son and heir of the purchaser, and hence he filed his Bill against his uncle and his co-feoffees. The defence made by George Mirfyn, the plaintiff's uncle, was, that his brother Robert had declared his will to be that the lands should be entailed on the plaintiff Robert his son and the heirs of his body, with remainder in default of issue to Katherine and Anne, the daughters of the said Robert the father, and sisters of the plaintiff, with remainder to the said George Mirfyn and the heirs of his body. The defendants did not, however, succeed, for in Trinity Term, 24 Hen. VI. (1446) a decree was made directing the defendants to convey the property to the plaintiff according to his prayer.

ROBERT MIRFYN, the son (the plaintiff in the above suit), appears to have sided with the Lancastrian party if, as appears probable, he is the same ROBERT MIREFYN, who, in the Patent Rolls of 2 Edw. IV. (1462–3), is referred to as a rebel, and whose hereditaments, "Vocat' Cobbeshole in Comitatu Kanciæ," were granted by the King to William Stanley. (*Cal. Rot. Patent, p.* 303.) The son of this Robert Mirfyn petitioned the King in Parliament, 12 & 13 Edw. IV., describing himself as "ROBERT MYRFYN the eldest son of Robert Myrfyn late of Anesworth in the Counte Kent Squyer," praying that the attainder of his father might be reversed. The prayer of the Petition appears to have been granted. See "*Rot. Parl. vol.* 6, 1472–1503," p. 32, and the original Petition in the State Paper Office, *Parliamentary Petitions, No.* 5,517."

I also find the will of Sir THOMAS MERFYN, Sheriff of London in 1511, and Lord Mayor 10 H. VIII. (1518), and who, at his death, left surviving children. The will is dated 2nd September, and proved 15th October, 1523. (APPENDIX I., p. vi.) Sir Thomas appears to have been a member of the Kent family, as he devised by his will his Manor of Downe in that county. His arms (which are recorded in the College of Arms) were, *Or, on a chevron sa. a mullet argent; on the dexter chief point of the shield a crescent of the second.* (*See also Harl. Ms., No.* 1,349, *fo.* 24*b.*) Weever (*Funeral Monts. fo.* 1631, *p.* 379) states that Sir Thomas was the son of George Mirfyn, of Ely, Com. Cambridge, and that he was entombed, (with his portraiture in alabaster,) in a chapel in St. Paul's, London, which was pulled down in 1549 by the Protector Duke of Somerset.

The name of MIRFIN occurs again in Queen Elizabeth's time; GEORGE MIRFINF, in 1580; and subsequently, ROBERT MIRFIN appears as one of the Defendants in a suit, 35 Elizabeth (1592—3), in the Court of the Duchy of Lancaster, relative to a dispute concerning property in Yorkshire. (*Ducatu. Lancastriæ, Cal. to Pleadings, &c., vol.* 3, *part* 4, *pp.* 103 *and* 283.)

See further notes as to the MIRFYN family, APPENDIX I. *p.* xv.

† Thomas Squerie, according to Philipott, descended from John de Squerie, who, temp. Hen. III., was seated at Squerie's Court, in the parish of Westerham, co. Kent. On this Thomas Squerie's death, an inquisition was held at Dartford on Monday in the third week of Lent, 17 Hen. VI., and the

co-heirs of their brother John Squerie, of Squerie's Court, in the county of Kent, who, according to Philipott, (*Survey of Kent, Lond., fo.* 1659, *p.* 359,) died s.p. 1463. The son of Richard Mervyn and Dorothy Squerie was RALPH MERVYN, also described* as of "Fountayne," who married a daughter of PARRE, by whom he had a son JOHN MERVYN, who became the owner of the Manor and Estate of Fountel-Giffard, and (as is stated*) married JOAN, daughter of Lord HUNGERFORD, of Heytesbury, a statement which cannot I think, for the reasons after set forth, be implicitly relied on.

The Manor of Fountel, or Fountel-Giffard, is situated in the parish of Fountayne, or Fountel, in the Hundred of Dunworth, in the county of Wilts. In Sir R. Colt Hoare's History of South Wilts (*Hun. of Dunworth, vol.* 4, *p.* 12, *et seq.*), the descent of the estate is given thus:—GIFFORD, the possessor, temp. Domesday Book; thence to MANDEVILLE and MAUDUIT; from the latter to MOLYNS, by marriage of EGIDIA, cousin and heir of John de MAUDUIT, with John de MOLYNS, who died 41 Ed. III. (1367), seised, *int. alia*, of the Manor of Funtell, leaving Sir William Moleyns his son and heir; who, dying 18 Hen. VI. (1439), left an only child, ALIANORE, who married Robert Lord HUNGERFORD, who thus became possessed of Fountel. It is added, that on the attainder of Lord Hungerford, his lordships and lands were granted to John Lord Wenlock, who was slain at the Battle of Tewkesbury, an°. 1471; and that "about this time the Manor passed into the Family of Mervyn."

Not being able to satisfy myself that this statement was correct, I applied to the Reverend Canon Jackson, of Leigh Delamere, in the hope that his well-known acquaintance with the antiquarian history of Wiltshire, and his knowledge of the genealogies of its families, would enable him to clear up the doubts I entertained of the accuracy of the above narrative. Canon Jackson very courteously examined the points which I suggested for his consideration, and came to the same conclusion as myself, viz., that there is something not quite satisfactory in Sir R. C. Hoare's statement The substance of the grounds on which he founded his opinion were as follows:—

"ROBERT, second Lord HUNGERFORD (who married MARGARET, daughter and "heiress of William Lord BOTREAUX), died 14th May, 1459, possessed† of the Fountel "Estate: In March, 1460, (being only a few months after his father's death, and, conse-"quently, after his own succession to the family estates,) his son, ROBERT, third Lord "HUNGERFORD, (more commonly called Lord MOLEYNS, from his marriage with Alianore, "daughter and heiress of the Baron of that name,) being one of the most prominent of "the Lancastrian Party, and having, apparently, in view the almost certain prospect of "attainder, in order to save his estates, made over to his mother, MARGARET Lady "BOTREAUX, such of them as would be likely to be confiscated. Now the estates which "came to him by his wife ALIANORE Lady MOLEYNS would *not* be of that number; in "fact, by the Act of Attainder, passed in the following year, which swept off the fortunes "of 500 noble and gentle-men, that particular class of estate is specially *exempted* from "forfeiture. We should not, therefore, expect to find,—nor do we in fact find,—ANY of "the known MOLINES estates conveyed away in anticipation for safety. Fountel *was* "amongst the number that Lord HUNGERFORD and MOLINES did so part with, which "leads to the suspicion that what Sir R. C. Hoare says, of its having come to the HUNGER-"FORDS *through* the MOLINES' heiress, is incorrect. The Deeds by which Lord

---

jurors found that he held in fee the Manor of Kestane, and property in the parishes of Farneburgh and Bromeleigh, and that John Squerie was his son and heir, and then aged 30 years. (*Inq. p.m.* 17 *Hen. VI., No.* 25.) John Squerie, on his death, 4 Ed. IV. (1463), left two sisters, his co-heiresses. Margaret, the elder, married Sir William Cromer, Knt., of Tunstal, co. Kent, and Dorothy, the younger, was, as above stated, the wife of Richard Mervyn. The property which the two ladies inherited was considerable; the portion which in the division fell to Dorothy Mervyn's share appears, however, to have been sold shortly after she became possessed of it. (*See Hasted's Kent, fo. ed., vol.* 1. *p.* 105, *&c.*)
* See Mervyn Pedigree:—*Ms. Coll. Arms,* "*Vincent's Coll., Sussex,* 121," *f.* 393.
† *Inq., post mort.* 37 *Hen. VI.—No.* 17.

"Hungerford and Molines conveyed his estates are ten* in number, and all bear date
"the same day, viz., 30th March, 1460. In one of these deeds he gives and grants to
"Dame Margaret Hungerford, his mother, all his lands, &c., in Fonthill Gifford,
"Stoppe, Fonthill Episcopi, Tisbury, and Farnhill in Fonthill, which he describes as
"*descended to him from his father*, (a statement corroborated by the fact, before mentioned,
"that, on that nobleman's death, those estates formed part of his possessions.) [*Inq. post
"mort. 37 Hen. VI., No. 17.*]

"It is therefore doubtful whether the Fountel estates passed from Molines to
"Hungerford, as stated by Sir R. C. Hoare. The next question is, How did Robert,
"*second* Lord Hungerford, acquire the property,—by inheritance, marriage, or purchase?
"Not, it would appear, by inheritance, for it is *not* included in the schedule of *his* father's
"(Walter, first Lord Hungerford) estates taken on his death in 1449 (*Inq. post
"mort. 27 Hen. VI., No.* 30). Nor, by marriage with the Botreaux heiress ; for then
"they would have been Margaret Lady Hungerford's already, *durante vitâ*, and there
"would have been no occasion for her son to make them over to her for safety. The
"only remaining presumption is, that Robert, second Lord Hungerford, purchased
"them. From whom, does not appear ; but the conjecture that he bought the estate
"from the family of Inge, is a probable one. Fountel, in 21 Edw. III. [1347], belonged
"to John Mauduit (*Inq. post mort., No.* 40), and although, as general representa-
"tives, the Molines succeeded Mauduits, it does not appear that Fountel passed to that
"family ; for, two years afterwards, viz., 23 Edw. III. [1349], it is found to belong to
"John Inge (*Inq. post mort., No.* 68), and, in the Wilts Institutions, A.D. 1442, the
"Patron of the Advowson is Thomas Inge.† The next presentation [in 1458] is by
"Robert Lord Hungerford and Moleyns. The supposition that Robert, second Lord
"Hungerford, purchased Fountel from Inge is further corroborated by the fact that, in
"the year 1435, he *did* purchase from Thomas Inge an estate included in the before-
"mentioned deeds of Robert Lord Hungerford and Molines, called Colmans, in the
"parish of Knoyle Episcopi."‡

The case still appearing to me to be not free from obscurity, I made a
further examination of the Inquisitions, which has led me to think that some
(though not all) of the difficulty connected with the acquisition by the Hungerford
family of the Fountel property is removed if we disconnect the *manor* of Fountel-
Giffard from other property in the parish. That Robert, second Lord Hungerford,
possessed lands and tenements in the *parish* of Fountel, and that those lands descended
to his son Robert, third Lord Hungerford, is clear; (*Inq. p. m.*, 37 Hen. VI.,
No. 17); that those lands were purchased by the second Lord from the Inge family, as
suggested by Mr. Jackson, is probable ; or they may have been acquired in part from
Inge, and in other part from the representatives of Sir Thomas West, who, in 1386, also
died seised of lands and tenements in the parish of Fountel-Giffard (*Inq. p. m.* 10 Ric. II.
No. 52), and from the Priory and Convent of Wytham, for whom, in 1391, lands in
Fountel were held by William Stourton and others (*Inq.* 15 Ric. II.).

But neither Robert, second Lord Hungerford, nor Inge, West, nor Stourton, seems to
have possessed either the *manor* of Fountel-Giffard, or that of Farnehyll, in Fountayne (both
of which, according to Hoare, descended to Eleanor Moleyns, who married Robert, third
Lord Hungerford), inasmuch as I find that, in 1287, Robert Mauduit died seised of the
manor of Funtel § ; which, in 1382, was held by Johanna, wife of Roger Dove ‖ ; that, in
1424, William Moleyns died possessed of it, and of the manor of Farnhyll ¶ ; and that, in
1429, *both* manors are included in the lands of William Moleyns, his son.**

---

* See *Cott. Mss., Brit. Mus., Julius B.* xii., *fo.* 237. See also *Sir R. Hoare's Hist. Wilts,* for
an abstract of these Deeds.
† See *Hoare's South Wiltsh.,* vol. 4, "*Hund. of Dunworth,*" *pp.* 195-6.
‡ Mr. Jackson informed me that he had in his possession an Abstract of Deeds confirming this
statement.

§ *Inq. p. m.* 16 Ed. I. No. 30. ‖ *Inq. p. m.* 6 Ric. II. No. 34.
¶ *Inq. p. m.* 3 Hen. VI. No. 29. ** *Inq. p. m.* 8 Hen. VI. No. 38.

If my supposition be correct, that the manors in question did accrue to Robert, third Lord Hungerford, by his marriage, the question is, how they became vested in Margaret Lady Botreaux. They certainly are not, by specific words, included in the conveyance to her from her son.

The steps, before alluded to, which were taken by Robert Lord Hungerford and Moleyns to avoid sequestration and to secure his property, proved ineffectual. In the Inquisition taken on his death in 1464 (*Inq. post mort., 4 Edw. IV., No.* 56), the deeds which he had executed to his mother in 1460 were treated as nullities, so far as they purported to vest his lands in her; for we find in the schedule of estates of which he died seised, the very lands, including Fonthill, which he had conveyed to her. The lands were seized by the Crown, and in 1468 were granted by EDWARD IV. to his brother RICHARD, Duke of GLOUCESTER,* a fact, it may be remarked, at variance with Hoare's statement that the lands of Lord Hungerford and Moleyns were granted to Lord Wenlock. The grant to the Duke of Gloucester did *not,* however, include the *manors* of Fountel-Giffard or of Farnehyll, which strengthens the supposition that they did not form a portion of the forfeited lands.

Margaret, Lady Hungerford and Botreaux, made arrangements with the Crown and the Duke of Gloucester, by which she obtained possession of some of the lands that had been forfeited; portions of which she sold, in order to raise money to redeem the remainder, and otherwise to assist in restoring the fortune of her House,† and it would appear probable that the lands at Fountel were included in the arrangement with the Crown, and that they, together with the manors (which were ASSUMED to form part of them), were sold at that time to JOHN MERVYN, who was one of the confidential friends, trustees, and general managers of LADY HUNGERFORD AND BOTREAUX. This supposition is borne out by the statements contained in the answer of MERVYN to a Bill in Chancery,‡ filed against him and John Touke (12th Edw. IV., 1472-3) by SIR OLIVER MANYNGHAM, Knight, and his wife ALIANORE, widow of Robert Lord HUNGERFORD AND MOLEYNS. The Bill alleged that "the said ROBERT and ALIANORE were seized in theyre demene as " in fee, as in right and title of the said Alianore, of " [int. alia] " the manor of Farnehill in " Fountehill, and Founthill Gyfford, w⁴ theyre appurtenances, and of the advouson of " the Church of Fountehille Gyfford;" and that being "so seasid, made estate by fyne, of " alle the said manors," &c., unto "WILLIAM, BISHOP OF WINCHESTRE, PIERS ARDERN, " Knight, JOHN MERVIN, JOHN TOUKE, and JOHN WYNGE," " to the use and behoef of " the foresaid Alianore and her heyres, and to th'entent that they shoulde therof make " estate unto the forsaid ALIANORE, and to her heyres and assignes, *when they were thereto* " *required,* the whiche WILLIAM BISHOP OF WINCHESTRE and PIERS ARDERN aforesaid " have, by theyr dede, relesid and quite claymed alle theyr right and title that they made " in alle the aforesaid manors, londes and tenementes, with alle theyr appurtenances " above said, to the forsaid ALIANORE, and to her heyres for evermore, according to • " th'entent aforesaid, and ofte tymes your said besechirs have required the forsaid JOHN " MERVYN and JOHN TOUKE to make estate of, and in, alle the said manors, londes, " tenementes and advowsons abovesaid, with their appurtenanc', to the forsaid ALIANORE " and her heyres, according to the wille and entent abovesaid; whiche to doo they utterly " and either of them have refusid and it [yet] dothe."

The answer made by JOHN MERVYN is : That as to alle the manors, &c., in the Bill mentioned, "except the man's of Farnehill in Fountchill and Fountehill Gifford, and all " the landes and teñts w¹ thap'ten'nce in Farnehill in Fountell and Fountell Gifford," he

---

* See copy Grant, dated 25th Oct. 1468 ; *Cott. Mss., Brit. Mus., Julius B.* XIII., *p.* 113.
† See the very interesting " Laste Will of Margarete, Lady Hungerford and Botreaux," with " the wryting annexed," dated 8th August, 1476. Printed in Sir Harris Nicolas' " *Testamenta Vetusta,*" *vol. i., p.* 310.
‡ The Bill and Answer are printed *in extenso* in the " *Calendars of proceedings in Chancery,*" *vol. i., p.* xci., *et. seq.* A note is appended, stating that there was a rejoinder by the plaintiffs, but that only part of it remains.

had at all times "seyn the said fyñ levied, been redy and yet is to make therof astat, to "the said ALIANORE and hur heires;" but, as to the Founthill estate, the answer proceeds : "And as to the seid man's of Farnehill in Fountehill and Fountehill Gifford, and to all "the seid londes and teñts in Farnehill in Fountehill, and Fountehill Gifford aforesaid the "seid JOHN MERVYN bi p'testacon, not knowing the same man's, londes, and teñts, to "be conteigned in the said fyñ, for answer saieth, that at the tyme of the same fyñ "leveed they that wer p'ties to the same fyñ no thyng hadde in the same man's, landes, "and teñts, ner any of them ony thyng had in the same; but MARGARET Lady HUNGER- "FORD AND BOTREUX at the tyme of the same fyñ leveed was thereof seased in "hur de** as in fee to hur owyn p'pr use, *whoes astat of and in the same Manrs, londes,* "*and teñts the seid John Mervyn hath to his own p'pre use.*"

The result of the dispute does not appear ; but it would seem that JOHN MERVYN continued in possession of the estates, including the manors of Fountel-Giffard and Farnehyll in Fountayne and the advowson, as the presentation to the living in 1550 was made by his great-grandson, SIR JOHN MERVYN, Kn', and a rent roll of his manor of Fonthill Gyfford, dated 20 Sep., 1559, is still existing.*

It should, however, as respects the presentation to the living of Fountel, be remarked that there were two vacancies between that which occurred in 1458, and to which Lord HUNGERFORD AND MOLEYNS presented, and the presentation made by Sir John MERVYN in 1550. These vacancies occurred in 1521 and 1547. In the institutions, no patron is named for the former, but the latter was filled up on the presentation of Sir Thomas Arundel, Kt.

As regards the marriage of JOHN MERVYN with ".JOAN," daughter of Lord HUN-GERFORD, the *sole* authority for it, so far as appears, is Vincent's pedigree.† It is not corroborated by any entry in the Hungerford pedigrees in the College of Arms, nor by any other documents relating to that family to which I have been able to refer. WALTER, first Lord HUNGERFORD, who died in 1449, had, according to Dugdale,‡ two daughters ; ELIZABETH, married to Sir Philip COURTENAY Kt., and MARGARET, wife of SIR WALTER RODENAY ; both of whom were mentioned in their father's will. ROBERT Lord HUNGERFORD (Walter's son), who died in 1459, mentions in his will a daughter MARY (who is also named in the will of her grandfather before referred to). Her marriage is not mentioned in Dugdale, nor is it noted in the Hungerford pedigrees. It, therefore, only remains to *conjecture*, that for "JOAN" is to be read "MARY ;" but it is somewhat difficult, in the event of this conjecture being adopted, to account for the omission of *her* name from the list of persons for whose souls prayers were directed, by Margaret Lady HUNGERFORD AND BOTREAUX, in the Foundation Deed of the Hospital at Heytesbury, to be offered up in the Parish Church of Heytesbury ; *especially* as one of the persons named was JOHN MERVYN, "*cum ab hâc luce migraverit.*" Again, the same MARGARET Lady HUNGERFORD and BOTREAUX, by her will (August 8th, 1476), appointed that in the Chapel which she had begun to build within the Cathedral Church of Salisbury, there should be founded a perpetual chantry for the daily celebration of divine service for the soules of divers of her family, and, amongst others, for the soul of "JOHN MERVYN, Esquire, after this "life ;" but no mention is made of his wife, as surely would have been the case if she had been a Hungerford. JOHN MERVYN was named one of the Trustees of the will of MARGARET, Lady HUNGERFORD AND BOTREAUX ; but the date of his death does not appear. Vincent's Pedigree gives him two sons:—WALTER, and HUGH ; but he must have had a third son, if the words "*Nepos Walteri Maruin de Fountaine in Com. Wilts Ar.*" (the description attached to WILLIAM MERVYN, with whom the Pedigree of the Pertwood branch of the family commences, as recorded in the Visitation of Wilts, 1623, *Ms. Coll.*

---

* *State Papers, Dom. Series Eliz., vol. vi., Case A., Eliz. No. 2.*
† *Ms. Coll. Arms, " Vincent's Sussex, 121," p. 393.*
‡ *Dug. Bar., fo. 1,676, vol. ii., p. 206.*

Arms "*I. C.* 22 ") are to be taken, as I have no doubt they are, to mean NEPHEW (and not Grandson as has been suggested) of Walter-Mervyn, as to which see "𝔓𝔢𝔯𝔱𝔴𝔬𝔬𝔡 𝔅𝔯𝔞𝔫𝔠𝔥."

HUGH MERVYN, the second son, married; but Vincent's pedigree does not name his wife. It, however, shows a match between his "daughter and co-heir" (whose Christian name is not stated) with . . . . . . "Bughton, of Cawsham" (Corsham).

WALTER MERVYN, of Fountel-Giffard, the eldest son, married twice; his first wife, JOAN, died without issue.* His second wife was MARY, daughter of John MOMPESSON,† or Mountpenson, of Bathampton, in the county of Wilts (by Isabel dau. and coh. of Thomas Drewe), who by his will,‡ dated 18th September, 1500 (and which, with a codicil, was proved at Lambeth on 5th October, 1502), made to his "son Walter Mervyn" the following bequest: "my russet gowne furred with old marterne" and "one of my dowbelettes of silk, and to my dowght' his wife "iij. goblettes with a cou'yng, and to hir xl' and the dettes that they owe me."

Walter Mervyn was possessed of the Manors of Fountel-Giffard and Farnehyll in fee, and died in possession of those estates on 12th July, 1512.* His will is dated 20th November, 2 Hen. VIII. (1510). By Mary Mompesson, he had two sons and three daughters.

I. JOHN MERVYN of Fountel-Giffard, the eldest son, of whom hereafter.

II. SIR EDMUND MERVYN, of Durford Abbey, in the county of Sussex (*See* "𝔇𝔲𝔯𝔣𝔬𝔯𝔡 𝔄𝔟𝔟𝔢𝔶 𝔅𝔯𝔞𝔫𝔠𝔥.")

    1. ALIANORA MERVYN, who was the first wife of Ambrose DAUNTESEY, of West Lavington, in the co. of Wilts, by whom she had issue, represented, in the male line in 1623, by Ambrose Dauntesey, then aged 13 years.§

    2. A DAUGHTER (whose Christian name does not appear) married . . . . . . FITZ-JAMES, of Redlinch, in Somersetshire.‖

---

* See Abstract of Inq. p.m., APPENDIX I., page iii. I have been unable, after careful search, to find Walter Mervyn's will, which is mentioned in the inquisition.

† There was a second marriage between the Mervyn and Mompesson families; Sir John Mervyn, as we shall presently see, had, for his second wife, Elizabeth Mompesson, the grand-niece of the above-mentioned "Mary."

‡ John Mompesson, the Testator, was Sheriff of Wilts, 18 Edw. IV. His father, Robert Mompesson, appears to have been the first of the family who settled in Wiltshire; he married Alice, the daughter and heiress of William Godwyn, of Gillingham, co. Dorset, by Elizabeth his wife, dau. and heiress of Thomas Bonham, temp. Hen. V. It is stated by Sir R. C. Hoare, that the Mompesson family are supposed to have descended from the Mounpynzon family, who flourished in Norfolk from a date shortly after the Conquest, until the reign of Edw. II. Sir Gyles Mounpynzon, of Norfolk, temp. Edw. I., had for his arms, "*Argent, a une lion sable, a une pinsion de Or en le espaudle*," a bearing corresponding with the Mompesson coat, viz., "*Argent, a lion rampant sable, charged on the shoulder with a chaffinch Or.*"

§ *Ms. Coll. Arm.* "*I.C.* 22" *Visit. Wilts,* 1623, 18*b.* The coat of Dauntesey, there recorded, is, "*Gules, a lion rampant argent, seizing a wyvern erect proper.*"

‖ I have been unable to trace this marriage, the authority for which is Vincent's pedigree. (*Ms. Coll. Arms,* "*Vin. Sussex,* 121," *f.* 392). The family of Fitz-James was seated in Somersetshire as early as the reign of Edw. III. (*Inq. post mort.,* 23 *Edw. III.,* No. 41). Richard Fitz-James, Bishop of London, 1505, who died in 1522, was the son of John Fitz-James (who died in 1476), by Alice, dau. of John Newburgh, of Dorsetshire, and grandson of James Fitz-James, who acquired the estate of Redlynch, in that county, by his marriage with Eleanor, daughter and heir of Simon Draycott. Sir John Fitz-James, the nephew of the Bishop, was, in 1526, Chief Justice of the King's Bench, and died circ. 1542. (See *Foss' Judges of England, Ed.* 1857, *vol. v., p.* 170, *et seq.,* where the pedigree of the family is very fully discussed). The Bishop had a brother Alored Fitz-James, who settled at Lewston, co. Dorset. (*Hutchins's Hist. Dorset, vol. iv., p.* 11.) The arms borne by Fitz-James the Chief Justice, as given by Dugdale, in his "*Origines Juridiciales,*" ed. 1671, *p.* 329, were "*Azure, a dolphin naient embowed argent between* 3 *mullets Or.*" The same arms are given for the name of Fitz-James, in Somersetshire. *Ms. Coll. Arms Alphabet of Arms, marked* "*I. K. L.*" *p.* 17.

3. JANE MERVYN married Edward BURLEY, of Writtle, in the parish of Potterne co. Wilts, eldest son of Thomas Burley, of Esterton, in the same county.*

JOHN MERVYN, the elder son of WALTER MERVYN and MARY MOMPESSON,

married ELIZABETH, daughter and co-heiress of John GREEN, of Stotfold, co. Beds, by Edith LATIMER,† by whom he appears to have had three sons and one daughter, and to have died during the lifetime of his father, who, 9th April, 1 Henry VIII. (1509), settled the Manor of Fountel-Giffard and Farnehyll, in trust for ELIZABETH, relict of his son JOHN MERVYN deceased, if she continued sole; with remainder to John Mervyn their son, remainder to settlor's right heir. Elizabeth Mervyn is mentioned in Inq. p. m. 4 Henry VIII. (1512), and was living at the date of her mother's will (1517).

The issue of the marriage of John Mervyn and Elizabeth Green were:—

    I. WILLIAM MERVYN, } ob. s.p.
    II. GEORGE MERVYN, } ob. s.p.

    III. SIR JOHN MERVYN, of Fountel-Giffard, Knt., of whom hereafter.

    1. ELIZABETH MERVYN, married Thomas HALL,‡ of Bradford, in the county of Wilts, by whom she had issue (See *Visit. Wilts*, 1565) represented at the Visitation of Wilts 1623 by Thomas Hall, æt. 22. (*Harl. Ms., No.* 1111; *Ms. Coll. Arm* "*I.C,* 22").

SIR JOHN MERVYN, of Fountel-Giffard, Knight, succeeded his grandfather WALTER. He married twice; his first wife being JANE, daughter of Philip BASKERVILLE, of Sherborne, in the county of Dorset (afterwards of Erdesley, in the county of Hereford), and widow of William Peverell, of Bradford Peverell, in the county of Somerset.

By Jane Baskerville, who was buried at Fountel, Sir John had thirteen children, five sons and eight daughters, viz.:—

    I. SIR JAMES MERVYN, Knt., of whom hereafter.

---

* This match is corroborated by an entry in the Burley Pedigree, which occurs in the Visitation of Wilts, Anno. 1565 (*Ms. Coll. Arms*, "*G.* 8," *p.* 17*b*), the representative of the marriage at that time being their son and heir George Burley of Writtle.

† Edith Latimer was daughter and one of the heirs of Sir Nicholas Latimer, Sheriff of Dorset and Somerset, 32 Hen. VI. and 11 Edw. IV., who died in 1505, *t. p. m.*, by Joan, daughter of Sir John Hody, Knt. Edith Latimer married three times; her *first* husband being John GREEN, of Stotfold, co. Bedford, by whom he had two daughters and co-heiresses, viz., Cicilie, who married for her first husband Richard Page, of Aylesbury; and Elizabeth, who was the wife of John MERVYN. Edith Latimer's *second* husband was Sir John Mordaunt, Knt. of Turvey, by whom she had issue two sons and one daughter, viz., John, created Lord Mordaunt, William Mordaunt, and Joan who married Giles Strangways, of Styanesford, in the county of Dorset. Sir John Mordaunt died in 1504, and his widow married again, her *third* husband being Sir John Carew, Knt., by whom she had not any children. (*Mss. Coll. Arms,* "*Vincent's Chaos*," *p.* 340. See also a carefully compiled and elaborate pedigree by Belts and Heard, "*J. P.* 87," *p.* 395.) By her Will dated 1st January, 1517, Edith, Lady Carew, then residing at Dawlish, in the parish of Buckland Abbot, in the county of Dorset, made bequests to her daughters Cecilie Page, Elizabeth Mervyn, and Joan Strangways, and appointed her son-in-law Giles Strangways, the sole executor, who proved the Will on 30th April, 1518, in the P. C. Cant. (*Regr. No.* 7, *Ayloff.*)

‡ The arms of Hall are "*Sable,* 3 *battle-axes argent.*" In the Visitation of Wilts, 1565, *Ms. Coll.*

C

II. EDMUND MERVYN, who married JANE, daughter of Sir Richard CATESBY, Knight, by his first wife, Dorothy, daughter of Sir John Spencer, Knight, of Wormleighton, co. Northampton,[*] and widow of Robert Gaynesford, of Carshalton, Surrey, at which place they were married 19 February, 1558–9;[†] and by her Edmund Mervyn, who was living in 1578,[‡] had three sons :—

    I. JOHN MERVYN,§ living 1578.[‡] He was tenant for life under his grandfather's will of his "*purchased estates*," including the manor of Compton Basset.

    II. EDMUND MERVYN, who is recorded by Vincent as having married ANN HUDLESTON, and is mentioned in his grandfather's will. He was living in 1578.[‡] Vincent gives issue of this marriage one son, viz. :—

        I. JAMES MERVYN.

    III. RICHARD MERVYN, living 1578,[‡] and mentioned in his grandfather's will.

III. JOHN MERVYN, stated by Vincent to have died s.p. He was living in 1578.[‡]

IV. PHILIP MERVYN, living 1578,[‡] he also is stated in Vincent's pedigree to have died s. p. He was appointed by his father's will (1566) one of the executors.

V. AMBROSE MERVYN, fifth son, but thirteenth child, married SUSAN, daughter of Geoffry UPTON,|| of Warmester, in the county of Somerset. He was

---

Arm, "G. 8," *p.* 48*b*, the arms of Hall, with four quarterings, are tricked, as are also the arms of Elizabeth Mervyn; but the coat there given for Mervyn differs from that borne by her brother, Sir John Mervyn, being "Argent, a demi lyon rampant sable," as used by the Pertwood branch, *except* that the fleur de lis is omitted.

* See the Catesby pedigree, *Ms. Coll. Arms*, "*Vincent's Northamptonshire* 114," *p.* 275. *Dugdale's Warwickshire, fo. ed.* 1730, *vol.* 2, *p.* 788, and *Manning and Bray's Surrey, fo. ed.* 1804, *vol.* 2.

† Register of Marriages, Carshalton, Surrey, where the following entry occurs, "1558–9, *Feb.* 19, *Edmond Marvin and Jane Gaynesford*." See also Funeral Certificate of Sir John Mervyn, APPENDIX I., p. xii.

‡ In 1578, Sir James Mervyn made a Deed relating to a portion of his property in the parish of Tisbury. The following is a copy of the abstract made by the late Mr. G. F. Beltz, *Lancaster Herald*, on his examination of Deeds and old writings, at Fonthill, in 1798. [*Ms. Coll. Arms.* "*A. xviii. J. P.* 18," *p.* 198.] "INDENTURE, 7th May, 20th Elizabeth, 1578; between Sir James Mervin, Knight, of first " part, and William Gibbs, of the Middle Temple, London, Gent., of the other part. Said James " Mervin hath limited Ashell's Down, or Ashell's Wood, in parish of Tysbury, Wilts, cum pt'in', which " said Sir James late had of Sir Mathue Arrundel, Kt., in exchange for other lands. Said Sir James " Mervin, in consideration of a marriage heretofore had between said Sir JAMES and Dame AMY now his " wife, and for love to JOHN MERVIN, EDMUND, and RICHARD MERVIN, nephews to said Sir James; viz[t]. " Sons of EDMUND Mervin, brother of said Sir James; and unto PHILIP, JOHN, and AMBROSE Mervin, and " to the said Edmund, brothers of said Sir James; said Sir James determined that the premises should con-" tinue in the name and *blood of the Mervins*. Ashell's Wood to continue to said Sir James Mervin and " Dame Amy, his wife,—remainder to such person to whom the Manor of Fonthill-Gifford,—and by Inden-" ture tripartite between said Sir James Mervin, by name of James Mervin, Esq., first part, John Ryves, Esq., " second part, Henry Mervin and Robert Hill, Esq., third part, the premises are conveyed to remain or " descend to the person who shall hold the Manor of Fonthill-Gifford."

In 1590, by Deed dated 3 Dec. 33 Eliz., Sir James (his wife Amy being then dead) revoked the above Deed, and settled the premises to his own use (*Beltz Abstract*); and they passed to his grandson, Mervyn, Earl of Castlehaven, and on his attainder, to the Crown, with the other Mervyn property which he possessed. (*Hoare's Wiltshire, Dunworth Hund., p.* 134).

§ It is probably this John Mervyn, who is mentioned in Willis' "*Notitia Parliamentaria*," as of the Middle Temple, and M.P. for Hindon, in the sixth and seventh Parliaments held at Westminster, 28 and 31 Eliz., 1586-88.

|| The Pedigree of the family of UPTON is entered in the Visit. of Somerset, 1591 (*Ms. Coll. Arms*,

named in his father's will (1566) as one of the executors, and he was also a legatee under the will and codicil of his brother Sir James Mervyn, dated 1st April, 1610, who requests that his adopted son Henry Mervyn, and his wife Christiana, will in respect of the love and bountye that he had bestowed on them, "bestowe meate, drink, and lodging" upon "his brother Ambrose as he (the testator) had theretofore done."

    I. PHILIP MERVYN (living 1610), son of the above Ambrose, was a legatee under the will and codicil of his uncle Sir James. who, however, declares that it is not his will that the said Philip should "fynger or have delivered unto him" the legacy, but that it should be employed to raise £10 yearly towards his maintenance so long as he should live.

1. ELEANOR MERVYN, Sir John's eldest daughter, was the second wife of Robert HILL, of Yarde, near Taunton, in the county of Somerset, and was living at the death of her father in 1566, at which time she had issue* as follows :—

    I. ROBERT HILL, ob. s.p.,   II. JAMES HILL, ob. s.p.
    III. GILBERT HILL. ob. s.p.   IV. JOHN HILL, ob. s.p.
    V. HUGH HILL married MARY, daughter of Sir John BONDE, of London, Knt., by whom he had issue. He is mentioned in the Will of his uncle Sir James Mervyn, who also names WINIFRED his (Hugh Hill's) daughter.
    1. JANE HILL married Thomas BREETON.
    2. ELIZABETH HILL, ob. s.p.
    3. MARGARET HILL married . . . . . . MARTIN, co. Devon.

2. EDITH MERVYN died unmarried.

3. MARGARET MERVYN, who married John COOK, of Underbridge, in the Isle of Wight, was living in 1566, and had the following issue:—
    I. John Cook, ob. s.p.   1. Ursula Cook.   2. Elizabeth Cook.

4. ELIZABETH MERVYN was the wife of John RYVES† of Damory Court, in the county of Dorset, who is referred to in his father-in-law Sir John's will, and appointed by it the guardian of the testator's grandchildren, John, Edmond, and Richard.

The issue of this marriage living at the date of the Visitation of Wiltshire in 1623 (Harl. Ms., No. 1,166), were:—
    I. JOHN RYVES.   II. GEORGE RYVES.   III. CHARLES RYVES.
    IV. HENRY RYVES.   1. ELIZABETH.   2. AMY.

"G. 19.," p. 106), from which it appears that they descended from John Upton, of Trelask, co. Cornwall, by Margaret, daughter and coh. of John Mulys, whose great-great-grandson, Geoffrey Upton, of War-mester, married Mary, daughter and coheir of Thomas Hone, of Mary St. Ottery, co. Devon. The Visitation of 1591 records the marriage of SUSAN UPTON with AMBROSE MERVYN.

* The names of the children of the marriage of ELEANOR MERVYN and ROBERT HILL, are taken from Sir John Mervyn's Funeral Certificate (1566). Ms. Coll. Arms, "I. 13," p. 75. See APPENDIX I., p. xii.
In the Visitation of Somerset in 1623 (Ms. Coll. Arms, "2 C. 22." p. 285) (57 years subsequently) the particulars of the family are recorded thus:—ROBERT HILL, of Yarde, near Taunton (the second son of Roger Hill, of Taunton, by Alice, daughter of John Towse) married two wives, first, Alicia, a daughter of . . . . . . Clarke, by whom he had one child, a daughter, who married William Symes of Chard, co. Somerset, who had issue: Secondly, ELEANOR MERVYN, by whom he had, I. Hugh Hill the eldest son (mentioned in his uncle, Sir James Mervyn's will) who married Mary, the daughter of Sir John Bonde, of London, Knt., and had issue; II. James Hill; III. John Hill, ob. s.p., 1, a daughter (Margaret) who was the wife of . . . . . Martin, co. Devon; 2, Jane, who married Thomas Breeton, and had issue. The arms of HILL, appended to the entry in the Visitation of 1623, as "allowed, under the hand of Robert Cooke, Clarencieux 1570," are, "Gules, a chevron engrailed ermine, between three garbs or, the whole within a bordure argent."

† There was a further marriage between the Mervyn and Ryves families. Elizabeth, the daughter of Robert Ryves, of Ranston, co. Dorset, and niece of this John Ryves, was the wife of George Mervyn, of Knoyle, the second son of George Mervyn, of Pertwood, by Melior Goldesborough. See Pertwood Branch.

5. MARGARET MERVYN, (a second daughter of this name,) being the tenth child of Sir John Mervyn and Jane Baskerville, is mentioned in her father's funeral certificate, and in his will is referred to as "my daughter, Mergarett the younger." She married Francis PERKINS, of Ufton, co. Berks.

6. ANNE MERVYN, wife of Edward CORDUROY, of Chute, in the county of Southampton, by whom she had issue a daughter, AMY, who is mentioned in Sir John's funeral certificate.

Two other daughters (whose Christian names are not given) are stated in Sir John's funeral certificate to have died without issue.

SIR JOHN MERVYN was knighted by Edward the Protector Duke of Somerset, at the camp at Roxburghe, in Scotland, 1 Edw. VI.* He survived his first wife, and

married, secondly, ELIZABETH,† daughter of John MOMPESSON, of Bathampton, in the county of Wilts, and widow of Sir Richard Perkins, of Ufton, in the county of Berks, Knt.; but by her Sir John had no issue that lived. In the second Parliament, 1 Mary ‡ (1554), Sir John Mervyn was returned as one of the Knights of the Shire for Wiltshire, and in the following Parliament (also 1554), he sat as member for Calne.‡ He died, as appears by his funeral certificate,§ "on Tuesday, the 19th day of "June, 1566, in the eighth year of the Queen's reign, at "his house at Fountayne Gifford, in the county of Wilts, "about 5 o'clock at night."

Sir John Mervyn added to his estates in Wiltshire by the purchase in 1553 for £952 2s. 2¼d. of the fee of the manor of Compton Bassett, which had previously been held by his family under lease, and which property had formed part of the jointure of Queen Catherine Parr. The purchase of this property gave rise, as will be after seen, to a very bitter litigation between Sir John's eldest son and his mother-in-law.

The manor of Compton Basset was conveyed to Sir John by grant from the Crown, dated at Westminster, 4th February, 7 Edw. VI.¶ He made his will,‖ which is stated to have been dated the 8th June, 1566; but that date would, if the day of his death is accurately stated in the funeral certificate, appear to be incorrect, as in the proceedings connected with the litigation,** the will is said to have been all written in Sir John's chamber on the forenoon of the day on which he died. By it the testator directs his body to be buried at Fountel, by the side of his first wife, and he instructs his executors to see that he and his Lady Elizabeth, "my wief that now ys," are buried "after a worshipfull sorte there, according to our estate." The directions as to the burial were evidently very strictly complied with; no doubt under the supervision of his widow. The Herald's certificate shows that it was attended with all due formalities; it gives a very detailed account of the proceedings previous to and at the funeral, including a note of the sermon preached in the church by Mr. Proctor, the Chancellor of the Bishop of Salisbury, in which the defunct was much commended for "his juste dealinge and for kepynge p'myses." The worthy Knight was followed to his grave by four of his five sons; by five daughters;

---

* Cott. Mss. Claude, C. III., fo. 169.

† Elizabeth, Dame Mervyn, was one of the four daughters (and eventually co-heiress) of John Mompesson, who was Sheriff for Wilts 24 Hen. VII., by Alice, daughter of Sir John Lye, Kt., of the Isle of Wight. She was grand-niece of Mary Mompesson, who was Sir John Mervyn's grandmother.

‡ Willis's "Notitia Parliamentaria."

§ See copy printed in APPENDIX I., p. xii.

‖ See copy Will, printed in APPENDIX I., p. ix.

¶ State Papers, Dom. Jas. I., Vol. 192, p. 7, where there is a copy of the Grant.

** State Papers, Dom. Jas. I., Vol. 192, pp. 7 and 8.

and by one daughter-in-law. His eldest son James was absent, and his place as chief mourner was filled by the second son Edmund. The absence of the heir, which unexplained would seem strange, no doubt resulted from his dissatisfaction with his father's will, or rather with the will which, as he maintained, was put forward as Sir John's, but which had in fact been made for him at the time he was almost *in extremis*, by his wife and the priest.[*]

The particular point of dissatisfaction with the Will appears to have arisen out of a bequest which it contained, entailing on the testator's grandsons John, Edmund, and Richard (the sons of Edmund), all the testator's " purchased lands," which included the Manor of Compton Basset ; a disposition which must have been annoying enough to Sir . James, on whom the Fountel-Giffard property was entailed, seeing that a portion of the park and grounds, including " the dairy, ponds, heronsewes, orchard, hopyarde, and his feeding " for beefe and muttons for his p'vicon, which his ancestors were driven to holde in lease " theise cc yeres which lieth intermyngled wᵗʰ his olde inheritans rounde aboute his house, " evyn to his doore, and for p'chase of wᶜʰ Sir John was dryven to selling a greate peece of " aunceient inheritaunce,"[†] were alienated from him. The feud waxed strong. Dame Elizabeth Mervyn and the priest William Gyll were proceeded against by James Mervyn for *forging* the Will, and John Ryves, the testator's son-in-law, for " bolstringe and mayn- " teyninge thereof."[†] There seems to have been hard swearing on the part of my lady's witnesses, who being for the most part " unlearned servingmen, handmaidds, ladds, and " girles," did nevertheless " skilfully and p'cisely depose, as learnedlie as utter barresters."[†] Whether or not their evidence they carried the day, and the Will remained undisturbed, does not appear ; but in 1607 Sir James Mervyn was in possession of the Manor of Compton Basset, as in that year the Attorney-General proceeded against him to recover, on the part of the Crown, some " assart " lands[‡] which Sir James claimed in Chippenham and Melksham Forests, as being parcel of the Manor.[†]

Dame Elizabeth Mervyn survived her husband fifteen years, having died 25th September, 1581,[§] in which year her will bears date. She appears to have altered her intention of being interred "after a worshipfull sorte," at Fountel, as she gives express directions for her burial at Ufton, near Richard Parkyns, her first husband. From her will it seems that a " *woeing*," which at the time of Sir John Mervin's death was going on between his daughter Margaret, " the younger," and my Lady's " ward and nephew," Francis Parkyns.[†] ended in matrimony, as they and their children were the principal beneficees under her will. [||] No other members of the Mervyn family are mentioned in it.

---

[*] William Gyll, then incumbent of Fountel.
[†] See *State Papers, Dom. Jas. I.*, Vol. 192, *pp.* 7, 8.
[‡] Woodlands cleared for cultivation.
[§] See " *Elias Ashmole's Antiquities of Berkshire*," 8vo., 3 vols., Lond. 1723, vol. 1, p. 27, " Ufton alias Uffington. Towards the east end of the Chancel, on the north side, is raised a fair and large " stone monument, where the statues of Richard Perkin, Esq., and the Lady Mervyn, his wife, were made " kneeling before a desk, but are now broken down." See also Abst. Inq. p. m., after Lady Mervyn's death. Appendix I., p. iv.
[||] See will of Dame Elizabeth Mervyn, late the wife of Sir John Mervyn, Kᵗ, dated 24th July, and proved 27th Sep., 1581. P. C. Cant. (*Reg. 32 Darcy.*)

SIR JAMES MERVYN, third child but eldest son of Sir JOHN MERVYN and JANE BASKERVILLE, succeeded on his father's death in 1566 to the Fountel-Giffard estate. He was born in 1529, and is described in Sir John's funeral certificate and in Inq. p. m. taken on Sir John's death, APPENDIX I. p iv., as "Esquire for the body of the Queens Majesty."* He married AMY, daughter of Valentine CLARKE, by his wife ELIZABETH, daughter and heir of ROLAND BRIDGES. In Sir John Mervyn's funeral certificate, Sir James' wife is described as being, at the time of the marriage, widow of . . . . . . Horne of Sarsdon in the county of Oxford, pensioner.† In the fourth Parliament of Queen Elizabeth, held at Westminster (1572) Sir James, then Mr. Mervyn, sat as representative for the county of Wilts.‡ From the " *Ducatus Lancastriæ* " (*Vol.* 2, *part* 3, *p.* 379), I find that in 1568 he was Steward of the Duchy lands (Kyngeston, Lacy Manor, Holt Chace and Park, and Wymborne Mynster), in the County of Dorset, an office of which he certainly was in possession in 1589-90; although in 1578-9 (21 Elizabeth) there seems to have been some dispute about it; as in that year a process was made by one Andrew Rogers, who claimed the bailiwick and keepership of the Chace of Kingston, Lacy Manor, &c., under a patent granted to Sir James Blunt, Kn[t], Lord Mountjoy. In 1574,§ Sir James received the honor of knighthood, and in 1592 he held the office of Collector of Customs at Dartmouth, as appears by two letters written by him to the Lord High Treasurer, Burghley, preserved in the British Museum. (*Lansd. Mss. No.* 70, *Arts.* 66 *and* 70.) The letters refer to the prize Portuguese Carrack, the " MADRE DI DIOS," which having in August, 1592, been taken by a fleet fitted out by Sir Walter Raleigh and others, aided by some ships belonging to the Earl of Cumberland, was brought into Dartmouth Harbour. Special Commissioners, as was usual in cases where prizes were taken by merchant adventurers, as they were termed, were appointed, to secure in the first place to the Queen her Custom dues, and then to make due division amongst the parties entitled to the prize.||

The Commissioners appointed to take charge of the " Madre di Dios" were Sir Robert Cecil, Sir Walter Raleigh, Sir Francis Drake, William Killegrew, Richard Carmaden, and Thomas Myddleton.

---

* See particulars of this now obsolete office in Pegge's Curialia, 4[to] Lond: 1791.
† I do not find any pedigree of Horne recorded in the Visitations of Oxfordshire, in 1566, or 1574; but there is entered in the former (*Ms. Coll. Arms,* " G. 5." *p.* 19) a pedigree of Bustarde, of Adderbury, which gives a marriage of Anthony Bustarde with Jane, daughter of " John Horne, of Saresden, in county Oxon, Esquire," and, at the time of the Visitation of the county, in 1574, the Herald, Richard Lee (*Portcullis,*) visited Sarsden House, near Chipping Norton, and examined the Arms found in the windows there; amongst others he notes a coat " *Argent, on a chevron engrailed gules, between three unicorns' heads erased azure, a crescent Or*," impaling " *Or, two bars azure, in chief three escallops ; in fesse a mullet gules*," and over it written " E. HORNE and AMYE CLARKE." (See " *Gatherings of Oxfordshire, Anno* 1574," published by the Harleian Society, 1871, from Lee's original Ms. in the Bodleian Library, *Wood's Colls.* 14 *D.*) In the list of the Band of Gentlemen Pensioners in 17 Hen. viii. (1526) printed in Pegge's Curialia, p. 27, appears the name of Edmund Horne. The HORNE arms, as given in the Bustarde pedigree above referred to, are " *Quarterly* 1 *and* 4, *Argent, on a chevron engrailed gules a crescent between three unicorns' heads erased azure*" (agreeing with those in the Sarsden windows); " 2nd and 3rd Ermine, three fleurs de lis within a bordure engrailed gules." (*Ms. Coll. Arms.* " G 5," *p.* 19.) This coat is also noted by Lee, who attributes it to " FABIAN," of Essex.
‡ *Willis'* " *Notitia Parliamentaria.*"
§ *Brit. Mus. Mss. Add* 5,482 *fo.* 14[b]. *Lansd. Ms.* 678, *fo.* 18.
|| See Notes upon the capture of " THE GREAT CARRACK," communicated by me to the Society of Antiquaries in 1850. *Archaeologia, Vol.* 33.

The appointment of the Commissioners was viewed with jealousy by the .regular appointed agents of the Customs, and a letter* to Lord Burghley, dated 12 Sept., 1592, intimates that some questions had then already arisen with the officers of the Customs at Dartmouth and Plymouth "touching the enteries and custome of suche goods of the Carrick as shall be dischardged in ether of the said ports."

Sir James Mervyn's particular difficulties and complaints on the subject will be best gathered from the following letter,† which he addressed to the Lord High Treasurer :—

"May it please your good Lordship to be advertized that the Carricke beinge heare " arrived wthin the Porte of Dartmuthe (where I am Customer and Collector of hir M^{ties} " receiptes), I have bin tolde by Mr. Midleton that he hathe warrant from hir M^{tie} under " hir owne hande, to collect and answer the custom thereof, affirminge that by his bonde " he woulde save me harmles for the custom dewe for all the goodes and merchandize that " showlde be discharged owte of the Carricke into other shippes to be transported into other " havens.

" I thinke (the matter beinge of an unknowen importance) that he can hardly wth his " bare bonde discharge the bonde wch I and my suerties have entred into, muche lesse the " oath wh^{ch} I have taken to the uttermoste of power and knowledge, for the beste advaunce- " mente of hir M^{ties} p'fites.

" Thearefore (my godd Lorde), havinge hir M^{ties} moste benefit in regarde, I hoape your " Lordship will take suche order as that I may not any wayes be indangered, nor incurr soe " greate disgrace, as that by passinge awaye a matter of soe great weighte to other ports, I " may be censured insufficiente for the trew and juste answeringe of hir Maties deuties in " hir custom, wch nowe (the goodes being heare in saftie) at my perill shall be suerly " answered.

" Your Lordship I dowbte not hath bin advertized that matters of very great valewe " have bin allredy sithence the comminge in of the goods imbeaseled by mariners and " others, whearby it may seeme probable that by often ladinge and unladinge and transport- " inge the same, it will much more be imbeaseled to hir M^{ties} greate disadvantage.

" There have bin divers merchants of the beste accompte in London whose factors " being heare have offered to deale for very great sommes, and to make suer paymente of " hir M^{ties} custome eather hear or in London, yf it shoud amounte to XX. or XL. thowsand " powndes, and at theyr owne hazardes to transporte the goods.

" And nowe forasmuche as divers shipes ar heare freighted and at this psente in " freightinge owte of the Caricke from Dartmuthe to London, some of two hundred tuns, " some of five hundred tunes, some more, some lesse, and doe take into them certayne " goodes, wares and marchandize, viz., in chestes, buts, pipes, packes and in divers other " formes of ladinge unknowen to the Customer for wante of Billes of Ladinge, by means " whereof hir M^{tie} may loose a greate parte of hir custom.

" And wheare alsoe certificats for every ship soe ladē will be required of the Customer " for the transportinge of the same to London, or els wheare, I shall be driven to make " uncertayne certificats contrary to the Statuts in theese cases p'vided, and contrary to the " orders in the Custom-howse, whiche I am bothe sworne and bownde in great bondes to " observe, beinge not able to expresse the qualitie nor quantitie of the contentes of a " number of chestes, packes, buts, pipes, canisters, cases, fardells and other pacchage.

" Thus cravinge your Lordshippes resolution what cowrse weare beste to be taken for " hir M^{ties} service and beste advantage before the dep'ture of the sayde shippinge owte of " this haven, I humbly take my leave. prayinge the Allmeighty to continewe your Lordship's " good helthe wth all happines. From Dartmuthe this seconde day of October, 1592.

" Yo^r Lo^p mowche bownd̄

" and ever redye at comandement,

" JAMES MERVIN.

" To the Reighte honorable
" my verye good Lorde
" the Lo. Burleighe, Lo.
" Heighe Tresorer of
" Englande.   " D.D. these."

---

* John Bland to Lord Burghley, Lansd. Mss. 70, Art. 40.
† Lansd. Mss. 70, Art. 66.

With Lord Burghley's reply I have not met; but it would appear from a further letter (*Lansd. Mss.* 70, *Art.* 70) from Sir James that a communication had been received directing him to continue the discharge of his duties as Collector of Customs and "to "courte the assistance of the Commissioners yf neede should soe requere." Further difficulties, however, arose, and if Sir James Mervyn's account as given in the following letter is to be credited, the fault did not rest with him, whose anxiety appears to have been to obtain payment of all dues "for hir Matie best advantage."

"My very good Lord, as I dought not but yor Lo^p will narolye loke (as greate reason "is you shuld) into everye man's acctions that hathe had dealing in the discharge of the "Carike here arrived, being a matter of soo great importance as it is, soo doo I assure "my selfe that yor Lo^p will looke for at my hands, being heere hir Matie Custom^r and "sooren to observe in like wyse the orders of the Custom howse set downe by your Lo: "direction, besyde yor comandem^t of late by yor letters sente hither to courte for the "assistance of the Comissioners (yf neede shuld soo requere) to have a trew and a p'fecte "reckoning for all hir Matie custom owte of the sayd Carike, wch by noo meenes wilbe "accomplesched as yt ought to be, or should have bin, yf I and the rest of the Officers of "Custome howse myght have ben suffered to have don that that appteynethe unto us and "owr office in all dewtye to have don.

"For ther is neyther custom^r, controuler, nor sercher but hathe bin tolde, being a ship "bord in the Carike, that that was noo place for him, but rather to be a shore, and there "to take a trew entree and note of all souche marchandice or other ware whatsoever shuld "be sett a land. And now som p'te thereof being sett a shore, the comissioners that ar "now at Dartmouthe, w^thowte cawling eyther the custom^r, or his deputye, the controwler or "sercher unto them, the seller doores (where mowche of thes marchandyce ar landed "being fast locte upon them) they breke up the chestes, and the packes, they sorte them "(as they saye), they sell them at ther plesure w^thowte the officers privitye. And for my "owne p'te I have bin sondry tymes denied (the seller doors being fast kepte) to cum among "them, or to be made accqueynted wth any of their doings. Alleging that they were busye, "praying me to spare them.

"Soo as I must be forced for hir Matie custom to accepte of as miche or as lyttell as "they lyst to make entre of, w^thowte myne owne privitie or my deputyes of ane thing.

"And what ther reson is whi they should in this sorte seclude me from being "accqueynted wth ther doings (yor Lo: letters inferring the contrary), I know not, nor can "imagen, unlesse yt be that I stand soren to see all things don uprightly for her Matie best "advantage, and they at ther lybertye upon ther awne discretion to doo what they seme "best. Thus having accqueynted yor Lo^p wth thes matt^rs, and having don, I protest my "best endevor for the advancement of hir Matie Custome, I hope I and the rest of the "Officers shalbe freed from blame, yf all things faule not owte as in right yt owte. And "soo, praying God for the p'servation of yor Lo^p helthe, I hu'bely take my leave. From "Dartmowthe this vj^th of Octobre, 1592.   "Yo^r Lo^p mowche bounden
"and ever redye at comandment,

"POSTSCRIPT.
"Mr. Midleton tellithe me that he will not only anser the custom above, of all suche "goods as ar to be transported from the Careke to London, but wold be his . . . . in "likewise (having made sale of as mich of the goods being sett at land as this comission "extendethe unto), and for the custom therof alsoo; wch must needs be a very great discredit "unto me yf yt shuld be all taken owte of my hands, that the wordle may thinke his bare "credit for ansering the custom of the goods leyed a shore to be in more securyte then

" upon my credyt and bonds, and therefore, unlesse yo[r] Lo[p] plesure be signefyed to the
" contrary I meene to make staye of soo miche of the sayde g>ods as shall amonte unto the
" custome of all the goods what soever soo landed.
" To the right honorable my verye good Lord, the
    " Lo. Burley, Lord high Tresorer of Inglande,
    " give thes at the Courte wth haste."

In a return made to the Privy Council, dated 28th November, 1595, of the names
of " Gentlemen of Accompte" not being citizens, lodging in London, I found that of
" S[r] James Marvyn, of the countie of Wilts, Knight," who appears to have been residing in
the Ward of Farringdon Without.*

In the year 1597 (39th Eliz.) Sir James again sat in Parliament as Member for
the Borough of Hindon. In July 1598 he was acting as one of the assistants at the
funeral of Sir Henry Knyvett, of Charlton, Wilts, as appears by the funeral certificate
of that Knight, to which he was a witness.†

In 1604 Sir James obtained a grant for life of the Mastership of Swans in the
Thames, together with the Bailliwick of Whittlesay Mere, and keeping of the swans there
and in the counties of Huntingdon, Cambridge, Lincoln, and Northampton.‡

After the death of his first wife, Sir James married DEBORA, daughter of James
PILKINGTON.§ Bishop of Durham, and widow of
Walter Dunche, of Little Wytnam, in the county of Berks.‖
By this lady he had no issue, and apparently she died
before him, as no mention is made of her in his will.

In the meantime the family estates had considerably
increased. To the property of Fountel and Compton
Basset had been added a considerable portion of the parish
of Tisbury, including the Manor of East Hacche ; and at
the time of his death Sir James Mervyn's landed property
must have been very considerable, both in extent and value.

There is, probably, no feeling more strongly im-
planted in the mind of a man who finds himself the
representative of an old family and in the possession of
an ancestral estate, than the desire that his name

---

* *Lansd. Mss.* **78**, *No.* 67, *Burghley Papers*; printed in Nichols' "*Collectanea Topographica et
Genealogica," vol. viii., p.* 207.
  † *Ms. Coll. Arm. "I. 16," fo.* 24.   ‡ *State Papers, Dom. Jas. I., vol. vi.*
  § In the Ms. Collections of John Charles Brooke, *Somerset Herald,* preserved in the College of
Arms ("*I.C.B., Yorkshire," vol. i., p.* 282), there are some particulars of the Pilkington family, from which
it appears that the Bishop, who was one of the six divines appointed for correcting the Book of Common
Prayer, was of the family of Pilkington, of Pilkington, co. Lancaster. He was appointed Bishop of
Durham by Queen Elizabeth, 1560, and continued in that See until his death on 23rd January, 1575-6.
In Surtees' *History of Durham* (*fo. ed.* 1816, *vol. i., p. lxxvj. et seq.*) there is a history of the Bishop and a pedigree
of his family, from which it appears that he was the son of Richard Pilkington, of Rivington, in the county
of Lancaster, and married Alice, daughter of Sir John Kingsmill, of the county of Hants. In a codicil to
his will, dated 21 Jan. 1575, the Bishop states that his daughter Debora is about to be married to Sir Thomas
Gargrave. The pedigree by Surtees gives him two daughters, Debora (bapt. at Auckland, 8 Oct.,
1564), who is there stated to have married Sir James Harrington, Knight, and Ruth, wife to Duntze, of the
county of Berks. This error is followed by Baines in his *History of Lancashire* (1836, *vol. iii., p.* 105).
According to Fuller, the two daughters, then children, were conveyed away in beggar's clothing at the
breaking out of the Northern Rebellion, to prevent the Papists killing them. " These," adds Fuller,
" afterwards were married with £4,000 a-piece ; the one to S[r] James Harrington, the other to Mr. Dunce
(Dunche), of Berkshire ; which portions the courtiers of that age did behold with envious eyes, for which the
Bishopric sped no whit the better."
  ‖ See Funeral Certificate of William Dunche, who died 11th May, 1597, printed in Nichols'
" *Collectanea Topographica et Genealogica," ed.* 1836, *vol. iii., p.* 293. See also Ashmole's "*Antiquities of
Berkshire," vol. i., pp.* 58 *et seq.,* for notices of the monumental inscriptions of the family of Dunche,
of Oke, in Little Wittenham Church, co. Berks.

and estate should be perpetuated; and especially does this passion rule, in cases where no male offspring exists to carry on, in the usual course of nature, the family descent. Sir James Mervyn possessed this feeling in its utmost intensity. His only child was a daughter, who had married into a noble house in whose name her's would be merged. The estates would, if given to her, devolve indeed upon those descended from him in blood, but the name, of which he was proud, would be lost. There would no longer be a "MERVYN of FOUNTEL-GIFFARD." To avert this almost certain contingency, every step was taken which could have been adopted. One of his name and near kindred (the son of Edmund Mervyn, his second cousin) was selected by Sir James as his "adopted son," and a marriage arranged between him and Sir James's grandchild, one of the daughters of his only child, Lucy, and to them a son was born in his lifetime, so that, when he died, his darling object appeared certain of accomplishment. He had lived to see a great-grandson on whom his estates would descend, and one bearing his own name and of his blood would again hold the broad acres of Fountel. But even yet there seemed in his mind a lingering doubt, a forecasting, as it were, of the future, for apparently not satisfied that the terms of the settlement which he had made on the marriage of Henry Mervyn with Christian Audley were sufficiently stringent, he called in aid all the legal acumen he could command in making his Will, in which he not only expressed in emphatic terms the object he had in view, but introduced provision upon provision which seemed to exhaust all possible contingencies, and provide for every adverse mischance. Humanly speaking, Sir James Mervyn had "tied up" his Manors, his lands, and his "chiefe house of "Fountel," and his household gods with them, so that they should remain "in the name and blood of Mervyn." However, "L'homme propose, mais Dieu dispose." Scarcely twenty years passed, before his house was the home of a stranger; its hearth knew a Mervyn no more; and at this day, no memorials remain of the family, not even the "comelie and decent tombe" which he directed his executors to erect over his father and mother. The house they inhabited, the "chiefe house," in which Sir James took such pride, has long since been levelled to the ground; and in its stead, three stately, but short lived piles, have succeeded each other. Even the ordinary parish records are wanting.

How it came to pass that the property was disposed of as it was, does not very clearly appear, inasmuch as the precise terms of the settlement made by Sir James on his granddaughter's marriage are not known; generally it is to be gathered from the will that the estates were settled in remainder, after his decease, upon Henry Mervyn and his heirs male. The terms of the settlement were evidently not restrictive enough to prevent Sir Henry selling Fountel, which he did in 1620,* to his wife's brother, Mervyn Lord Audley and Earl of Castlehaven, on whose attainder in 1631 it was granted by the Crown to Sir Francis Cottington, Bart., created Lord Cottington, in whose family it remained until sold to Mr. Alderman Beckford, whose son wasted fortunes in raising a magnificent fabric, of which, like its predecessor, the "chiefe house" of the Mervyns, not a vestige now remains.

---

* It has been previously mentioned that amongst the Ms. collections of the late G. F. Beltz, Lancaster Herald, preserved in the College of Arms. (*A. xviii. J. P.* 18), there are some Abstracts of Deeds which, in 1798, he made on examining them at Fonthill. The following is a transcript of one of those abstracts :—

"1 July, 18 James, 1620. Indenture between SIR HENRY MERVIN, of Fonthill, county Wilts, "Knight; SIR THOMAS THYNNE, of Longleate, county Wilts, Knight; SIR RICHARD NORTON, of "Rotherfield, co. Southampton, Knight; and HUGH HILL (*Sir James Mervyn's Nephew*), of Splott, "near Taunton, county Somerset, Esquire, first part; and the Right Honorable MERVYN, LORD "AUDLEY, EARL OF CASTLEHAVEN, and the Right Honorable ELIZABETH, LADY AUDELEY, "COUNTESS OF CASTLEHAVEN, wife of the said Earl, of the other part: Sir Henry Mervin, for con-"sideration of certain sums, hath granted to said Earl and Countess, and their heirs, executors, and "administrators, the Lordship and Manors of Fountell, which late were the messuage, lands, and "hereditaments of Sir James Mervin, Knight, deceased."

But I am somewhat anticipating events; Sir James' will,[*] bearing date the 1st April, 1610, was proved in the Prerogative Court of Canterbury on the 21st November, 1611, by the five executors therein named, viz.: Sir Mervin Audley (testator's grandson); Sir Thomas Thynne (husband of Mary Audley, one of testator's granddaughters, and grandfather of Mr. Thomas Thynne who in 1682 was assassinated by the agents of Count Kóningsmark); William Gibbes, of Parrat, Esquire; Henry Mervyn (testator's adopted son); and Hugh Hill (nephew to Sir James, being the son of his sister Eleanor, who married Robert Hill, of Yarde, near Taunton, in the County of Somerset).[†] By his will the testator directed that he should be buried in his Church of Fountel, in the tomb with his late wife Amye, then deceased, and he ordered his executors to erect a monument to the memory of his father and mother, who were buried in the Chancel of the said Church. Whether or not Sir James' requests were attended to, is not known, as Mr. Alderman Beckford, when he subsequently became possessor by purchase of the Fonthill Estate, pulled down the old Church, and destroyed, or, as some allege, *buried* [‡] the monuments which it contained !

Sir James Mervyn died 1st May, 1611, his only child Lucy having died in his lifetime, as appears by the Inquisition taken on his death.[§]

LUCY, or LUCIA MERVYN, daughter of Sir James Mervyn and Amye Clarke, was the wife of George Lord AUDLEY of Heleigh. Lord Audley, who

was born in 1551, was some time Governor of Utrecht in the Netherlands. He resided principally in Ireland, and was wounded at the Battle of Kinsale in December, 1601. (*Cal. Carew Mss.* 1601, *p.* 184.) In 1604, in consideration of his good services to " the late Queen" in Ireland, a grant was made to him of Crown lands of the clear yearly rental of one hundred pounds sterling current money of England. (*Cal. State Papers* "*Ireland*" 1603-6, *pp.* 258-9.) He was created EARL OF CASTLEHAVEN, in the peerage of Ireland, in 1617, in which year he died, aged 66 years. ‖

Lady Audley's mother, Amy Lady Mervyn, was, as I have mentioned, a widow when she married Sir James. By her first husband it would seem that she was mother of a daughter ELIZABETH, who married ANTHONY BOURNE, and by him had two daughters, Mary Bourne and Amy Bourne,¶ the latter of whom eventually married Fulke

* See APPENDIX *I. page* ix.
† *Ms. Coll. Arm.* " 2 *C.* 22," *p.* 285, Visit. Somerset, 1623.
‡ *Hoare's Hist. Wilts, vol.* 4. " *Dunworth Hundred," p.* 22.
§ *Inq. p. m. 27 June, 13 Jas. I.* (1616), *2nd part, No.* 130, APPENDIX I., p. iv.
‖ *Collins' Peerage,* ed. *Brydges,* 1812, *vol.* 6, *p.* 554. *Nicolas' Historical Peerage,* ed. *Courthope,* 1857, *p.* 35.
¶ Mary Bourne married Sir Herbert Croft, Knt. The following entries relating to this lady are from the Parish Registers of Sarsden :—
" Anno 1575. Quarto die D'bris, anno predicto, MARIA BOURNE baptizata."
" Anno 1591. Vicesimo quinto Maij Anno 1591. Herbertus Croft Mariam Bourne duxit, in facie " ecclesiæ: his testibus, Anthonio Bourne et Elizabetha uxore ejus, Sybilla Bushmede (or Burghende), " Elizabetha Parrye, Ezechiale Weston, et Gulielmo Bearde."
Herbert Croft (Mary Bourne's husband) was born about 1571, and was knighted at Theobalds on 7 May, 1603. He was the eldest son of Edward Croft, by Ann, dau. and heiress of Thomas Browne, of

Conway,* the second son of Sir John Conway, Kn^t (by Eleanor, daughter of Sir Fulke Greville, Kn^t), and brother of Edward Lord Conway.†

Anthony Bourne ‡ was the son of Sir John Bourne of Battenhall, in the county of Worcester, Knight, one of the principal secretaries of Queen Mary. He appears to have been an extravagant worthless man, who deserted his wife and children and went with a paramour to live abroad. Apparently Sir John Conway was a friend of the Bourne family, and interfered very actively to settle the spendthrift's pecuniary affairs. There are amongst the State Papers, *Dom. Series Elis.* (1582 *to* 1590), a great number of documents relating to the transactions between Sir John, and Anthony Bourne and his family. Our interest in them is, however, limited to some letters which passed between Lucy Lady Audley and her half-sister Elizabeth Bourne, which show the existence of much affection between them, and are interesting specimens of domestic letters of the period. They are three in number, commencing with one from Lucy Lady Audley, which shows her character in a pleasing light; it is dated 13th August 1584, from Fountel, where she was then living, and is as follows:—

"Nature (my good syster) shulde be greatlie weakened of her wonted fforces yf I
" shulde not by full convenient meanes, desire to knowe of yor well doynge, and good
" contentment; and ffor that all occasions of assurance are taken awaie by yor straunge
" aboades; Thees are to desire yo^n in regarde of my satisfaccon, and other more of
" yor well lovinge ffrendes, to returne me some ffew lynes to wyttnesse vnto vs what state
" yo^n nowe remaine in, and what course of liffe yo^n haue resolued one; yf to abandon
" yo^rself ffrom yor well wishinge ffrendes, then greeved shall wee be, to fforsee howe
" straungers, that loves and lyves wth spoille, will in the ende reiect yo^n. Yet thus muche,
" sweete syster, I am to lett yo^n vnde^rstande, that my home shall euer be to yo^n as
" yor owne, and if yo^n wolde but putte one the mynde sure to make triall of me and yt, I
" doubte not then but bothe wolde answere yor expectacon. And wth all yo^n shall doe me
" a greate curtesie; whoe am ffayne, for wante of a househoulde companion, to goe the
" oftner abrode; wch is the onlie impairinge of my good housewifferie. Thus wishinge in
" yo^n all good effectes, I ende, unsatisfiede till I see yo^n. Fountell this xxviii^th of
" Auguste, 1584.

" Yo^r assured ffrend
" and lovinge Syster,

" To my very lovinge Syster   " LUCYA AUDELEY.§
  "Mrs. BOURNE, geve thees."

Attlborough, co. Norfolk; and grandson of Sir James Croft, Privy Councillor and Comptroller of the Household of Queen Elizabeth, by Alice daughter and eventually co-heiress of Richard Warnecombe, of Ivington, in Herefordshire. Sir Herbert Croft (who became a monk, and died at Douay in 1622), by his wife Mary Bourne, had issue four sons, viz :—Sir William Croft, Knt., who was born in 1593, and was Gentleman of the Privy Chamber to Charles I.; Sir James Croft, Knt.; Herbert Croft, Bishop of Hereford; and Robert Croft, of Varpole, county Hereford. Bishop Croft's son was created a Baronet in 1671. (See *the Retrospective Review ; Lond.* 1827, *Second Series, vol.* I, *p.* 469, in which there is an interesting account of the Croft family.) The representative of the family and title is now (1873), Sir Herbert George Denman Croft, Bart.

* There does not appear to have been any issue of the marriage of Fulke Conway and Amy Bourne, whereupon her sister Mary, who, as before shown, was the wife of Sir Herbert Croft, became the sole heiress of her father Anthony Bourne. *Ms. Coll. Arms*, "*Vincent's Warwickshire," p.* 151.

† Letter, Council of State, dated from Oatlands, 11 Sep., 1587, to Sir John Conway, on behalf of Mrs. Elizabeth Bourne, who had complained against Lady Conway (Sir John's wife) for "wrongfully" matching her eldest daughter to Sir John's second son, and getting into her hands Mrs. Bourne's younger daughter (Amy) with the purpose to marry her to Sir John's youngest son. (*State papers, Dom. Series Elizabeth, vol.* 203, *No* 40.) It would seem that Anthony Bourne had assigned the guardianship of his daughters to Sir John Conway, upon the understanding that his eldest daughter was to be married to Edward Conway, Sir John's ELDEST son. See letter, Bourne to Conway, dated 1 March, 1583. (*State papers, Dom. Series Elizabeth, vol.* 159, *No.* 2.)

‡ *Ms. Coll Arms*, "*C.* 30," *p.* 54. He is also described in the Conway pedigree, given by Vincent in his Warwickshire (*Ms. Coll. Arms, p.* 51) as Anthony, son and heir of Sir John Bourne, Knt.; and Sir Harris Nicolas, in his notice of the Croft family (*Retrospective Review, New Series, vol. i., p.* 493), calls him "Anthony Bourne, of Holt Castle, in Worcestershire.

§ *State Papers, Dom. Eliz., vol. clxxii., No.* 116

The following would seem to be the answer to Lady Audley's sisterly letter :—

" To the Right Honorable her very loving sister Lucia Ladie Audley.

" My good Sister,

" I give you a million of thanks, that you would vouchsafe to enquire after my " well-doing. Amongst all my misfortunes, nothing had increased my grief so much " as the unkindness of my natural friends, of whom I have allways deserved well, and " find the contrary. When I was distressed, and forced and constrained by necessity to " seek the aid of friends to resist the injuries my unkind husband offered me himself, and " my children, to the utter overthrow of us all, I first sought my refuge amongst those which " by nature were most bound to have yielded me counsel and comfort, friendship, suc- " cour and assistance. Being refused through no ill deserts in myself, but through want " of good will in themselves, I was forced, my dear sister, and could not otherwise, to " accept aid amongst strangers who had some reason to offer it, and I more to take it, I " hope by such degrees as neither in my proceedings and government I have purchased any " disgrace to myself, loss to my children, or discomfort to my kin. I wish my hard fortune " and extremity had been harder and my relief less, so I had found my aid and comfort " amongst you. My life wears with no secret grief, neither have I any corrosive which con- " tinually consumes my health and quietness; but only the wickedness of my husband, and " of my nearest friends (that should be) in nature and alliance, which wrong me in my due " just deserts, and yll grace themselves in their unjust speeches and actions against me and " my reputation. If those well hoping friends which you now say foresee the harm and " spoil likely to grow to me in time by strangers, would accept me and mine into their " friendly care and protection, upon my earnest suit and reasonable offer to have done " mie good, and themselves no hindrance, I should now have been free from the danger they " fear and foresee, and I more near my comfort and safety amongst themselves. I wish " my fortune had been so favorable and my friends so loving. Sure the fault is not mine in " judgment of the world. It is unlikely I should ill deserve amongst my natural kin that " have behaved myself to gain good opinion, good grace, and friendship amongst strangers. " They are bound to yield me nothing of right. I can challenge nothing but by desert, and " I find nothing amiss (I thank God) in my life and fortune; but the lack of love in my " husband and mine own natural friends and allies. Now, I have discovered unto you, " sweet sister, the woe of my life. Let me tell you I live at Sarisden, where I mean to " secrete myself and my sorrows, until God give me a better estate. To whose Divine pro- " vidence I commend your health and safety, desiring you to recommend my humble duties " to my mother, to receive my friendly commendations to yourself, and my thankful heart " into your bosom.

" Saresdon, November, 1584. Yoʳ loving sister and assured friend, though most " unfortunate. " E. B."[*]

Lady Audley appears to have combined much kindness of heart with shrewd business-like views, if we may judge from the following letter to Sir John Conway in reply to one from him written at the instance of her worthless brother-in-law, claiming from her payment of a sum of money :—

" I vnderstand by yoʳ lʳre (Sʳ John Conway) as also by my brothʳ Bornes, that he " is fallen to repentance of his good dedes for the mayntennce of his baill, and therefore " wold have me to send hym the mony, wᵃ voluntaryly he gave me, and I unwillinglie " kepte. The wᵃ as I denye not, but that owte of hundreds wᵃ (in brotherly sorte as I " toke it) he offryd me, I receiveyd by way of lone the smale some he nowe challengethe. " So I assure yoᵘ on my credit, that I offringe to render the same wᵃ in one weke after, he " refusyᵈ to take it at my hands, and gave it me frelye, not wᵗowte challenge of greate " unkyndnes for the profer. And therefore can not be pᵉswaydyd but that this demaund is " rather to make me the blaser of his liberallytie, then that he will iustefie on his credit " that I owe it hym. Nevᵗhelesse, I acknowledge in curtesie to owe hym as fryndly a " tourne, wᵃ I mean to resᵗve, but tyll I see hym bent to ymploy it better then nowe " I knowe he will, by what tyme I fear he will have more neade than nowe he hathe. " And, therefore, I pray yoᵘ tell hym from me, that he hath treasure in store, wᵗʰ the

* State Papers, Dom. Elis., vol. clxxv. No. 15. Mrs. Elizabeth Bourne would seem to have died in 1599. as I judge by the following entry in the Sarsden Register :—" Anno 1599. Augusti vicesimo-quinto. Elizabetha Bourne, sepulta."
* State Papers, Dom. Elis. vol. ccxxxiii., No. 42.

F

22

" increase. But it is dedicatyd to so holy a use as he may not have it to profhane vpon so
" badd an Idoll as he dothe nowe vowe all his offrings to. And so wth my frindly
" comendacons and well wyshing to yo' self and yo' good wyf I ende.
"·Ffountehill the 13 of August,
" To my good frynd   " Yo' redy ffrinde,
    " Sr John Conway. Knyght."

Lucy Mervyn Lady Audley had seven children, two sons and five daughters, viz.:
    I. MERVYN Lord Audley and second Earl of Castlehaven, who was attainted of
felony, whereupon his title and estates (including the Fountel property) were
forfeited to the Crown. At his death in 1631, he left by his first wife
ELIZABETH, daughter and co-heiress of Benedict BARNHAM, three sons and
three daughters, viz. :—
        I. JAMES, who, by Letters Patent, 3rd June, 1634, had a new creation
to the title of Baron Audley and Earl of Castlehaven, and was,
in 1678, by a special Act of Parliament, restored to the Barony
of Audley, which had been forfeited on his father's attainder, and
was the third Earl of Castlehaven. It would seem that there
was some difficulty connected with the grant of the Fountel
Estates by the Crown to Lord Cottington, as I find that
this Lord Castlehaven, in 1633, confirmed it by a deed of
arrangement, in consideration of being allowed to retain the
Manors of Bishopstrowe in Wilts, and of Stalbridge in Dorset,
with other property in Ireland.* Lord Castlehaven distinguished
himself under the Duke of Ormond, in Ireland, and, in 1649,
was chosen General of the Irish forces against Cromwell. He
subsequently, on the reduction of the Kingdom by the Parliamentary Army, went to France, where he remained until the
restoration of Charles II. He died at Kilcash, in Ireland, 11th
October, 1684, s.p., and was succeeded by his brother Mervyn.†
        II. GEORGE, who, being a Benedictine monk, was passed over in the
Act of Restoration of 1678.
        III. MERVYN, who, on his brother's death, succeeded as 21st BARON
AUDLEY, and 4th EARL OF CASTLEHAVEN, died in 1686.‡
        1. LUCY, married *first* to John ANKETELL, of Compton, co. Wilts, and
of Newmarket, co. Cork; *secondly*, to Gerald FITZMAURICE,
brother of Lord Kerry.
        2. DOROTHY, the wife of Edmund Butler, Viscount MOUNTGARRET.
        3. FRANCES, married Richard BUTLER, brother of James, Duke of
Ormond.
    II. SIR FERDINANDO TOUCHET, who was made Knight of the Bath at the
creation of Henry, Prince of Wales§, and is mentioned in his grandfather's

* *Hoare's Hist. of Wilts, vol. iv., Dunworth Hundred, p.* 134.
† *Collins' Peerage, by Sir Egerton Brydges, ed.* 1812., *vol. vi., p.* 555.
‡ The Earldom of Castlehaven became extinct on the death, in 1777, of John, sixth Earl, and the
Barony of Audley is now (1873) dormant between the two daughters and co-heiresses of George Baron
Audley, who died 18th April, 1872.
§ *Collins' Peerage, ed. Brydges, vol. vi., p.* 554.

(Sir James Mervyn) will. He was a staunch Roman Catholic, and a "suspected" person. From a letter written by Sir Edward Dering,* Lieutenant-Governor of Dover Castle, to Secretary Dorchester, 17 February, 1630, it appears that Sir Ferdinando had landed at Dover, and attempted to pass into England disguised as a servant, in order to avoid taking the oath of allegiance; he was, in consequence, arrested and imprisoned in the Fleet Prison, from which place he presented a petition to the Privy Council praying that he might be set at liberty, and the prayer of his petition was granted. He married the widow of Sir John Rodney, of Pilton, in the county of Somerset, Knight.

1. ANNE, the eldest daughter of the Earl of Castlehaven and Lucy Mervyn, married Edward BLOUNT, of Harleston, county Derby.

2. ELIZABETH, married, *first*, Sir John STAWELL. of Stawel, co. Somerset, Knt. *Secondly*, Sir Thomas GRIFFIN, of Dingley, co. Northampton, Knt.†

3. MARY, the third daughter, was the first wife of Sir Thomas THYNNE,‡ of Longleat, co. Wilts.

4. CHRISTIAN, who married SIR HENRY MERVYN, of Petersfield county Southampton, Knt. See the 𝕯𝖚𝖗𝖋𝖔𝖗𝖉 𝕬𝖇𝖇𝖊𝖞 𝕭𝖗𝖆𝖓𝖈𝖍.

5. ELEANOR, who *first* married Sir John DAVIES,§ Knight, the King's Attorney-General in Ireland, and *secondly* Sir Archibald DOUGLAS, Knight. By her first husband she had a daughter, LUCY DAVIES, who married Ferdinando, sixth Earl of Huntingdon.

---

* *State Papers, Dom. Series, Ch. I.*

† The grandson of this marriage, Sir Edward Griffin, was created, in 1688, Baron Griffin, of Braybroke Castle, co. Northampton, which title became extinct on the death without issue of Edward, third Baron, in 1742. (*Edmondson's Baronagium Genealogicum, vol. vi., p. 48.*)

‡ There were three sons issue of this marriage, two of whom died s. p.; the third, Sir Thomas Thynne, was the father of Thomas Thynne, of Longleat (who was murdered at the instance of Count Konigsmark), and of two daughters; Stuart, who married Sir Edward Baynton of Bromham, Baynton, co. Wilts, K.B.; and Elizabeth, the wife of John Hall, of Bradford, co. Wilts.

§ The family of Davys or Davies were settled at Chicksgrove, in Tisbury (a parish adjoining Fountel-Giffard), co. Wilts, *temp.* Edw. VI. Sir John Davies was a distinguished member of the family. He was born 1569, and died 1626, having been Attorney-General for Ireland from 1603 to 1616. (See *Chalmers' Biog. Dict.*) There was a subsequent connection between the Mervyn and Davies families. Matthew Davies, of Shaftesbury and of the Middle Temple, and M.P. for Whitchurch (Sir John Davies' nephew), having married Anne (daughter of Edmund) Mervyn, who died in 1657, and was buried in Tisbury church.

CORRIGENDA.

DURFORD-ABBEY BRANCH.

Page 25, line 20.   After " Reader in " insert "the," and after " Autumn " insert " of."

Page 32, line 34.   " £3,100 " should be " £3,500."

Page 32, line 39.   After " the French ships which were " delete " engaged " and substitute " employed."

Page 35, line 9.   After " did not " delete " return " and substitute " reach."

      „   line 19.   The words " durst hazard " should be " *dursn't*" (durst *not*).

DALLAWAY, in his History of the Western Division of the County of Sussex (*4°* *Lond.* *1815. vol. 1 pp. 212, 213*) states that the Abbey of Durford was founded in 1160 by Henry Hosatius, or de Horsé, for Monks of the order of Præmonstratensians, or Canons of St. Augustine, and that their endowment was valued at the suppression (when the Abbey was surrendered by John Simpson, the Abbot), at £98 4s. 5d. [*Dugdale*] or £108 13s. 9d. [*Speed*] and in 1538 the site, &c., was included in grants made to William, Earl of Southampton. Upon the death of Lord Southampton the Crown resumed, and re-granted the demesnes of the Abbey to Sir EDMUND MERVYN, *in capite;* and, the Sussex Historian adds, " from his descendants it passed to the Bettesworth family." It has been before shewn* that HENRY MERVYN, the great-grandson of Sir EDMUND, sold the estate (possibly to his brother-in-law Peter Bettesworth, who had married his sister Elizabeth Mervyn) and invested the purchase-money in property connected with the Fountel estate. Mr. Dallaway states that at the date of his History (1815) little could be traced of the original buildings of the Abbey, all of which had been applied to the purposes of a large farm ; but he adds that the house was still capacious and that the pointed windows had been walled up when it became the residence of Sir Edmund.

SIR EDMUND MERVYN, Knt., second son of WALTER MERVYN of Fountel Giffard, by ELIZABETH MOMPESSON, and grantee from the Crown of Durford Abbey, was brought up to the Bar, and according to Mr. Foss,† received his legal education in the Middle Temple, where he was elected Reader in Autumn, 1523, and again in Lent, 1530, and was raised to the degree of the Coif in the Michaelmas Term of the following year. Henry VIII., on February xi, 1539, made him one of his Serjeants, and on November 23, 1540, constituted him a Judge of the King's Bench.‡ By some letters addressed to him by the Council, he seems to have been then resident in the neighbour-hood of Racton, in Sussex. § Little (adds Mr. Foss) is told of him by the reporters, either as an Advocate or a Judge ; but he was continued in his seat on the accession of Edward VI. ; and is frequently named in that reign in the criminal proceedings which have

---

     * *Will of Sir James Mervyn,* APPENDIX I., p. ix.

     † " *The Judges of England,*" by Edward Foss. *Lond.: Murray,* 1864.

     ‡ *Dugdale's Orig.* 216, *Chron. Ser.*   Sir Edmund was knighted at the Parliament 33
Hen. VIII.   *Cott. Ms. Claud. C.* 111. *fo.* 134ᵇ.

     § *Acts Privy Council, vii.* 175, 179.

been preserved in the *Baga de Secretis*. Dugdale does not introduce him as a Judge under Queen Mary, but it is evident that she continued him in his place, as he is one of the Special Commissioners named upon the trial of Sir Andrew Dudley and others for High Treason, on August 18, 1553.[*]

It may be inferred, therefore, (continues Mr. Foss), that he was in no way concerned in the attempt to change the succession of the Crown. His name was not attached either to King Edward's will, or to the other instrument which Northumberland required the Councillors to subscribe. It is possible, however, as Sir James Hales is always noticed as the only Judge who refused to affix his signature, that Mervyn was at the time prevented by illness from attending; for though named in the Commission of August 18, it does not follow that he was present at the trial, and he is certainly never mentioned after that date.

Sir Edmund married twice, his first wife being, as appears by the Visitation of Sussex taken in 1530[†] (Ms. Coll. Arm. "D. 13"), ELEANOR, daughter of Thomas WELLES, by whom he had issue five sons and three daughters.

I. WILLIAM MERVYN, named in the Visitation, is also mentioned in his father's will, at the date of which (1550) he was married and had issue, as the testator directs his then wife, Elizabeth, to make a new lease to his "son William Mervin and *his* son, of the house in which he now dwelleth." In Vincent's Pedigree,[‡] William Mervyn is made the fourth son.

II. EDMUND MERVYN, also named in the Visitation of 1530. He was appointed one of his father's executors, and is in the will called "Parson of Bramshot." Vincent places him in the Pedigree as eldest son.

III. EDWARD MERVYN, named in, and living at the date of, the Visitation of 1530; but not mentioned in Vincent's Pedigree, nor in his father's will. He is probably the Edward Marvyn who is stated by Willis (*Notitia Parliamentaria*) to have sat in Parliament as Member for Petersfield, co. Southampton in the fifth Parliament of Elizabeth (1586-8.)

IV. FRANCIS MERVYN, was living at the date of the Visitation before referred to, and he is inserted by Vincent as the second son. No mention of him is made in his father's will.

V. NICHOLAS MERVYN, appears in the Visitation of 1530, and is also named by Vincent, who places him as third son. Sir Edmund's will is silent as to any son of this name.

1. ELIZABETH MERVYN, living at the date of the Visitation of 1530. Vincent gives Sir Edmund Mervyn two daughters of this Christian name—one by each wife; and the daughter of Elizabeth Pakenham, he states, was married to John Rous, of Devonshire. The *latter* statement, however is incorrect, as Sir Edmund in his will mentions his daughter "Eleanor" as being the wife of Rous.

2. ELEANOR MERVYN, named in the Visitation of 1530, appears by her father's will (at the date of which, 1550, she was living) to have married Richard ROUS, of Rogate, co. Sussex, second son of Roger Rous, of Modbury, Devon, whom Sir Edmund by his will appointed an executor; an appointment which, however, he revoked by a codicil. This marriage and its issue are recorded in the original Visitation of Sussex, in 1570, Ms. Coll. Arm., "G. 18," p. 73[ᵇ] (See also Westcote's Devon, p. 581.)

3. AGNES MERVYN, named by Vincent, and mentioned in, and living at the date of, the Sussex Visitation of 1530; but not referred to by name in her father's will.

Sir EDMUND's second wife, who survived him and is named in his will, was

---

† See APPENDIX II., p. iv.   [*] 4 *Report Pub. Rec. App.* ii., 218—235.   ‡ Ms. Coll. Arm.: "*Vincent's Coll. Sussex*, 121," p. 393.

ELIZABETH, third daughter and co-heiress of Sir Edmund PAKENHAM, Knight,* by

whom, according to Vincent, he had three children—two sons and one daughter.‡
The Visitation of 1530 only records the two sons, viz². :—

> I. HENRY MERVYN, who appears to have succeeded his father at Durford
> and of whom hereafter.
> II. GEFFERY MERVYN, living at the date of the Visitation of 1530, but no
> mention is made of him in his father's will.

The will§ of Sir Edmund is dated 24th July 1550, and he thereby desires to be
buried in the south aisle of Bramshot church (in the county of Southampton) where
" Sir Edmund Pakenham, Knight, and my Lady late his wife lye."‖

The testator mentions his wife Elizabeth, his daughter Edith, wife of his son Henry,
to which son he gives " all the plate that I had with the marriage of his wife, that was
Sir Anthony Windsor's." He also gives to his son Henry his " Wiltshire gelding." The
will names testator's daughter Elenor Rous ; his cousin, Nicholas Tichborne ; his cousin,
Mary Burleigh, to whom he gives a legacy of 20 marks " for her marriage" ; his cousin,
Sir John Mervyn, Knight, whom he appoints supervisor of his will, with a direction that
he is to take testator's books of law, for his " cousin James Mervin, in recompence of
such reckoning as be between him and me." Sir Edmund also mentions his son William
Mervyn, and *his* son. The will appoints testator's " cousin, William Mervyn," " Edmund
Mervyn, Parson of Bramshot," and Richard Rous, executors ; but, by a codicil, after
reciting that he had appointed his " nephew William Mervyn," and his (testator's) son
Edmund, executors, revokes the appointment, and names his " nephew, John Mervyn,"
his " nephew, William Mervyn," and his son, Edmund, executors ; adding, " my said
son Rowse not to be one, because not of blood unto me, and of myne own name."

---

* A full pedigree of the Pakenham family will be found in the College of Arms Mss. " *Vincent's
Baronage,* 20."

† These shields are facsimiles of drawings illustrating the Pakenham pedigree in " *Vincent's Baronage*"
in the College of Arms, and represent three of the four coats which Lady Mervyn was entitled to quarter
with her paternal arms. The first is CREKE (*Sable, a hand ppr. in a maunche arg. and or grasping a fleur
de lis of the last*) impaling GLANVILLE (*Arg. a chief indented az.*) The second, the coat of BLUNDUS
(*Lozengy or and sa.*)

‡ Vincent mentions a daughter, ELIZABETH MERVYN: who, he states, married John Rous, of
Devonshire, but of whom there is no mention in the Visitation of 1530. Vincent has evidently mistaken her
for Eleanor, the daughter of Sir Edmund's first marriage, who was the wife of Richard Rous. Dallaway
(*Hist. Sussex, vol. i., p.* 212), on the authority of Vincent, gives a daughter Elizabeth, sister to Sir Henry,
married to Peter Bettesworth, of Fyning, Rogate ; but this is also a mistake for Elizabeth, the daughter
of Edmund Mervyn, of Petersfield, hereinafter mentioned.

§ See APPENDIX II., p. ii.

‖ On application to the Rector of Bramshot, for information as to the existence of any monumental memorial, the Reverend Mr. Bellas replied that there was not anything in the church or register
book (which commenced in 1560) likely to lead to the discovery of the burial of any members either of the
Mervyn or Pakenham family.

Sir Edmund's will was proved in London on the 16th November, 1553. On his death he appears to have been succeeded at Durford by

HENRY MERVYN, his elder son, by his second marriage with Elizabeth Pakenham. This Henry Mervyn married EDITH, daughter of Sir Anthony WINDSOR,

Knight, (the brother of Andrew Lord Windsor, of Stanwell,)* by Elizabeth, daughter of Sir Henry Lovell, of Harting, co. Sussex, Kn[t] The only recorded issue† of the marriage of Henry Mervyn and Edith Windsor was a son, Edmund Mervyn, who died in his father's lifetime, and of whom hereafter.

Henry Mervyn married secondly JANE, daughter of . . . whom he appointed sole executrix of his will, dated 6 March, 1609, and proved in London 20 May, 1614. (*See* APPENDIX II., p. iii.).

EDMUND MERVYN, son of Henry Mervyn and Edith Windsor, was of Durford Abbey, and subsequently of Petersfield, co. Hants. He is mentioned in the

will of Sir James Mervyn, of Fountel-Giffard, as his " cozin Edmund Mervyn," then deceased. By the inquisition taken after his death it was found that he held the site of the late monastery of Durford, with the demesne lands of Durford, in Hartinge and Rogate, and other property in Petersfield. (*See Inq. p.m.* 2 *Jas. I.* (1604–5), *Part* 12, *No.* 187, *and* 12 *Jas. I., Part* 2, *No.* 175‡)

He married ANNA, daughter of William JEPHSON, of Froyle, in the co. of Southampton (by Mary, the daughter of John Dannett, of Dannett's Hall, in com. Lancaster, and widow of Thomas Wotton, of the co. of Kent), and grandson of William Jephson, to whom Henry VIII. granted the Manor of Froyle ; and which Anna Mervyn was the sister of Sir John Jephson, of Froyle, who, for his first wife, married Elizabeth, daughter and heir of Thomas Norris, son of Henry Baron Norris, of Rycote. (*Visit. Hants* 1622–1634, *Ms. Coll. Arm.*, " *C.* 19," *p.* 82.)

By his will,‡ dated 8 Sept., 1604 (proved 20 Feb., 1605) Edmund Mervyn devised all his estates in Sussex and Hants to his wife Anna for life, to enable her to bring up his children then unmarried, and to pay them 400 marks as marriage portions, and he devised all his said estates to his " son and heir," Henry Mervin, after the death of his wife. She survived him, and made her will,§ dated 31 May, 1625, and proved in July, 1628.

---

* See Ms. Coll. Arm.: "*Philipott's Mullett*," *p.* 174[b] where there is a full Pedigree of the Windsor family.

† There would, however, appear to have been other issue of this marriage, as in the Parochial Registers of Rogate, co. Sussex, appear the following entries :—

BAPTISMS. 1562, May, Jane, daughter of Henry Mervyn, Esquire.
           1563, November 10, Henry, sonne of Henry Mervyn, Esquire.
           1565, April 19, John, sonne of Henry Mervin, Esquire.
           1567, November 23, Catherine, daughter of Henry Mervin, Esquire.
BURIALS. 1563, November 27, George, son of Henry Mervyn, Esquire.
           1565, April 19, John, sonne of Henry Marvyn, Esquire.
           1570, January 9, Jane Mervin.
           1570, January 16, Catherine Mervin.

Ex. rel[e]. Rev[e]d. J. S. Barrow, of Rogate, 3 *Oct.* 1872.

‡ See APPENDIX II., p. ii.   § See APPENDIX II., p. iii.

The issue of the marriage of Edmund Mervyn (who died 9 Sept. 1604) and Anna Jephson were :—

I. SIR HENRY MERVYN, baptized at Rogate, 26th December, 1583, and of whom hereafter.

II. WILLIAM MERVYN, baptized at Rogate, 16 Feb.; buried there 9th March, 1586.

III. EDMOND MERVYN, baptized at Rogate 15 Nov.; buried there 20 Dec., 1593.

IV. FRANCIS MERVYN, baptized at Rogate 23 May, 1599, and buried the same day.

V. EDMUND MERVYN. According to the pedigree preserved in Ulster's Office, Dublin, amongst the Mss. of the late Sir William Betham, there was a second son of this name who is described as of Fonthill and Dublin, and buried in St. John's Church, Dublin. (See his Funeral Certificate, APPENDIX II. p. iv.) Betham states that his will was dated 11 August, 1634, and he died the 14th of the same month. He married MARY, the daughter and heir of Sir Alexander CLIFFORD*, of London, Kn⁺ and had issue two children :—

    I. CLIFFORD MERVYN.

    1. FRANCES MERVYN, who is stated in her father's funeral certificate to have been then living in London.

VI. PHILIP MERVYN.†

VII. RICHARD MERVYN.†

1. BLANCHE MERVYN (mentioned in her mother's will, 1625), was the second wife of JOHN EVATT, Dean of Elphin in Ireland. He died in 1634. There was issue of the marriage three sons and two daughters, all unmarried at their father's death‡.

2. ELIZABETH MERVYN, baptized at Rogate 2 April, 1582, and mentioned in her mother's will as the wife of Peter BETTESWORTH, to whom she was married at Rogate 29 July, 1600.

3. ANNE MERVYN, baptized at Rogate 17 Oct. 1585.§

4. DOROTHY MERVYN, baptized at Rogate 19 March, 1594 ; buried there 14 Feb. 1598.

5. CATHERINE MERVYN, baptized at Rogate 7 Sept. 1600.

SIR HENRY MERVYN, son and heir of EDMUND MERVYN and ANNA JEPHSON, born in 1583, was, as we have seen,‖ the cousin and "adopted son" of Sir James Mervyn, of Fountel-Giffard, to whose principal estates, including Fountel, he succeeded, by virtue of a settlement made on his marriage with Sir James' grandchild, CHRISTIANA, one of the daughters of George, Baron AUDLEY and Earl of Castlehaven, by Lucy Mervyn. In 1614, Sir Henry sat as M.P. for Wotton Basset,¶ and in October, 1617, he, being then of Fountel, obtained a grant from Charles Howard, Earl of Nottingham, K.G., Lord High Admiral, of the office of Admiral and Captain-General of the Narrow Seas, from the Thames to the Scilly Islands, which appointment was, eight months afterwards, confirmed by Letters Patent under the Great Seal.** For this office, Sir Henry, following what appears to have been the very general practice of that period, paid upwards of £3,000.†† The

Seal of Sr. Henry Mervyn impressed on Letter from him to the Admiralty Commissioners, 13 Nov. 1636.‡‡

---

* Sir Alexander Clifford's will is dated 18 May, 1621, and proved by his relict, Dame Jane Clifford, 1621-2. He refers to his daughter Mary and her husband Edmund Mervyn, and gives directions to be buried in Bobbing Church, co. Kent. (P.C.C. Regr. 4 Savile.)   † Betham's pedigree.

‡ See his Funeral Certificate in Betham's Irish Funeral Certificates preserved in the College of Arms, London, vol. vi, p. 187. See APPENDIX II., p. iv.

§ Possibly this Anne Mervyn was the wife of Sir Richard Aldworth, of Newmarket, co. Cork, Knᵗ and Provost Marshall of the Province of Munster, who died at Dublin 21 June, 1629. His Fun. Cert. states that he "had to wife Anne Mervyn," and had no issue. See Betham's Fun. Ent. preserved in Coll. Arm., London, vol. iv. No. 145.

‖ See ante, p. 18.   ¶ Willis " Notitia Parliamentaria."

** State Papers, Dom. Jas. I., vol. xli.   †† State Papers, Dom. Ch. I., vol. vi.   ‡‡ See p. 35.

emoluments of the office were a fee of twenty shillings a day, and wages for sixteen men at ten shillings a month, "without check or muster." The investment does not appear to have been a particularly good one, if we are to understand that the emoluments were limited to his pay, which, as will be hereafter -seen, was by no means regularly met; but there is no doubt that the indirect gains attaching to the position he held, from prize money and other sources, were considerable; for later on, we find him writing that if the East India Company desire a convoy from Sicily, where one of their vessels had put in, he begs that he "may be thought of," and again, in recommending one John Fortescue, for a vacant gunner's place on board one of the ships of his fleet, he thinks it necessary to accompany his recommendation by a very pointed assertion, " I vow to you that my recommendation has no price," as though the rule which then prevailed were the converse of that which he had adopted in the particular instance. I fear the adage "*Qui s'excuse, s'accuse,*" was applicable.

At the time when Sir Henry Mervyn obtained his office, James I. was paying considerable attention to the increase of the Navy of England, which, in Elizabeth's time, consisted of thirty-three ships, besides pinnaces, to which the King, between 1618 and 1623, added nine or ten new ships. Some authorities have gone so far as to assert that the English naval power at that time was little inferior to the Dutch, who, however, possessed a very much larger quantity of shipping, although probably of inferior burthen to that belonging to the English. ·

The first record I find of Sir Henry Mervyn's exploits at sea is in 1622, when he took a Dutch East Indiaman (said to be worth a hundred thousand pounds). His excuse for this act of hostility against a friendly power, was the fact that the Dutchman did not, upon being challenged, "strike sail." Upon the request, however, of the States Ambassador, the prize was restored; so that the capture at all events did not prove profitable to the Admiral, who did not long remain undisturbed in the exercise of his duties; for, in March 1623, he got into difficulties with his Government, in consequence of a Rochelle vessel having captured a Dunkirk ship laden with treasure from Spain, and bound for Calais. The duty of conveying the Rochelle ship; having on board the celebrated Huguenot leader Benjamin Soubise, the brother of the Duke de Rohan, had been confided to Sir Henry, against whom the accusation made, both by the French and Spanish Ambassadors, was, that he had not only connived at the capture by Mons'. St. Ravie, who commanded the Rochelle ship, but that he had participated in the booty.

So persistent were the demands of the two Ambassadors to the Government, that Sir Henry and his Vice-Admiral, Sir William St. John, might be punished for the part that they had taken in the business, that a Commission was appointed to inquire into the alleged breach of violence towards countries with whom England was at that time in friendly alliance. The Commission commenced its inquiries, and Sir Henry left his command, giving out that he was going to Newmarket (where the King then was), in order to justify himself to his Sovereign; but the Vice-Admiral remained on board his ship.

Instead, however, of going to Newmarket, Mervyn made his way to Portsmouth; and as the authorities had some fear of his escaping, a special Privy Council summons was sent to him by Secretary Sir Edward Conway,[*] directing him to leave his ship, the " Garland," in charge of his officers, and proceed to London, to answer the complaints made against him; and a similar communication was sent to Sir William St. John, who was in command of the "Adventurer"; and on the 15th March both Admirals were in a messenger's "*care*." Sir Henry applied for leave to make a voluntary confession to the King, which he alleged would be much fuller than could be extorted from him by examination. He was not, however, allowed to have the audience with James which he desired, in consequence of the renewed application by the French and Spanish representatives that

---

* Sir Edward Conway was the son of Sir John Conway, who is referred to in connection with Lucy Mervin, Lady Audley, (See ꬵountel-Ꝿiffarð branch, p. 20), whose grandniece, of the half-blood, Amye Bourne, married Sir Edward's younger brother, Fulke Conway. Sir Edward was created, in 1624, Baron, and subsequently, Viscount Conway, and became Lord President of the Council; he died in 1630.

justice should be done on the offenders. Accordingly several preliminary steps were adopted by the Government with a view to bring the case before the Admiralty Court; and in the meantime the two Admirals were committed to the Marshalsea on Privy Council warrants. Apparently, however, the steps which the Government had taken were not satisfactory to the French Ambassador; for we find him, in May, 1623, again applying to Secretary Calvert, and requesting "that His Majesty may be reminded to punish Sir " Henry Mervin and Sir William St. John." Notwithstanding the Ambassadorial urgency, nothing was in reality done in the trial beyond preferring Articles, to which Sir Henry put in his answer, and thereupon claimed to be released on bail. This claim was remitted by the Judge of the Admiralty Court to the consideration of the King, on the ground that if it was to be understood that he had been committed for *punishment*, the allowance of bail depended on the King's pleasure, adding that if he was only retained for *safe custody*, then he was entitled to bail. The appeal to the King resulted in an authority to the Admiralty Judge to discharge the prisoners on "good bail." During the two years, 1623 to 1625, Sir Henry remained suspended, if not actually removed, from his office; but no steps were taken to bring him to trial.

In the meanwhile the position of England towards Spain had materially altered. The Duke of Buckingham had, by the exercise of his all powerful influence over James and the Prince of Wales, succeeded in breaking off the intended marriage of Charles and the Infanta, and with it all friendly alliance with her country; whilst an effort was made to induce the French King to enter into a league with England for an avowed war against Spain. This effort resulted in an expedition in 1625 under Captain Pennington, made with the ostensible purpose of enabling the French King (who had at that time no naval force) to make an attack upon the Genoese, who were the firm allies of the Spanish monarchy.

The failure of the effort made to place an English naval force at the disposal of the French Government, arose, as is well known, from a suspicion on the part of Captain Pennington, and the sailors under his command, that they were in fact intended to operate, not against the Genoese but against La Rochelle, the stronghold of the Huguenots, whose extermination the French King Louis and his minister Richelieu were bent on effecting. Whether or not the suspicion was well founded is an historic doubt, for the solution of which a new chapter in English history has to be written.[*] The desire which prevailed in March, 1623, on the part of the English Government to maintain good relations with Spain had therefore ceased. The representations of the Ambassadors of that country no longer met with a subservient respect; the influence which had obtained the imprisonment of Sir Henry Mervyn had ceased, and with it any desire on the part of the Government to prosecute the accusation which had been made against him.

Influenced, probably, by considerations arising out of the altered circumstances, Sir Henry Mervyn, in September, 1625, petitioned the King, alleging that he had given £3,500 for the office from which he had been suspended without any known cause; and stating that he was suffering under the want of necessary food and raiment, "accompanied " with shame and dishonour;" concluding his petition by praying that the King would not appoint any one else in his place, without ordering the repayment of the money the petitioner had so paid. The petition appears to have been referred to Secretary Sir John Coke, the draft of whose report of " The true state of Sir Henry Mervyn's case " is preserved[†] in which he states that the Admiral was charged by the French Ambassador with having assisted the Rochellers in spoiling the French, and with having participated in the

---

[*] It would be beyond my province, here, to enter upon the consideration of the arguments whether Charles and Buckingham deliberately gave over the ships for use against the Protestants; or whether, they were dealing double with the French Government; but those who feel an interest in the question, will do well to consult the version given of the expedition by Mr. John Forster, in his Life of Sir John Elliot, and the counter view put forward by Mr. Samuel R. Gardiner, in a communication addressed by him to the " Athenæum " newspaper of the 14 December, 1872, under the head of " The True Story of the Ships lent by Charles I. to serve against the French Protestants."

[†] *State Papers Dom. Ser., Chas.* I, *vol. viii.*, 18.

booty; that King James, after enquiry, had removed Sir Henry from his employment, and directed a judicial proceeding; but that, the Lord Treasurer Middlesex not supplying the necessary money, the business was not further prosecuted.

Apparently no relief was afforded to Sir Henry upon his petition, for we find him again petitioning* the King, entreating that, after twenty years spent in the service of the King and his father, "he be not suffered to perish under the King's displeasure," adding plaintively that "bereaved of friends by the King's frown," and "defrauded of an estate "by a disobedient son,"† he beseeches the King to preserve him "and his three daughters" from dishonorable wants by bestowing on him £200.

Whether it was the effect of the petitions, or some influence brought to bear on the Duke of Buckingham (probably the latter), does not appear; but we find that, early in 1626, his restoration to office is discussed. Sir Henry Palmer had, it would seem, been appointed Admiral of the Narrow Seas in Mervyn's stead; and, in April of that year, he is evidently in fear of being displaced; for, writing to Secretary Nicholas, he says that he has heard rumours that Sir Henry Mervyn is to be restored to his place; but that he disregards those rumours, "having confidence in the Duke." Palmer's ‡ confidence in the Duke was, however, ill-founded. Sir Henry Mervyn was again admitted to the King's sea service: the precise date does not appear; but in October 1626, one Wood, the master of the "Entrance," writes to him that that ship is ready, and furnished with provisions for 160 men for fourteen weeks; but that the men refused to sail without being paid their past sea wages; and, in the same month of October, we find him giving a certificate of competence to one Cooper to command a ship. Sir Henry again entered upon the command of a ship; but was not, apparently, immediately reinstated in his old office, for in May 1627 he writes to the Duke of Buckingham from "aboard the Happy Entrance," in the Margate Roads, thanking him for his appointment to a ship, and soliciting to be employed as Admiral of the Narrow Seas.

About the time that Admiral Mervyn was reinstated in his office, Buckingham had determined that England should break with France, and, with this end, encouraged the English ships of war and privateers to seize French merchant vessels, and we find Sir Henry taking part in this warfare. In July 1627, he reports to Secretary Nicholas his recapture of an English ship taken by the French, adding significantly, that he understands that the Admiralty Judges count English goods no prize; but he wishes the merchants to know that he shall expect "salvage." Indeed, as before remarked, Sir Henry's investment of £3,100 in the purchase of his office would not prove a very good venture, unless we are to suppose that, during his tenure of office, his indirect gains (in the shape of captured prizes and booty) were very considerable; for in December 1628 we find that he petitioned the Privy Council, alleging that there was then due to him for wages and disbursements a sum of £8,160. He does not, however, get paid anything on account of his arrears until 1630, when a warrant is issued for payment to him of £500, to be "defalked" off his demand for £3,110 alleged to be due to him, but the accounts whereof "are not yet cast up."

In the autumn of 1627 there was a threatened attack by the French on the Channel Islands, the defence of which Sir Henry Mervyn claimed by right of his warrant as Admiral of the Narrow Seas; and his claim seems to have been admitted, as in August he presents to Lord Holland an account of the French fleet prepared for the attack on Guernsey and Jersey, and points out the inadequacy of the fleet appointed for the defence of those islands. On his return from the Channel Islands he was directed to intercept two ships which had been built for the French at, and were coming from, Amsterdam.

Sir Henry Mervyn was in frequent communication with the Duke of Buckingham.

* State Papers Dom. Ser., Chas. 1, vol. xiv. 73.
† Who this disobedient son was, whether Captain James Mervyn or Audley Mervyn, does not appear.
‡ Sir Henry Palmer was compensated for the loss of the office which he held during Mervyn's disgrace by an appointment of Comptroller of the Navy. (State Papers Dom. Ser., Ch. 1 : 1631, March.)

In December, 1627, he wrote his Grace, reporting the reasons why he has not been able to put to sea, but "hopes not to merit a room in the list of those whom the " Duke names dull and slothful seamen." Buckingham, finding that the provocation given to the French did not culminate in an open breach between the two countries so rapidly as he wished, entered into negotiation with the Duke de Rohan and his brother, Monsr. de Soubise, the leaders of the French Protestant faction, to aid them in resisting the attacks on their liberty which were threatened by the French King and his cardinal minister.

Preparations were accordingly made for an invasion of France; but money supplies were scarce, and there was consequent delay in victualling the ships: men were wanting, and great and infectious sickness (resulting principally from the absence of proper food and clothing) broke out among the seamen, who, notwithstanding their sickness, were obliged to be kept on board the ships, as the country refused to billet them on account of the infection. Sir Henry Mervyn, writing to Buckingham and to Secretary Nicholas, from Plymouth, in December, 1627, protested that unless the Duke take it speedily into consideration, the King "will have more ships than sailors;" the men, he reported, " have neither shoes, stockings, nor rags to cover nakedness ;" the ships are all so infectious that he fears, if they hold the sea one month more, they will not bring men home enough to moor the ships: he eulogizes the patience of " the poor men," and earnestly urges that a supply of provisions and clothes should be sent. And again, writing to the Duke in January, 1628, he reiterates the deplorable state in which the seamen were, and concludes by begging pardon for communicating such harsh news, adding, " but it is " better your Grace should know it, than believe things better than they are."

In February, 1628, Sir Henry Mervyn was appointed one of the Members of the Council of War, and in the summer of that year, the ill-fated expedition against the French was undertaken. A fleet of 100 ships, and an army of 7,000 men, were fitted out and sailed under the personal command of the Duke, to invade France. When the fleet arrived before La Rochelle, so ill-concerted had been the arrangements that the Rochellers refused to admit the troops, which had arrived for the purpose of acting as their allies against the French Government, and accordingly the Duke turned his force against the Island of Rhé, which he attacked ; but such was his incapacity and inexperience that the expedition proved an utter failure, and having lost two thirds of his land forces, he was compelled to return to England in October, 1628, totally discredited.

The effect of the attempt made by the English to assist the Huguenots having thus failed, the French Government were encouraged to adopt open measures against them, and accordingly took steps to besiege La Rochelle. The Earl of Denbigh (Buckingham's brother-in-law) was despatched to its relief, and Sir Henry Mervyn accompanied him ; but the fleet returned without having effected anything, and having, it is said, refused to engage the French ships which were engaged in the blockade. Buckingham, furious at the imputation of cowardice which was made against the English, proceeded personally to Portsmouth to superintend the outfit of a new force, but, before it was ready, the knife of the assassin, Felton, had laid low the ambitious spirit which at that time governed the destinies of Great Britain.

The year 1629 opened on a period of great embarrassment in the finances of the country ; the expenses which the expedition to Cadiz and Rhé and Rochelle entailed, were such that no funds were forthcoming to carry on further offensive measures ; indeed, they barely sufficed to keep a few ships afloat for the protection of the Narrow Seas. Sir Henry was at that time fully occupied in cruising in the Downs in his ship, the " Lion," and in transporting various persons of note to and from England, amongst others, Don Carlos de Colonna, Sir Henry Vane, and two of the Lord Treasurer's sons.

In December, 1629, Sir Henry applied for leave from the Admiralty to proceed to Ireland to settle some private affairs. This application for leave of absence arose out of a letter which he had received from Sir William Ryves (the Attorney-General for Ireland), written at the request of Lady Christian Mervyn (Sir Henry's wife), to apprize him that in consequence of failure in passing the patent and paying the fines for certain lands in Ireland, and also because the articles enjoined on the Earl of Castlehaven, his brother, had not been performed, Sir Henry's lands were all forfeited to the Crown ; and that Captain John Lee, brother of Sir Daniel Lee, who held lands under Sir Henry, was going to England to procure a separate grant from the King.* The leave applied for, was accorded, as we find a letter in January, 1630, to Secretary Nicholas, thanking him, and hoping one day to give him some testimony of a respectful honest gratitude " *quod jam* " *fata negant.*"

In April, 1630, the Admiral is back at his post, writing to the Lord of the Admiralty from Yarmouth Roads, on board the " Reformation." The expedition against Spain and France came to an end after the death of Buckingham and the surrender of Rochelle, and this fact may probably have led to Sir Henry entertaining the notion of quitting the Naval Service. It is certain that in the autumn of 1630 he had some conference with Sir Kenelm Digby, one of the Commissioners for the Navy, in reference to the surrender of his patent office as Admiral of the Narrow Seas, a step which he did not seem to have however contemplated taking except for good considerations. He required payment of his arrears, which he stated amounted to £10,000, or £5,000 of those arrears and £3,000 for the place, that being the sum which it had cost him.†

The year 1631 must have been an anxious period for Sir Henry in connection with family affairs, for it was at that time that his unhappy brother-in-law, the Earl of Castlehaven, was brought to trial, condemned, and executed, for crimes which could only have been the result of insanity.‡ Some members of his family, indeed, treated the accusations as unfounded, and as the result of a conspiracy, as appears from a petition presented to the King by Lady Christian Mervyn and her sisters, the Ladies Amy Blount and Elizabeth Griffin.§

In the three following years Sir Henry was actively engaged in matters connected with the Admiralty. He was called on to advise the Board as to the number of men to be allowed for manning each of H.M.'s ships, and as to the dimensions of ships about to be built, &c. I find him, also, strongly advocating the erection of lighthouses on the North and South Forelands.

In 1635 the presence in the English Channel of a combined Dutch and French fleet, although both of those countries were at that time at peace with England, gave an excuse for the King to make a display of the naval force of Great Britain, the outfit of which had been provided for by the first levy of the then newly-invented tax of ship-money ; and accordingly a fleet, under the command of Robert Earl of Lindsay, with instructions " to preserve his Majesty's honour, coasts, jurisdictions, territories, and subjects within the extent of his employment," cruised in the Channel with great ostentatious display from May till October.

Sir Henry Mervyn does not appear to have had service with this fleet ; but in the following year, 1636, when the second payment of ship-money came in, the fleet was again

---

* *State Papers Dom. Series Chas.* i *vol.* 153. 90.
† *State Papers Dom. Series Ch. i.* 1630, *Sep.* 4.
‡ Insanity in the Touchet family is evidenced by a very mad letter addressed by Lady Eleanor Davies, signing herself Eleanor Tickett, to her sisters Lady Amy Blount, Lady Elizabeth Griffin, and Lady Christian Mervin, in which she comments on a passage in the 75th Psalm. " In the hand of the Lord there is a cup and the wine is red," which she applies to the destruction of London, and assures the persons addressed that this construction was sealed on her mouth with a kiss by Him who made her and heaven and earth. She subscribes herself " Your sister in the Lion's Den." (*State Papers, Dom. Series, vol. cclxxxiii.* 14.) This Lady Eleanor, who, after the death of her husband, Sir John Davis, in 1616, married Sir Archibald Douglas, was a religious enthusiast. She published a pamphlet—" The Restitution of Prophecy, that buried talent to be revived." 4ᵐ 1651. During the Commonwealth she was harshly treated, and is said to have been confined in Bethlehem for several years. She died in 1652, and was buried in London in the Church of St. Martin's-in-the-fields. *Hoare's Mod. Wilts, vol.* 4 *p.* 154.
§ *State Papers, Dom. Series, vol. clxxxix.,* 69.

fitted out under the command of Algernon, Earl of Northumberland, Sir John Pennington being nominated to the Vice-Admiralty, and Sir Henry Mervyn being named Rear-Admiral, with the charge " to guard his Majesty's seas." The vindication of the English sovereignty of the seas, appears to have been very disproportionate to the means adopted to assert it, being limited to compelling the Dutch fishermen to accept and pay for licenses to ply their trade in the Narrow Seas ; a step which led the Dutch to intimate very plainly that a renewal of such a course would infallibly produce a breach between the two nations. When the Earl returned, a portion of the fleet remained under the command of Sir Henry, and did not return home until March 1637.

The following is a letter, preserved in the State Paper Office *(Dom. Ser. Chas.* 1., *vol. cccxxxv., No.* 52), addressed about this period to the Commissioners of the Admiralty :—

" May it please y' Lo**.

" I have endeavoured w** what diligence the same would permitt to give an account of " y' Lo** commands, And my former letters to Mr. Secretarie, if they have not miscarried, " intimate as much as heere is certified in effect. If there had been anie iust cause of " complaint against the victuallers in diligence I should have beene much to blame not to " have given y' Lo** notice of it as an iust excuse for my staye. But the extremitie of " weather, w** has beene the cause thereof, can not bee prevented. Here are at the Cowes " about 90 saile of ships, bound all to the eastwards, who all this time durst hazard the " danger of putting to sea. I beseeche y' Lo** bee of opinion y' that my care shall faile in " all diligence to put to & keepe the seas when my maister and officers dare undertake " the chardge. Thus I humbly rest y' Lo** most humble seruant.

He: Mervm

" Stokes Baye on bord the
" St. Andrewe, No. 13**, 1636.

" To the Right Ho*** the Lords Com** for the Admiraltie."

During this period of winter service, it would seem that an alarm was raised that the Turks were committing depredations upon our coasting vessels, and an order was accordingly sent by the Admiralty to Sir Henry, directing him to range the western coasts, and to free the same from Turks and pirates ; and having scoured those coasts for a fortnight, he was to repair to the Downs to his Admiral for further instructions. Sir Henry does not appear to have given much credit to the alleged Turkish raid, as, in writing from Dover in January, 1636-7, to acknowledge the receipt of his orders, he adds, that he has not heard of any Turks or others that molest the freedom of trade in those parts, but that it is usual with the inhabitants to fancy the crescent in all colours, as they did last year by the King's ships, which were employed for their safety, and fled from them, filling the country with acclamations that the Turks had chased them *

In May, 1637, a new commission for a Council of War was issued "to consider such particulars as concern the security of His Majesty's realms, the assisting his allies, and all other matters concerning war," and Sir Henry Mervyn was one of the commissioners therein named.

Sir Henry was that year again actively employed under the Earl of Northumberland, to whom he was reappointed Rear-Admiral. The Earl on his return complained to the Council against the state and management of the Navy, and in the articles which he adduced in that respect he was supported by Sir Henry Mervyn, Sir John Pennington, and others in the fleet.

In June, 1637, Sir Henry was directed to carry over the Prince Elector Palatine to

---

* *State Papers Dom. Series, vol. cccxlv.,* 70.

Holland. The "Great Fleet" of 1637 did about as much as its two predecessors, which in fact amounted to nothing at all.

In 1638, Sir Henry again served as Rear-Admiral in the "Victory," but in the following year he made up his mind to quit the service, as is gathered from a paragraph in a letter from one Thomas Smith, to the Vice-Admiral Sir John Pennington, in which he writes that:—"Sir Henry Mervin has now given in his resolution to my Lord (Earl of Northumberland) that he cannot go in this summer's fleet, and desired to be excused, wherewith my Lord is very well contented, and I believe he will not come into our fleet again in haste; he is now suing to His Majesty to have £1,000 in money or £500 per annum for 7 years, and then he will relinquish all his claims to the Admiralty of the Narrow Seas, but I believe he will get nothing."*

It appears that Sir Henry Mervyn carried out his intention, as in March, 1639, he is referred to as being out of all command, "having to go to Ireland."

Sir Henry died in 1646, having made his will, wherein he is described as "of the City of Westminster, Knight," on the 29th May in that year; and the will was proved in the following month of June. In it † he mentions his son Audley Mervyn, and his daughters Deborah Lady Blenerhassett, Lucy, and Elizabeth Mervyn, Frances Coach, and Katherine Messar. He does not refer to his wife nor to his elder son James Mervyn, who had both predeceased him.

I. JAMES MERVYN, the eldest son of the marriage of Sir Henry Mervyn with Christian Touchet, was living in 1610, at the date of the will of his maternal grandfather, Sir James Mervyn of Fountel-Giffard, in which he is mentioned. James Mervyn appears to have followed his father's profession, for in 1626 I find him in command of the King's ship the "St. Claude,"‡ and in 1627, Sir John Coke writing to Secretary Conway that he had despatched letters to Sir Henry at Portsmouth, adds, but that neither he "nor his son" were there, and again in the same year, Sir John Jephson,§ writing to Conway, states that he has sent a letter to Captain Mervyn from his father, in which Sir Henry directs his son to take three Dutch East India ships. In December 1627|| Captain James Mervyn writes to Secretary Nicholas, alleging that his men were sick, and asking leave of absence "to follow a business he has in London and Wilts."

Apparently he did not again join the fleet. I find no further mention of him in the State Papers, and at one time I was under the impression that he had met with his death by violence in London a few months after the date of his letter; for in July, 1628,¶ Secretary Conway instructs Sir Robert Heath, the Attorney-General, "to take knowledge of the Inquisition of the Coroner "of the Verge on the death of Captain James Mervyn," with directions "if "it be found manslaughter to prepare a pardon for Thomas Stradling."

It would seem, however, that the Captain James Mervyn referred to was not the son of Sir Henry, as he went over to Ireland, and apparently settled there; for I find a funeral entry in Ulster's Office, recording, upon her husband's information, the death of his wife, ELIZABETH, the daughter of Sir John PHILIPOTT, of Thruxton, co. Southampton, who died 13th May, 1640, and

---

* The letter is dated 21 Feb. 1638/9. (*State Papers, Dom. Series, vol. cccxiii.*, 56.") Probably the opinion expressed by the writer was verified by the fact, inasmuch as at the date of Sir Henry's will (1646) there was about £12,000, "long since due to me from His Majesty," and this sum appears to have been his sole property. See APPENDIX II., p. iii.
† See APPENDIX II. p. iii.
‡ *State Papers,* "*Dom. Ser. ch. 1. vol. xxiv.*, *p. 71.*"
§ Captain James Mervyn's great-uncle, the brother of his grandmother Anna Jephson.
‖ *State Papers,* "*Dom. Ser. ch. 1 vol. lxxxvi., p. 56.*"
¶ *State Papers,* "*Dom. Ser. Chas. I.*, 1628, 110," *No. 71.*

was buried at St. Werburgh's in Dublin,* where also Captain James was buried on 12th July in the following year, 1641,† leaving no issue.

II. SIR AUDLEY MERVYN, (see Notes as to the Irish Branch.)

1. LUCY MERVYN, was living at her father's death, unmarried.

2. DEBORAH MERVYN, who married first Sir LEONARD BLENERHASSET, and secondly RORY MAGUIRE, son of Bren Lord Maguire ; she was mentioned in her father's will as living in 1646.‡

3. ELIZABETH MERVYN, living at her father's death, unmarried.

4. FRANCES MERVYN, who at her father's death was the wife of . . . . COACH.

5. KATHERINE MERVYN, also living in 1646, and then the wife of WILLIAM MESSAR.

---

* See copy Funeral Certificate, APPENDIX II., p. iv.
† See copy Funeral Certificate, APPENDIX II., p. iv.
‡ Betham's Mss. (Ulster's Office) vol. xii., pp. 215—19.

THE

PERTWOOD BRANCH

OF THE

𝕸𝖊𝖗𝖛𝖞𝖓 𝕱𝖆𝖒𝖎𝖑𝖞.

A third branch of the Mervyn family settled at Pertwood, a small parish situate in the hundred of Warminster, but locally in that of Mere, in the county of Wilts. The whole parish consists of one estate, comprising about 450 acres. It now, with other property formerly appertaining to the Mervyn family in the adjoining parish of East Knoyle, belongs to Mr. Alfred Seymour, M.P., by whose father, the late Mr. Henry Seymour, it was purchased about forty years since.

Sir R. C. Hoare[*] states that the Mervyns acquired Pertwood in the early part of the 16th century, by the marriage of William Mervyn with Margaret, the daughter and heir of William Fletcher and his wife Joan, the daughter and heir of John Brether. In 1471[*] William Fletcher presented to the living, and in 1477[†] he and his wife Joan presented. The first presentation by Mervyn occurs in 1539,[†] when John Marvyn and Robert Temmys and Joan his wife presented, and from that date down to 1670 the patronage appears to have been vested in the Mervyn family.[†]

Whilst the pedigree of the Mervyns who settled at Pertwood is entered in three[‡] out of the four Wiltshire Visitations, it is somewhat remarkable that there is not any record in either of them, of the Fountel-Giffard family, although at the dates at which the three earliest Visitations were made (1530, 1565, and 1623) its Representatives held important positions and were large landed proprietors in the county.

The original note book of the Visitation of 1565 is preserved in the British Museum (*Harl. Ms. No.* IIII., *p.* 58), and contains a pedigree of four generations, commencing with "Willyam Marven of Pertwood, com. Wilts, Gent. 'nefewe' to Walter Marvyn of Fown-"teyne in com. Wilts, Esquire." This description is followed in the fair copy returned by the Heralds for registration in the College of Arms.[§] The next Visitation was held in 1623; but the entries in the original note book (*Harl. Ms. No.* 1165, *p.* 5) do not extend so far back as William Mervyn. The record of this Visitation in the College of Arms ("*C.* 22," fo. 23ᵇ) includes, however, the entries made at the previous Visitation, and brings down the pedigree to the members of the family living in 1623; but the Heralds made their return in Latin, and translated the word "nefewe" by "nepos." In a certified extract in English from

---

* Hist. Modern Wilts.
† See "*Phillipps' Wiltshire Institutions.*"
    1631. Patron Thomas Mervyn, of Pertwood, Gent.
    1638.   „   George Mervyn, Esquire.
    1660.   „   John Mervyn, Gent.
    1662.   „   ditto.
    1670.   „   ditto.
‡ See APPENDIX III. pp. iv. and v.   § See APPENDIX III. p. iv.

the Visitation of 1623 now before me, made 16 November, 1723, by Richard Mawson,* *Portcullis Pursuivant*, he has retranslated the word "nepos" as "grandson," and this error has given rise to some discussion as to the precise connection between the Pertwood and Fountel-Giffard families. The late Mr. William Courthope, *Somerset Herald*, considered that the translation given by Mawson was probably correct, on the ground that the word "*nepos*" was often used to designate a grandson,† and that there was no record of Walter Mervyn of Fountel having had any brother except Hugh Mervyn, who left only daughters, whilst there were two entries in Vincent's pedigree (*Ms. Coll. Arm.* "*Vin. No.* 121," *fo.* 392) of grandsons of Walter named William; Mr. Courthope, however, omitted to notice that the same authority mentions that one of those grandsons died s.p.; but even if that

---

* Richard Mawson was appointed Portcullis in 1717, and Deputy Registrar of the Coll. of Arms in 1733. On 2 Sep., 1745, he was nominated Windsor Herald, but he died on the same day. *Ex. rel:* Sir Albert Woods.

† This suggestion of Mr. Courthope's led me to consult some authorities as to the meaning generally given to the word "nepos," and I find that classic writers almost invariably used it to designate a grandson. Virgil in referring to Ascanius, Venus' grandson, writes " Dardanius que nepos Veneris, " *Æneid iv.* 163. Ovid however uses the word for grand-nephew, "Cæsar ab Æneâ qui tibi (Cupidini) fratre nepos" (*Pont iii.,* 3, 62); as does also Suetonius, "Sed novissimo testamento tres instituit heredes, sororum nepotes." *Cæs.* 83. The word "neptis" is generally used for grand-daughter: "Metellum enim multi filii filiæ nepotes neptes in rogum imposuerunt" (*Cic. Tusc. i.,* 35): but Ælius Spartianus has neptis in the sense of niece. *Hadr.* 2. " Nepos," in the sense of descendants generally, is to be met with, *ex. gr.,* "Tarda venit seria factura nepotibus umbram" (*Virgil, Georgic* 2), " Pugnent ipsique nepotesque." (*Æneid iv.,* 629). In the Latin law records, "nepos" seems to have been used indifferently for "nephew" or "grandson"; thus in Fine Roll 13 Edw. I, (1285), it occurs in the former sense: " Rex cepit fiedlitatem Rogeri Papyloun *nepotis* et heredis Willielmi Papyloun defuncti de omnibus terris et tenementis que idem Willus *avunculus* suus tenuit." So also 'in an inquisition post mortem 36 Hen. VIII. (1545): "Symeon armiger, est *nepos* et proximus hæres dicti Radulphi Symons, viz., *filius* Johannis *fratris* dicti Radulphi jam defuncti." An instance of the use of the word as meaning grandson will be found in Fine Roll 33 Edw. I. (1305): " Rex cepit homagium Johannis de Grey *nepotis* et heredis Isabellæ de Grey defunctæ de omnibus terris et tenementis, etc., de quibus prefata Isabella *avia* sua fuit seisita." See also *ante* Appendix I., p. v., Inq. p. m. Sir James Mervyn. In like manner "neptis" is used to designate either a niece or a grand-daughter. In the former sense it will be found in the Inquisition 24 Edw. I. (1296) de Clerbek : " Johanna, *filia* Roberti de Clerbek fratris Henrici de Clerbek, et Elizabeth Soror ejusdem Johannæ, et Alicia Soror ejusdem Johannæ, sunt hæredes dicti Henrici. Johanna *neptis* predicti Henrici est una hæredum, et Elizabetha Soror predictæ Johannæ alia hæres et *neptis* ejusdem Henrici, et Aliciæ tertia hæres Soror predictæ Johannæ et *neptis* dicti Henrici.

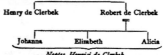

Neptis Henrici de Clerbek.

As referring to a grand-daughter, "neptis" occurs in the Retour of Service, dated 20 March, 1588-9, printed in the documents connected with the Mar Peerage Case now before the House of Lords (Appendix, No. 27, p. 184, of the case of J. F. E. Goodeve Erskine): "Joannes nunc Comes de Mar, est legitimus et propinquior heres dicte quondam Isobelle Comitisse de Mar, respectu habito quod ipsa erat *neptis* quondam Donaldi Comitis de Mar eius, avi fratris quond Domine Helene de Mar," etc. The pedigree being:

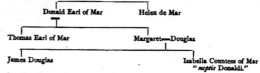

It results therefore, that the true interpretation of "nepos" or "neptis" depends on the context with which it is used.

had not been the case, it is impossible that he could have been Sheriff of Dorset and Somerset in 5 Hen. VII. 1489-90, (which William Mervyn of Pertwood was*), seeing that his brother, John Mervyn, the son of Walter's eldest son, and who succeeded his grandfather at Fountel was only nine years old in 1512,† and that the other grandson William, was living in 1550 at Durford in Sussex. I have no doubt that the founder of the Pertwood family was a nephew and not a grandson of Walter, on the grounds, first, that the original entry by the Heralds so described him; secondly, that the word "nephew" was correctly written "nepos" when the pedigree was translated into Latin; and thirdly, that the dates are inconsistent with any other conclusion.

In the Visitation of London made in the year 1664‡ (*Ms. Coll. Arms.* "*D.* 19," fo. 87*b*) there is entered the pedigree of John Mervyn of London, merchant, the grandson of John Mervyn of Pertwood and Melior Gouldsborough, and in the Wiltshire Visitation of 1677§ (*Ms. Coll. Arm.* "*D.* 28" *fo.* 31) the descent of Edward Mervyn of Salisbury, from George Mervyn of Pertwood, is recorded. There is also in the College of Arms (Ms. "8 D 14" p. 115) a modern pedigree‖ registered in 1801, of the descendants of John Mervyn of Pertwood and his wife Anne Toppe, who are mentioned in the Visitation of 1623. It is principally from the above sources, supplemented by documentary evidence, which I have specified, and personal information of facts within their knowledge, derived from living descendants of this branch of the Mervyn family, that I have compiled the following pedigree.

I should mention that I have in some instances been guided to sources of information by the pedigree which will be found printed in Sir R. C. Hoare's Hist. of Wilts (*Mere Hundred, p.* 180). compiled, as I believe, about 1799 by the late G. F. Beltz, *Lancaster Herald,* and which so far as it extends appears to be substantially correct, with however one important error as regards Richard Mervyn, the Chancellor of Exeter Cathedral and the founder of the Devonshire branch of the family, who has been inserted by Beltz a generation lower than that in which he was born.

WILLIAM MERVYN, nephew of Walter Mervyn of Fountel-Giffard, settled at Pertwood¶ on his marriage with MARGARET, daughter of William FLETCHER, by Joan, the daughter and heir of John BRETHER of Pertwood. He was Sheriff of Somerset and Dorset, 5 Hen. VII. (1489-90),* and on his death, according to the Wiltshire Visitation taken in 1565, left two children, viz. :—

JOHN, his son and heir.
ELIZABETH, a daughter who died unmarried.

JOHN MERVYN, the son, was of Pertwood, and married AVIS, daughter of

---

* *Hutchins' Hist. Dorset, vol.* 1., *Introd. p.* 66.
† *Inq. p. m.* 4 *Hen.* VIII. See APPENDIX I., p. iii.
‡ See APPENDIX III., p. v.
§ See APPENDIX III., p. v.
‖ See APPENDIX III., p. vi.
¶ Unfortunately the early Pertwood Registers are not to be found. Mr. Alfred Seymour informs me that at the time the estate was purchased by his father, the Church was used as a cattle shed, and he recollects when it was cleared out for the purpose of service being performed in it, the farmer's wife protested against the pulpit being interfered with, on the ground that her best brood of geese would be disturbed.

John COCKERELL, of Stoughton, co. Wilts, by whom he had three children, two sons and a daughter.*

   I. JOHN MERVYN, of whom hereafter.

   II. PHILIP MERVYN, who is recorded in the Visitation of 1565, and mentioned in his brother John's will (1599). He married, but the name of his wife does not appear, and had two sons and a daughter, all of whom are mentioned in his brother's will, viz. :

      I. ANDREW MERVYN, a legatee under his uncle John's will (1599), and living at the date of his brother William's will (1620), in which he and his two children are mentioned, the two children being at that date under age, viz. :

        WILLIAM MERVYN.

        KATHERINE.

      II. WILLIAM MERVYN, also a legatee under the will of his uncle John, was a citizen and brewer of London, and married, 1stly, ANNE . . . . , by whom he had two daughters.

        I. ELIZABETH } Both mentioned in their father's will, and then
        2 SUSAN   } (1620) under age.

He married, 2ndly, ELEANOR, daughter of Edward NEWMAN, by whom he does not appear to have had any issue. His will is dated 22 Feb. 1620,† and was proved 13 April 1621, by Eleanor Mervyn, his widow and sole executrix. He desired by his will to be buried in St. Sepulchre's without Newgate.

      I. FRISETTE married to John ADAMS, and both mentioned, with their children in the will of her uncle John Mervyn (1599), and in the will of her brother William (1620). Frisette and her husband were living in 1632 (the date of her cousin Thomas Mervyn's will), and then residing at Hindon.

   I. MARGARET MERVYN, who was the wife of Adelme WHITAKER, of Edington, co. Wilts.

JOHN MERVYN, of Pertwood, the elder son and heir of John Mervyn and Avis Cockerell, was married on 14 Sept. 1561,‡ to MELIOR, the daughter of Robert GOLDSBOROUGH, of East Knoyle, a parish adjoining Pertwood. He was possessed of considerable landed property in Wiltshire, including the Manor of Pertwood, and lands in Fountel-Bishop, Stopp, Hyndon, Fountel-Giffard, and Chicklade, as appears by an Inquisition§ taken after his death, which records that he died on 24 June, 1601. His will was dated 8 May, 1599, and was proved 13 April 1621, by his son Thomas, on the 13 November, 1601.|| By his wife Melior Goldsborough, who survived him, John Mervyn was the father of

   I. CHRISTOPHER MERVYN, who is mentioned in the Visitation of 1565, and is recorded in that of 1623 as having died without issue.

   II. JOHN MERVYN is mentioned in the Visitation of 1565 as the second son and then living ; but he is not recorded in the Visitation of 1623, and he evidently died without issue before his father, as in the Inquisition his next brother is found the heir.

   III. THOMAS MERVYN, of Pertwood, who in the Inquisition§ taken on his father's death is described as his son and next heir, and as then (1601) of the age of 34 years and upwards. He is mentioned in his father's will (1599), under which he was devisee of a house at Hindon, and was appointed residuary legatee and executor, and proved the will. Thomas Mervyn was one of those gentlemen who preferred to pay a money composition

* See Visitation, Wilts, 1565, APPENDIX III., p. iv.
† See Abstract Will of William Mervyn, APPENDIX III., p. vii.
‡ See Par. Reg., East Knoyle, APPENDIX III., p. ix.
§ See APPENDIX III., p. ix.
|| See Abstract Will of John Mervyn, APPENDIX III., p. vii.

rather than be knighted at the coronation of Charles I. The patronage
of the Rectory of Pertwood was vested in him and in 1631 he exercised it
in favor of his nephew, Richard Mervyn, afterwards D.D. and Chancellor
of Exeter Cathedral, the founder of the 𝔇𝔢𝔟𝔬𝔫𝔰𝔥𝔦𝔯𝔢 branch of the family.
He married, MARGARET, daughter of John EDWARDS, of Westbury, co. Wilts,
but appears to have died without leaving any children. His will* is dated
13 February, 1632, and was proved in London in the following year. In it
he mentions his brother William and *his* son Thomas; also his brothers
Austin and Ambrose. He devised an estate at Chicklade, co. Wilts in
settlement upon John, Mathew, Richard, and Thomas, sons of his brother
George, who he appointed sole executor and residuary legatee.

IV. GEORGE MERVYN, 4th son, of whom hereafter.

V. WILLIAM MERVYN,† the 5th son, who is recorded in the Visitation of 1623,
and mentioned in his father's will (1599). He is also mentioned, with his
son Thomas, in his brother Thomas Mervyn's will, (1632).

VI. AUGUSTINE MERVYN, the 6th son, was of East Knoyle. He is mentioned in his
father's will (1599), and recorded in the Visitation of 1623, and is also mentioned in the will of his brother Thomas (1632). His will* is dated 20 April,
1634, and was proved in London 17 Nov. 1637. In it he mentions his wife,
who was PRISCILLA, daughter of Francis SAMBORNE, of Mayden Newton, in
the county of Dorset. Augustine Mervyn, like his elder brother, declined the
honour of knighthood at the Coronation of King Charles I., and consequently
had to pay a composition of £10. He was a donor to the church of East
Knoyle, where he lived, and his gift, a silver Paten, still exists, bearing the
following engraved inscription:—"*Amoris ergo donum hoc moriens pie generosus
Augustinus templo huic Mervinus reliquit* 1637."‡ The children of Augustine
Mervyn and Priscilla Samborne appear to have been nine in number, viz.:—

I. AUGUSTINE MERVYN, the eldest child, was baptized at Tisbury,§ 17
Nov., 1617, and was buried at East Knoyle‖ 11 December, 1617.

II. AUGUSTINE MERVYN, a second son of that name was baptized at
Tisbury,§ 30th March, 1619, and is recorded in the Visitation of 1623
as then of the age of four years.

---

* See Abstract of the Will, APPENDIX III., p. vii.

† This William Mervyn was possibly the "Rector of the church of Boyton Corton Magna and Parva,
and the chapel of Rhodden," whose will is dated 1 Aug. 1647, and was with a codicil of 1 Aug. 1651
proved in London 26 April, 1652, by his son, George Mervyn, of Salisbury (*P. C. C.* 77 *Bowyer*). The will
mentions Testator's wife Joane, then deceased, his son Thomas (who in the codicil, (1651), is stated to
have died since the date of the will), a son William, and his children; another son Henry, and his
children; a third son George of Salisbury, and his children; also three daughters, viz., Cicely, wife of
Edward Olden; Constance, married to George Dyer; and Anne, the wife of Alexander Cray. The testator
appointed Mr. Matthew Mervyn, of Upton, one of the overseers of his will. I take it that the third son
"George," referred to in the will, was George Mervyn, of Salisbury (described in the Ledger of the
Corporation of that City as "Mercer"), who in 1662 invested two sums of £100 each with the Mayor and
Commonalty of Salisbury in consideration of an annuity, the interest of the money after his death being
distributable amongst the poor of the City, including a payment of twenty shillings to the Clergyman of
St. Edmund's parish for a sermon to be preached on the anniversary of his death. See *Hoare's Wilts-
Salisbury, Vol. 2, pp. 828 & 448*) Mr. Charles M. Lee, *Town Clerk* of Salisbury, informs me (1873) that a
Deed exists, dated 3rd March, 1661, which gives "Margery" as the Christian name of this George Mervyn's
wife, but I have not met with any further particulars of their family.

I find (*P. C. C. 22 Ruthin*) a will of another William Mervin, of East Knoyle, "Clerk and
Batchelor," dated 1st January, 1651, administration to which was granted by the P. C. C. on 21st January,
1656, to testator's brother-in-law, Robert Dominicke, one of the trustees named in the will which mentions
testator's sisters,—Lucy Dominicke and her children, Mellyer Gundery and her children, and Mary Grove,
and also testator's kinsman Thomas Mompesson and his brother Henry Mompesson, and his kinswoman
Mrs. Ellen Mompesson. I cannot identify this testator. See Abstract APPENDIX III., p. vii.

‡ *Ex-relatione* Rev. R. N. Milford, Rector of East Knoyle, 1873.

‖ See Par. Reg., East Knoyle, APPENDIX III., pp. ix. & x.

§ See Par. Reg. Tisbury, printed in Hoare's Wilts Dunworth Hund., pp. 150-1, probably from the

III. CHRISTOPHER MERVYN was baptized at East Knoyle* on 26th September 1626, and was mentioned in his father's will (1634).

1. DOROTHY, mentioned in the Visitation of 1623, as then of the age of twelve years. She would appear to have married at East Knoyle* on 5 June, 1628, Francis TOOPE.

2. MARY, recorded in the 1623 Visitation as aged nine years. She was mentioned in her father's will (1634).

3. VERTUE was baptized* 22 July, 1621, and entered in the Visitation of 1623, and also referred to in her father's will.

4. PRISCILLA, who is recorded in the Visitation of 1623, was baptized at East Knoyle* 17 May, 1623, and mentioned in her father's will.

5. ANN, baptized* 1 March, 1624, and mentioned in her father's will.

6. KATHERINE, baptized* 8 Oct., 1631, and mentioned in her father's will.

VII. AMBROSE MERVYN, the seventh son of John Mervyn and Melior Golds-borough, was a legatee under his father's will (1599) as tenant for life of the testator's house at Hindon, and is also mentioned in the will of his brother Thomas (1632); he is recorded in the Visitation of 1623, as also his wife ELIZABETH, daughter of John WILLOUGHBY of West Knoyle, with their three sons, viz.:—Nicholas, John, and Christopher. He is also recorded with his wife Elizabeth and son John in Visit. of London (1664). Ambrose Mervyn's wife Elizabeth died 24th December, 1645, and was buried at Chicklade.† Her husband survived her, and died . . . November, 1656, and was also buried at Chicklade.†

I. NICHOLAS MERVYN,† the eldest son, married MAGDALEN . . . . . who survived him. She is described in her will, dated 20 May 1687 (APPENDIX III., p. viii.), as " of Founthill Episcopi," and thereby directed that she might be buried at Chicklade, near her husband. The issue of the marriage were—

I. JOHN MERVYN, mentioned in the will of his uncle John Mervyn, of London (1686), as " my nephew John Mervyn of Founthill," and was named one of the executors in his mother's will (1687), and was also sole executor of his brother Nicholas's will (1689). It is probable that John Mervyn married, as his brother Nicholas, in his will, mentions his " sister-in-law Ann Mervyn," and on the gravestone of John there are the remains of an inscription which may possibly have recorded the death in 1714 of his widow; he died 11 January 1712, and was buried at Chicklade.†

II. NICHOLAS MERVYN was, with his brother John, executor

---

following notes by the late G. F. Beltz, *Lancaster Herald*, (who assisted Sir Richard C. Hoare in his history,) which were made on visiting Tisbury Church, 13 Sep. 1799, and are preserved in the College of Arms. (Ms. A. xix., J.P. 19, fo. 445):—

" On a small square brass plate in Tisbury Church :—' Here lyeth interred in hope of a joyful
" ' resurrection, ANN the daughter of Edmond Mervin of Founthill, in the county of Wilts, Esq., and
" ' the loving wife of Matthew DAVYS of the Middle Temple, London, Esq., who was born at Chicks-
" ' grove in this Parish. She dyed in the month of November, 1657.'

I have not been able to trace the parentage of this Anne Mervyn. See ped. of the Davys family, Hoare's Wilts—Chalk Hund. p. 36.

" The TISBURY REGISTERS were examined 14 Sep. 1799.
" *The Baptisms begin* 1563.
" 1567. Oct. Dorothy the daur. of Thomas Mervyn."
" 1617. Augustine, son of Mr. Augustine Mervin, was bapt. 17 Nov."
" 1619. Augustine, son of Augustine Mervin, Gent., was bapt. 30 day of March."
" *Burials begin Jan.* 1563."
" 1657. Anne, wife of Matthew Davys, Esq., burd. 9 Nov."

* See Par. Reg. East Knoyle, APPENDIX III., pp. ix. & x.
† See Foot Note * on next page.

of his mother's will (1687). His will is dated 4 July 1689 (APPENDIX III., p. viii.), and he died, apparently unmarried, on the 2 April 1692, and was buried at Chicklade.[*]

III. THOMAS MERVYN, married MARY . . . . ; both of whom are named in his mother's will (1687), and in his brother Nicholas' will (1689), and had issue a son.

    I. AMBROSE MERVYN, who is named in his great uncle's (John, of London) will (1686), who describes him as his "godson;" and in his grandmother Magdalen's will (1687), as also in that of his uncle Nicholas (1689).

    1. JANE, a daughter, described in the will of John Mervyn of London (1686) as "my niece Jane Mervin." She is also mentioned in the wills of her mother, and her brother Nicholas.

    2. MELIOR, who married Francis TURVILLE, both of whom, together with their children Francis Turville and Melior, are mentioned in Magdalen Mervyn's will (1687), and in will of Nicholas Mervyn (1689).

    3. ELIZABETH, married Wilks HIBBERD. She is mentioned in her mother's will (1687) as then dead; her husband and children John Hibberd and Jane, are also mentioned in the will of her brother Nicholas Mervyn, (1689).

II. JOHN MERVYN, the second son, migrated from Wiltshire and settled in London, where he married FRANCES, daughter and sole heiress of

---

[*] I was at one time in doubt whether it was Nicholas Mervyn, or his brother Christopher, who was the husband of Magdalen Mervyn of Fontel-bishop, and who by her will desires to be buried in the church of Chicklade, "near my late husband." (See APPENDIX III., p. viii.) I accordingly applied for information to the Rev. J. C. Faber, the Rector of Chicklade, who, in reply, informed me that the parochial registers only reach back to 1721, and that he could not, on any monumental stone, find mention or record of any member of the Mervyn family. Mr. Faber subsequently, however (20 Sept. 1873), very courteously wrote me, that in preparing the churchyard for enlargement, there had been found under the turf several gravestones belonging to the Mervyn family, of which he sent me the following particulars :—

Inscriptions on Tombstones in the Churchyard of Chicklade, co. Wilts.

HERE LIETH THE BODY OF ELIZABETH MERVIN, WIFE OF AMBROSE MERVIN, WHO DIED DECEMBER 24, 1645.

The "BETH" in Elizabeth is nearly illegible.

. . . . . OF AMBROSE MERVIN, WHO DIED . . . . . DAY OF NOVEMBER, IN THE YEARE OF OUR LORD 1656.

The first part of this inscription, and the upper portion of the words "OF AMBROSE MERVIN WHO," are broken off.

HERE LYETH THE BODY OF NICHOLAS MERVIN, SON OF NICHOLAS MERVIN, WHO DEPARTED THIS LIFE YE 2 DAY OF APRILL, ANNO DOM. 1692.

. . . . . MR. JOHN MERVIN OF FOUNTHILL, WHO DIED JANy. 11, ANNO DOM. 1712.

The words previous to "MR. JOHN" are illegible, and the upper portion of "HILL" in Founthill is broken off.

. . . . . OF JOHN MERVIN, WHO . . . . . JULY 1, ANNO DOM. 1714, AGED . . . .

The rest of this inscription is broken off.

    The two last inscriptions are on the same stone. There are also two other tombstones, which, judging from their position, in all probability belonged to the Mervin family; the inscriptions, however, are erased, with the exception of the date "1638" on the one, and "LIFE THE" and "SEPTEMBER" on the other.

    The fact of the record on the gravestone of the death of Nicholas, who was no doubt Magdalen's son, describing him as "son of Nicholas Mervin," satisfied me that her husband was Nicholas, and not Christopher.

Richard SIMONDS, by whom he had issue living in 1664 (*Visit. London*, 1664*), two sons and a daughter. His will† is dated 11th December, 1686, and was proved in London 25th March 1689, by his son Francis.

    I. FRANCIS MERVYN, son and heir, aged 10 years in 1664. He was appointed the executor of his father's will (1686). His will,‡ in which he is described as of Eltham, co. Kent, is dated 25th April, 1702, and was proved P. C. C. by his brother James on 16th May following.

    II. JAMES MERVYN is mentioned in his father's will (1686), and was appointed executor, and proved his brother Francis' will in 1702.

    1. MARY. This child is not mentioned in her father's will, so that she was at its date (1686) probably dead.

III. CHRISTOPHER MERVYN, third son of Ambrose Mervyn and Elizabeth Willoughby, mentioned in the Visit. 1623.

    1. PRISCILLA m . . . . . BOWLES, and was living (1689). She is referred to in the will of her brother John Mervyn (1686) as "my sister Priscilla Bowles." In the will of her nephew Nicholas (1689) she is mentioned as "my aunt Boles;" he also mentions his "cozin Elizabeth Boles."

GEORGE MERVYN, the fourth son of John Mervyn and Melior Goldsborough, became heir to his brother Thomas Mervyn. He is mentioned in his father's will (1599) as then married and having children, and is also, with his sons John (and *his* son John), Matthew, Richard, and Thomas, named in the will of his brother Thomas Mervyn (1632), by which he was appointed sole executor and residuary legatee, and is registered in the Visitation of 1623, and in 1677 as of Pertwood; in 1638 he presented to the living of that parish on the resignation of his son Richard, who had been appointed by his uncle in 1631. George Mervyn, like his two brothers Thomas and Augustine, was amongst those country gentlemen who paid a composition for not taking the order of knighthood at the coronation of Charles I.§ He married ELIZABETH, daughter of Robert RYVES, of Ranston in the county of Dorset, who was buried at East Knoyle, 30th November, 1624,‖ having had four sons and three daughters, all of whom were entered in the Visitation of 1623.

    I. JOHN MERVYN, of Pertwood, eldest son and heir, of whom hereafter.

    II. MATTHEW MERVYN, who was 24 years old in 1623. He is mentioned in the will of his uncle Thomas (1632), and was living in 1634, at which date he is mentioned in the will of his uncle Augustine, of which (with his brother John) he was appointed overseer. He married¶ KATHERINE, daughter of Edward PIKE, [of Maiden Newton, co. Dorset?] by whom he had issue a son and a daughter.

        I. GEORGE MERVYN, who married DOROTHY, daughter of John WILLOUGHBY, of Baverstock, co. Wilts, by whom he had issue three sons and two daughters.

---

* See APPENDIX III., p. v. † See Abstract of the Will APPENDIX III. p. vii.
‡ See Abstract of the Will, APPENDIX III. p. viii. § Ex. auct! Sir Thomas Philipps.
‖ See Par. Reg. East Knoyle, APPENDIX III., pp. ix. & x.
¶ The marriage of Matthew Mervyn with Katherine Pike and the particulars of their issue are given on the authority of a Ms. note apparently in the handwriting of Richard Mawson *Portcullis*, which I found amongst the family papers of my late aunt Mrs. Frances Drake.

I. PHILIP MERVYN, who married SARAH, daughter of William KNAPTON, of Brokenhurst in Hampshire, by whom he had issue one son.

II. GEORGE MERVYN, }
III. JOHN MERVYN, } ob. s.p.

1. MARY, who married John ORD, of Longleat.
2. HENRIETTA, who married Anthony WARTON, Prebend of Horningsham, co. Wilts.

1. ELIZABETH, who married William BURLTON, of Knoyle, co. Wilts.

III. RICHARD MERVYN, D.D., of Devonshire. (*See* "**Devonshire Branch**.")

IV. THOMAS MERVYN, mentioned in the Visitation of 1623 as then 10 years old. He is also named in the will of his uncle Thomas Mervyn (1632). He was of East Ensild, co. Wilts, married* ANN (widow of . . . . . WHITE), to whom, as his relict, administration was granted by the Prerogative Court of Canterbury, 14 March 165⅘.

1. MELIOR, living in 1623, and recorded in that year's Visitation as married to John HAYTOR, of Little Langford, in Wilts.
2. ELIZABETH, living 1623, married* Nathaniel FREAK, Counsellor, of Shaftesbury, co. Dorset.
3. MARGARET, baptized at East Knoyle,† 16 May 1605, and living in 1623, married* Christopher BARON, of Mere, co. Wilts.

JOHN MERVYN of Pertwood, the eldest son and heir of George Mervyn and Elizabeth Ryves, was baptized at East Knoyle† 3rd August 1595. He is mentioned in and signed the Pedigree taken at the Visitation of 1623, and was then aged 28. He sold his estate of Upton‡ in East Knoyle to his brother Richard, and in 1635 was living at Motcombe, co. Dorset. He is mentioned in the will of his uncle Thomas Mervyn (1632), and also in the will of his uncle Augustine Mervyn (1634), of which (with his brother Matthew) he was appointed overseer. He married in 1622 ANNE, daughter of John TOPPE of Stockton, co. Wilts, and sister of John Toppe of Lincoln's Inn. She is mentioned in the Visitation of 1623§ and also in the Visitation of 1677 apparently as then living, and if so, of the great age of 80 years. I have not any note of John Mervyn's death, but he presented to the living of Pertwood in 1660, 1662, and 1670. The children of his marriage ‖ with Anne Toppe were nine, three sons and six daughters, viz. :

I. JOHN MERVYN, of whom hereafter.
II. EDWARD MERVYN, who settled at Salisbury, and of whom also hereafter.
III. GEORGE MERVYN.

1. MARGARET, who was baptized at East Knoyle 31 April 1623,† and is recorded in the Visitation of that year as the then only issue of her father's and mother's marriage. She married . . . PERRY, of Hindon.
2. MARY, baptized 25 April 1625,† married Dᵣ William CREED,¶ Regius Professor of Divinity at Oxford.

---

* My authority for these several marriages is the Ms. before referred to.
† See Par. Reg. East Knoyle, APPENDIX III., pp. ix. and x.
‡ The sole remnant (as I believe) of the Mervyn landed property in Wiltshire now held by any descendant of the family, is an annual rent charge issuing out of this estate, and now belonging to my cousin Major John Mervyn Cutcliffe Drake, R.E. See **Devonshire Branch**.
§ Ms. Coll Arms, " *C. 22*," *p. 23b*, APPENDIX III., p. iv. The arms of Toppe are recorded in the pedigree of that family taken at the Visitation of Wilts in 1623 (Ms. Coll. Arm., " 1 *C. 22,*" *p. 59*), which gives the marriage of Ann Toppe with John Mervyn. The coat of Toppe being " *Arg. on a canton gules, a fist in antique mail couped ppr.*," with the following note underneath the tricking, "A patent confirmed to John Toppe, of Stockton, in the county of Wilts, by Edmond Knight, Norroy King of Armes, 1592, as his ancient armes." Quartered with the above coat are the following arms, "Argent semée de lis, a lyon rampant sable; " for Archbold. (See also Ms. Coll. Arm. " *I. 23,*" *p. 67*.)
‖ The particulars of the children of John Mervyn and Anne Toppe, except so far as they are supplied by the pedigrees set out in APPENDIX III., pp. iv., v., & vi., are taken from Mawson's Ms. previously referred to.
¶ Dr. William Creed was a native of Reading co. Berks, born about 1615, elected a scholar, and subsequently became a Fellow of St. John's College, Oxford. He entered the church, and became a noted

3. ANNE, married   . .   FLOYD of London.
4. HONOR, married   . .   HANSFORD of London.
5. ELIZABETH, baptized 29th November 1629 ;* died young.
6. A daughter, who married   . . .   BRADFORD, Minister in Devon.

JOHN MERVYN (of Fountel-Giffard), the eldest son of John Mervyn and Anne Toppe, was baptized at East Knoyle 20 April 1624.* He is mentioned in the will of Thomas Mervyn (1632), and married 11 August 1655† (before a Justice of the Peace at Gillingham), REBECCA, daughter of Christopher DIRDOE, of Gillingham. He was buried 1692. Letters of administration were granted by the Prerogative Court of Canterbury, on 12 December 1692, to his widow and his son Thomas Mervyn. His widow was buried 1693. The issue of the marriage were two sons.‡

    I. WILLIAM MERVYN of Pertwood ; barred entail in 1685.

    II. THOMAS MERVYN, who purchased Bourton House, near Wincanton, co. Dorset, 10 November 1702. He married MARY . . . . , who was buried 27 November 1728. He was buried 12 June 1745. The issue of his marriage being four sons

        I. HENRY MERVYN, who was admitted tenant 1 October 1745, and sold the Bourton property in 1752. He was buried 15 June 1753, having married MARY SUTER, who survived him, and was buried 8 May 1768.

        II. THOMAS MERVYN, living 1719, died before 1750.

        III. JOHN MERVYN, baptized 1704, married 30 Sept. 1724, ELEANOR, daughter of the Reverend Thomas LAMBERT, Rector of Boyton and Sherrington (by Jane, daughter of Sir Henry Coker), baptized also in 1704. John Mervyn died in 1765, and his widow in the following year. The issue of their marriage were eight children— two sons and six daughters.

            I. LAMBERT MERVYN, born 12th, bapt. at Kingstone Deverill,‖ 24th July 1725 ; died 15 Aug. 1750, unm

            II. JOHN MERVYN, born 24 January, 1726-7, bapt. at Kingstone Deverill,‖ 2 July 1726 ; died 15th, bur. at Kingstone Deverill,‖ 20th May 1805, unmarried, and, in the notification of his death in the newspaper,§ was described as the last male issue of the family.

---

preacher. He was a staunch Royalist, but during the Commonwealth held the Rectory of East Codeford or Codeford St. Mary, co. Wilts. After the Restoration (in June 1660) he was made Regius Professor of Divinity in the University of Oxford, and shortly afterwards became Archdeacon of Wilts and Rector of Stockton in that county. He died at Oxford, aged 47, on the 19th July 1663, and was buried in Christchurch. *See* Wood's Athenæ Oxoniensis (*Bliss' edition, Lond.* 1817 *vol.* 3, *pp.* 637-8.) No mention is made in the Memoir or Monumental Inscription of his marriage.

* See Par. Reg. East Knoyle, APPENDIX III., pp. ix. and x.

† " John Mervian, son of John Mervian, of Pertwood, in the county of Wiltshire, Gent., and Rebecca " Dirdoe, daughter of Christopher Dirdoe, of the parish of Gillingham, in the county of Dorset, Gent., were " three several Lord's days published in the parish church of Gillingham aforesaid, at the close of the " morning exercise ; to wit, on the 8th, 15th, and 22nd days of July 1655, that the said John Mervian the " son, and Rebecca Dirdoe intended to be joined in the holy state of matrimony; to which no exception was " made, and the 11th day of August 1655, were married by John Still, Esquire, one of the Justices of the " Peace of the said county of Dorset." *Ext. from Register of Marriages at Gillingham.*

‡ My authority for the statements as to the issue of this marriage is a Ms. pedigree furnished to me by Sir Henry Mervyn Vavasour, Bart., which appears to have been compiled in 1842 with great care, and, so far as I can judge, with accuracy by the late Col. Lambert White, of Yeovil, the son of Nelly Mervyn and William White ; but unfortunately the places of baptisms, marriages, and deaths are not given, thus materially diminishing the practical value of the pedigree, the earlier part of which is printed in Hoare's Modern Wilts, Heytesbury Hundred, p. 203. See also Lambert pedigrees Mss. Coll. Arm., " I. C. 22," *p. 52b,* and " J. P. 43," *pp.* 489-90.

§ Extract from the" Salisbury and Winchester Journal," Monday, 20 May 1805:—" On Wednesday, " died at his house at Kingstone Deverill, aged near 80 years, John Mervin, Gent., the last surviving " male issue of the ancient and respectable family of that name, formerly of Fonthill in this county."

‖ See Par. Reg. Kingstone Deverill, APPENDIX III., p. x.

1. MARY, born 23 Feb., bapt. at Kingstone Deverill,* 6 March 1728–9; died 7 January 1783.
2. JANE, born 24 August, bapt. at Kingstone Deverill* in Sept. 1732; buried 2 March 1737.
3. BETTY, born 24 Jan.ʳ 1734; married 11 Dec.ʳ 1769, James BRICE, and died s.p.
4. NELLY (eventually, on the death of her brother John, coh. of her father), born 10 June 1737; married 15 July 1766, William WHITE, who was born 8 August 1726, and died 1 May 1810. She survived her husband and died 31 July 1816, leaving issue.†

    I. WILLIAM LAMBERT WHITE, of Yeovil, Lt.-Col. of the East Somersetshire Yeomanry Cavalry, b. 1 June 1767, and d. 17 April 1845, having married 25 June 1789, ANNE dau. of Moulton MESSITER, of Wincanton, who was b. 25 May 1761, and d. 20 March 1852, leaving one child Lætitia Messiter White, b. 15 March 1790, and d. unmarried 15 May 1868.

    II. JOHN MERVIN WHITE, who was b. 22 Aug. 1770, and d. unmarried 10 May 1793, æt. 22.

    III. FREDERICK WHITE, b. 6 March 1772, and d. 25 Feb. 1845, having married ELLERY, dau. of the Rev. Peter BEAVIS, who d. 19 Nov. 1828; the issue of their marriage being

        I. WILLIAM WHITE, b. 23 Jan. 1805, and d. unmarried 25 May 1844.

        II. FREDERICK WHITE, b. 17 Feb. 1806, and married in 1842 to MARY JANE KING, but died without issue.‡

        1. ANNE, b. 10 Dec. 1803, and died 18 July 1826.

        2. FRANCES, b. 20 Feb. 1809, and died 23 Sept. 1872, having married T. RODHAM, who pre-deceased her.‡

        3. JANE, b. 20 April 1814; *living* unmarried 1873.‡

    IV. JAMES WHITE, b. 4 March, 1774; d. 5 June 1852, unmarried.‡

    V. ALBINUS WHITE, b. 23 June 1779; d. 4 April 1808, unmarried.‡

    1. NELLY MARIA, b. 11 April 1767; married John DYER, and died 4 March 1799, s.p.

    2. JANE, b. 3 June 1776, and died 3 Dec. 1779.

5. JENNY MERVYN, eventually co-h. of her father, born 1 Nov.ʳ 1739; married John PARRATT, and died 29 Dec.ʳ 1824.
6. REBECCA MERVYN, eventually co-h. of her father, born 5 April 1744, and died 2 June 1800, having married, 1767, Joseph KIDDLE, who survived her and died 1824.

IV. JAMES MERVYN, born 1706; buried 1707.

---

* See Par. Reg. Kingstone Deverill, APPENDIX III., p. x.
† Some of the particulars of the issue of Nelly Mervyn and William White were furnished to me by Mr. Henry Messiter, of Wincanton, whose aunt, Anne Messiter married William Lambert White.
‡ Ex relⁿ Mr. H. Messiter, 1873.

EDWARD MERVYN, the second son of John Mervyn and Anne Toppe, signed the pedigree entered at the Wiltshire Visitation of 1677, wherein he is described as being then of the age of 37 years, (which would give 1640 as the date of his birth). He settled at Salisbury, and is recorded as having died before 1691.[*] He married, about 1665, FRANCES, daughter and heiress of Francis SHELDON, of Manston, co. Dorset, (who survived her husband, and on 4th May 1690,[†] re-married John Nicholas, and was living in 1716 at the date of her daughter Frances' will.) Their issue were seven children, four sons and four daughters.

I. SHELDON MERVYN, the eldest son, was eleven years old at the Visitation of 1677. He inherited the Manston Estate, which he sold to Peter Walter, of Stalbridge, and afterwards resided at Hanley in the county of Dorset, where he died unmarried 6 December 1734, and was buried at Pertwood.[‡] His will[§] was dated 3 Dec. 1725, and proved in London 11 March, 1734.

II. EDWARD MERVYN, the second son, mentioned in Visitation 1677, and in Pedigree of 1801, died unmarried in 1716.

III. JOHN MERVYN, baptized at St. Martin's, Salisbury, 26 Dec. 1667. [‖]

IV. JOHN MERVYN, (after referred to) fourth son.

1. FRANCES, the eldest daughter of Edward Mervyn and Frances Sheldon, was living in 1725. She died unmarried, leaving a will[§] dated 28 June 1716, by which she appointed her brother Sheldon residuary legatee and sole executor. Administration of the effects of the testatrix, unadministered by the executor, was granted by the Archdeaconry Court of Dorset to her sister Mary Pouldon, then of Stalbridge co. Dorset, widow, on 3 November 1737.

2. MARY, the second daughter, born in 1673, married at Manston, 11 February 1703, Richard POULDON, of Hanley in the county of Dorset, but had no issue. She survived her husband, and resided at Ringwood co. Southampton. She died 27 March 1747, aged 74,[¶] and was buried at Pertwood. Her will, dated 6 Oct. 1744, was proved 5 May 1747.[**]

3. ANN, the third daughter, married the Reverend John TRIPSACK, whom she survived, and is recorded in the pedigree Coll. Arms 1801,[††] as having had issue two sons, one of whom, Henry Tripsack, is a legatee under the will of his aunt Frances Mervyn.

4. ELIZABETH, the youngest daughter, was baptized at St. Martin's, Salisbury, 11 Dec. 1680,[‖] and was living in 1725. She married Paget WALTER,[‡‡] the

---

* See Ped. 1801, APPENDIX III. p. vi.

† Manston Par. Reg.: "M[r]. John Nicholas & M[rs]. Frances Mervyn were marryed Maij 4[to]. A[o]. D[ni]. 1690."

‡ "Here lies the body of Sheldon Mervin, son of Edward Mervin, Esq., and Frances his wife, sole daughter and heiress of Francis Sheldon, Esq[re] of Manston in the county of Dorset, who departed this life December the 6th 1734, in the 68th year of his age." (*Monumental Inscrip. Pertwood Church*.)

§ See Abstract of the Will, APPENDIX III., p. viii.

‖ Par. Reg. St. Martin's, Salisbury, APPENDIX III., p. x.

¶ *Monumental Inscrip. Pertwood Church:*—"Here lies the body of Mrs. Mary Pouldon, relict of "Richard Pouldon, Esq., and sister of Sheldon Mervin, Esq., who died 27 March 1747, aged 74."

** See Abstract of the Will, APPENDIX III., p. viii.

†† It is somewhat remarkable that Frances Mervyn in her will of 1716 refers to Mrs. Pouldon and Mrs. Walter as her "sisters," but describes Mrs. Anne Tripsack as her "sister-in-law."

‡‡ For particulars of the Stalbridge Estate (the original house on which was built by Mervyn Earl of Castlehaven) and the Walter family, see *Hutchin's Hist. of Dorsetshire*, Lond. 1813, vol. iii., p. 239.

only child of Peter Walter* (who bought the Manston Estate from her brother Sheldon). Mr. Paget Walter died in his father's lifetime, leaving by his wife, Elizabeth Mervyn, 3 sons,† Peter, b. 1715, Edward, and Sheldon, b. 1721 (neither of whom left male issue), and four daughters, viz.:—Jane (of whom hereafter), Diana, born 1714, married George Anne Buckett, Mary, who died unmarried 1751, and Elizabeth, born 1719, who married Matthew West,‡ of Cranborne.

> EDWARD WALTER, the second son of Elizabeth Mervyn and Paget Walter, who was born in 1727, and died in 1780, left (by his wife HARIOT, 2nd daughter of George, 5th Baron Forester), a daughter and heiress, Harriot Walter, who married James Bucknall, 3rd Viscount Grimston, created Baron Verulam, the grandfather of JAMES WALTER, 2nd EARL of VERULAM, born in 1809, and now (1873) *living*.

> JANE WALTER, the eldest daughter of Paget Walter and Elizabeth Mervyn, (who is mentioned in her aunt Frances Mervyn's will, 1716), was born in 1710, and died in 1801 at the advanced age of 91, having married (at Hanley, 1 Oct., 1741) William COLES, of Salisbury, by whom she was mother of Jane Coles,§ an only child, who was born at Hanley, in 1744, and married in Salisbury Cathedral 16 Sep. 1766, to Thomas Hutchings, of Sherborne, Dorset, who took the name of MEDLYCOTT, by whom she was grandmother of Sir WILLIAM COLES MEDLYCOTT, Bart., of Ven House, Sherborne, born in 1806, and now (1873) *living*.

JOHN MERVYN, the fourth son of Edward Mervyn and Frances Sheldon, settled at Sturminster Newton Castle co. Dorset. He was baptized at St. Martin's church, Salisbury 4th May 1679,|| and buried at Manston, 18 May 1733,¶ having married BRIDGETT DARLING (who was also buried at Manston, on 29 January 1734 |); their issue being one son and two daughters.

> I. The Rev. EDWARD MERVYN, sometime Fellow Commoner of Balliol College, Oxford, admitted 15 Feb. 1728,** and became B.A. 17 Jan. 1731. He had a living in ,Somersetshire, where he married, but died without issue in the lifetime of his father. (*Ped. Coll. Arm.* 1801.)

---

* Of whom Pope wrote—

> "What's property, dear Swift? you see it alter
> From you to me, from me to Peter Walter."

See some notes on the Walter family in "*The Herald and Genealogist*," vol. viii. p. 1.

  † The Mervyn Pedigree of 1801 (APPENDIX III., p. vi.) states that there were three children of the marriage between Paget Walter and Elizabeth Mervyn, "one son and two daughters," but from the pedigree furnished to me by Sir W. C. Medlycott the above statement would appear to be accurate.

  ‡ Sir W. C. Medlycott informs me that there were issue of this marriage, a son, Rev. Edward Mathew West of Bradford co. Dorset, who married Ann Coates, and had issue, the Rev. Edward Walter West, Vicar of Milborne Port; the Rev. Mervyn West; Capt. Henry West, R.N.; and four daughters, of whom two (Harriet and Ann) died at Milborne Port, unmarried.

  § Mrs. Jane Medlycott was much interested in the history of the Mervyn family, and corresponded on the subject with my venerable friend, the late Mrs. Dorothy Mervyn of Ashford, Devon. I have now before me, one of Mrs. Medlycott's letters to Mrs. Mervyn, in which she gives several family particulars. The letter was written from Bath, where she then resided, in May 1823, just a year before her death at the advanced age of 79.

  || Par. reg. St. Martin's Salisbury, APPENDIX III., p. x.

  ¶ "John Mervin (of) Sturminster Newton Castle (buried) May 18th 1733." "Bridget Mervyn (of) Sturminster Newton Castle (buried) Jan'y. 29 1734." (*Extracted from Par. Registers of Manston.*)

  ** Ex. rel. Robert Scott, Master of Balliol, in letter to Sir H. M. Vavasour, 12 Nov. 1864.

52

1. **BIDDY**, the elder of the two daughters, (and on their brother's death, co-heirs of their father,) married† at Sturminster Newton Castle, 14 April 1735, Henry NOOTH, eldest son of the Reverend James Nooth, Prebendary of Wells Cathedral. She died in 1769,‡ and was buried at Manston. Mr. Nooth survived her, and was buried at Dorchester in 1784. Henry Nooth and Bridget Mervyn had with other issue§

I. JOHN MERVYN NOOTH, M.D., baptized at Sturminster Newton Castle, 5 Sep. 1737. In 1801, he verified by his signed attestation the accuracy of the pedigree registered in the College of Arms in that year.‖ He was at that time residing at Quebec, but he subsequently settled at Bath, where in 1807 he married the widow of Mr. WILFORD, by whom he had no issue.¶

II. HENRY NOOTH, the second son, born at Sturminster Newton Castle, 1 June 1741, was Lieut.-Colonel 4th Dragoon Guards. He married in 1766, at Fulham, co. Middlesex. ANNE ASSHETON, the eldest daughter and co-heir of Mail or Maghull YATES, of Spaldington, co. York, by his wife Elizabeth Trafford,** and in 1791 took, by royal licence, the name and arms of VAVASOUR, in pursuance of the will of his wife's ancestor, Thomas Vavasour, of Spaldington.¶ In 1801 he was created a Baronet, died 15 March 1813, and was buried in the family vault at Bubwith, co. York, on the 22nd of the same month. Anne Lady Vavasour survived her husband Sir Henry, and died at York 9th January 1818, and was also buried at Bubwith. The issue of the marriage were two sons.**

  I. EDMUND TRAFFORD NOOTH,** born at Chippenham, 14th February 1766, was a Captain in the 76th Regt. of Foot, and died at Calcutta, 5th Nov. 1796, unmarried.

  II. SIR HENRY MAGHULL MERVIN VAVASOUR, who was born 19 July 1767, and baptized at Blandford, 18 Aug. 1767.** He succeeded as 2nd Baronet on the death of his father in 1813, having previously married, in Dublin on 14 July 1807, ANNE, elder daughter of William VAVASOUR, of Dublin, L.L.D., the representative of the Vavasours of Spaldington in the male line. Sir Henry, who entered the army

---

* The Arms here given as those of Nooth are inserted on the authority of Sir H. M. Vavasour, who states that he has in his possession evidence that the Coat was borne by his grandfather, Lt.-Col. Henry Nooth, previous to his taking the name and arms of Vavasour.

† The statements as to the descendants of the marriage between Bridget Mervyn and Henry Nooth have been supplied to me by their great-grandson, Sir Henry Mervin Vavasour, Bart., who has inherited from his grandmother, Anne Assheton Lady Vavasour, a taste for genealogical researches. Lady Vavasour, between the years 1780 and 1818, collected with great care information connected with her own and her husband's families. The notes so collected form two Ms. volumes, the contents of which, so far as they bear upon the Mervyn connection, have been courteously placed at my disposal by Sir Henry in addition to the materials which he has himself collected in continuation of Lady Vavasour's compilation.

‡ "Biddy Nooth (of) Sturminster Newton (buried) Oct. 4th 1769." (*Extracted from Par. Reg. Manston.*)

§ See Pedigrees, APPENDIX III., pp. ii. and vi.

‖ See APPENDIX III., p. vi.

¶ *Ex rel.* Sir H. M. Vavasour, Bt.

** See Pedigree *Ms. Coll. Arms D.* 14, *pp.* 12, 13, verified in 1787 by Elizabeth Yates (née Trafford) and Anne Assheton Nooth (née Yates.)

as Cornet in the Horse Grenadier Guards March 1783, attained the rank of a Lieutenant-General, and was an active Magistrate for East Yorkshire, and an eminent agriculturist. He died 4th January 1838, and was buried at Bubwith. Lady Vavasour who survived her husband, died 7th June 1845, and was buried at Netherex co. Devon. The issue of the marriage of Sir H. M. M. Vavasour and Anne Vavasour, *living* in 1873, are an only son and three daughters* viz:

I. SIR HENRY MERVYN VAVASOUR of Spaldington co. York, 3rd Baronet, who was born 17 June 1814, at Melbourne Hall in the parish of Thornton, in the East Riding of the county of York, was for many years Major in the East York Militia, and married 30 June 1853, at St. James's Church Piccadilly co. Middlesex, the Honorable LOUISA ANNE NEVILLE, second daughter of Richard 3rd Baron Braybrooke, by whom he has had issue.

  1. BLANCHE, b. 6 June 1854, bapt. St. George's, Hanover Square, 9th, d. 14th, and bur. at Littlebury co. Essex, 19th July in the same year.
  2. CONSTANCE, born at Hatherton Hall co. Stafford, 16 March 1856, baptized in the ecclesiastical parish of Cannock in the same county 11 April 1856 ; *living* 1873.

  1. ANNA MERVYNIA, born 11 September 1812, at Elvington Hall in the East Riding co. York, and married in 1839, at Monkstown, co. Dublin, the Reverend Joseph DUNNINGTON, M.A., of Thicket Priory in the East Riding, co. York, who has taken the name of JEFFERSON, and has issue, *living* 1873, three sons and three daughters.
  2. CAROLINE SUSAN, born 21 July 1816, at Melbourne Hall, and married, firstly at St. George's, Hanover Square in 1841, her cousin William Thomas VAVASOUR, only son of the Reverend Richard Frederick Vavasour, Rector of Stow co. Gloucester ; and secondly, at Bath, in 1868, the Reverend William WIGGIN, now (1873) Rector of Hampnett, also in the county of Gloucester, *living* 1873.
  3. EMMA MATILDA, born 26 Sep. 1818, at Melbourne Hall, married in 1852 at Brompton. in the North Riding co. York, Whitehall DOD, of Llannerch Park co. Denbigh, (only child of John Whitehall Dod, of Cloverley, M.P. for North Shropshire,) both *living* 1873, but without issue.

III. JAMES NOOTH, baptized at Sturminster Newton Castle, 28th September 1744, and living at Bath in 1801; he married ELIZABETH, daughter of . . . . . BINDLEY, sometime one of the

---

* Ex rel. Sir H. M. Vavasour, Bt.

Barons of the Cinque Ports. She was living in 1792. The issue of the marriage were one son and one daughter.

    I. HENRY STEPHEN NOOTH, baptized at Bath, 22 June 1795. Died s.p.*

      1. CHARLOTTE, born 15 April 1783, baptized at Dorchester. Died unm.*

  IV. EDWARD NOOTH, born at Sturminster Newton Castle, 28 May 1747, and died at Verdun unmarried in 1767.

    1. MARY, baptized at Sturminster Newton Castle, 13 January 1743, married John JAMES, of Bristol. She died and was buried at Bristol, leaving one son.

      I. JOHN MERVYN JAMES, mentioned in will of Robert Prower,† (1792).

    2. FRANCES MERVYN, second daughter and co-heir of JOHN MERVYN and Bridgett DARLING, married‡ Robert PROWER, of Cranborne, co. Dorset, surgeon, who, in 1786, obtained the diploma of M.D. from the University of Aberdeen. She died 9th January 1789,§ and was buried at Cranborne, as was also her husband, who died on 30 August, 1793,§ aged 68, having made a will dated 31 August 1792.† The surviving issue of the marriage‖ were three children, one son and two daughters.

      I. The Rev. JOHN PROWER, after mentioned, born Nov. 7 1747, baptized at Sturminster Newton, 16 March 1751.¶

      1. FANNY, born Sept. 10th, 1746, baptized at Sturminster Newton, 16 March, 1751,¶ married to the Rev. Henry RIGBY, also after mentioned.

      2. BIDDY or BRIDGET, baptized at Cranborne, 2 Oct. 1755; and married in 1788 to the Rev. William STOREY, as after mentioned.

---

* *Ex rele.* Major Prower.

† See Abstract of the will APPENDIX III., p. viii.

‡ I have been unable to trace the place of marriage which apparently took place about 1745, and is recorded (as is also the place and date of Mrs. Prower's death) in the pedigree registered in 1801 at the College of Arms before mentioned (APPENDIX III., p. vi.); but in it Dr. Prower's christian name is, by mistake, inscribed as "*John*" instead of "*Robert*;" his identity is, however, established by the statement appended to his name "*now M.D.*" It will be seen by the text that Dr. Prower followed the profession of a surgeon before he obtained his diploma as Doctor of Medicine.

§ *Inscriptions on Monument in the Chancel of Cranborne Church:*—"Near this place, in the vault "of Robert Prower, M.D., are deposited the remains," "of Fanny Prower, wife of Robert Prower, M.D. "She died the 9th January, 1789." "Of Robert Prower, M.D. He died the 30th of August, 1793." The Parochial Registers of Burials at Cranborne contain the following entries viz :—"Fraces (*sic*) Prower, "aged (*sic*) of this Parish, wife of Robert Prower, M.D., was buried Jan. 17th 1789." " Registered "Jan. 17th by me Henry Donne, Vicar." "Robert Prower, M.D., aged 68, of this parish, was buried "Sept. 7th, 1793." "Registered by me H. Donne, Vicar."

‖ The particulars of the children of this marriage and of their descendants were furnished to me by Major John Elton Mervin Prower, of Purton House, Wilts (Dr. Robert Prower's great grandson), and by Miss Charlotte Sophia Story-Maskelyne, of Basset Down House, co. Wilts (the granddaughter of Biddy Prower, who married the Reverend William Storey).

In the Registers of the parish of Sturminster Newton there is, as above shown, an entry of the baptism, on the 16th March, 1751, of "William, son of Robert Prower, was born 12 February, 1750," and in the Cranborne baptismal registers there are the following entries :—"Robert, of Robert "Prower, Gent., Aug. 12, 1751." "Betty, of Mr. Robert Prower, Aug. 29, 1752." And "William, of "Robert Prower, Gent., June 25, 1754." from which it would seem that there were other children; but Major Prower informs me that he never heard his grandfather allude to them, and he considers that they must have died in their infancy, a conclusion corroborated by the fact that Dr. Prower does not mention them in his will.

¶ Extracts from Baptismal Registers of the parish of Sturminster Newton, co. Dorset, certified by the Rev. R. Lowndes, Vicar, 1874 :—"1751, Mar. 16. Fanny, daughter, John and William, sons, of Mr. "Robert Prower and Frances his wife. Baptisms for 1751. Fanny, daughter of Robert Prower, was born "Sept. 10th, 1746. John, son of Robt. Prower, was born Nov. 7, 1747. Wm., son of Robt. Prower, was "born 12 February, 1750."

55

I. The Rev⁴ JOHN PROWER, M.A., Vicar of Purton, co. Wilts; b.
7 November 1747; collated to the living of Purton 22 Dec. 1771,
mentioned in his father's will (1792); d. 29 November 1827, æt. 80,
and buried at Purton.* He married, 1st July 1777 at Great
Hallingbury, Essex, ANNE, daughter of Christopher LIPYEATT of
Marlborough,† who died 25 July 1811, aged 64, and was also buried
at Purton.* By her he had three children, two sons and one daughter.

    I. JOHN MERVIN PROWER, b. 14 January 1784, bapt. at Purton,
7 March 1784;‡ Honorary Canon of Bristol, December
1844; succeeded his father as Vicar of Purton in February
1828, which preferment he held until his death on 2 April
1869.‡ He married at Purton, 20 September 1809,‡
SUSANNAH, only child§ of John COLES,‖ of Codoxton
House, Neath, co Glamorgan, who died 15 Oct. 1811,
aged 25 years, and was buried in St Michael's church at
Gloucester. The only issue of the marriage of John Mervin
Prower and Susannah Coles was:—

        JOHN ELTON MERVIN PROWER, of Purton House,
b. 11 Oct., and bapt. at St. Michael's church,
Gloucester, 20 Oct. 1811, formerly Captain in the
67th Regiment, and late Major in the Royal
Wilts Militia. Major Prower was High Sheriff
of Wilts, 1862-3, and married 5 July 1844,
at Cookham, Berks, HARRIET, daughter of William
PAYN, of Kidwells, Maidenhead, by whom he has
had issue:—

           I. MERVYN PROWER, b. 2 May, and bapt. at
Purton, 6 June 1847, died at Oxford,
28 November 1867, from the effects of
injuries which he received in attempting

---

* *Mon. Insc. Purton Church-yard.* "Sacred to the memory of the Rev⁴. John Prower, M.A., who
"died the 29th of November 1827, aged 80. For 56 years the highly respected Vicar of this parish, endeared
"to his parishioners by an almost unequalled kindness of disposition and attention to their spiritual welfare.
"In this Vault likewise repose the remains of Anne his beloved wife daughter of Christopher Lipyeatt Esq.
"of Marlborough in this county. Most exemplary as a wife, mother and friend. She died the 25th July
"1811 aged 64. And also those of their youngest son Thomas Prower Esqre. who died the 27th of October
"1823, in the year of his age 37."

† The Lipyeatts were long settled at Marlborough, of which town Christopher Lipyeatt was Mayor
in 1674. Jonathan Lipyeatt, the last male of the name now living, resides at the Hermitage, Dawlish,
with an unmarried granddaughter, the sole survivor of the family.—*Ex rel⁴.* Major Prower.

‡ *Extracts from Purton Parochial Registers:*—
Baptisms 1784. "John Mervin, son of Reverend John, and Ann Prower, privately baptized 7 March
"1784, and publicly baptized October 23." Signed "J. Prower, Vicar."——*Marriages* 1809. "No. 318."
"John Mervin Prower, of the Parish of "Quatt, in the county of Salop, and Susannah Coles of this parish;
"married in this church by license this 20th day of September, in the year 1809, by me John Prower,
"Vicar."——*Burials* 1869. "John Mervin Prower (Vicar) Purton, April 7, age 85. Resident Vicar
"of this parish for 41½ years."

§ *Mon. Insc. Purton Churchyard.*—"Sacred to the memory of the Rev⁴ʸ John Mervin Prower, son of the
Rev⁴. John Prower, Honorary Canon of Bristol, and 41 years Vicar of this Parish. He died April 2nd 1869,
aged 85. Also to the memory of Susan his wife, only child of John Coles, Esq., of Codoxton House,
Glamorganshire. She died Oct. 15 1811, aged 25, and is buried in St Michael's Church, Gloucester."

‖ The family of COLES were seated at Thrupp, near Faringdon, co. Berks, in which church there
are some monumental records,—John Coles was married on 12th Dec. 1785, at the parish church of
Newent, co. Gloucester, to Susan ELTON, sister to John Elton, of Newent, the last male representative of
the ancient family of Elton, of the Hazles, co. Hereford. On the deaths of John Elton (at Gloucester)
without issue, and of Elizabeth Elton his unmarried sister, Major John Elton Mervin Prower became the
heir-at-law of his uncle, and inherited his property, other than the Herefordshire estate which he had sold
in his lifetime. Monumental records of members of the Elton family will be found in the churches of
Ledbury and Newent, and in the Cathedral at Gloucester. *Ex rel⁴.* Major Prower.

to rescue a fellow collegian in a "Town and Gown" Riot. A monumental slab of black marble to his memory was placed by his fellow collegians on the wall of the Chapel of Brasenose College, bearing the following inscription :—

"In Memoriam MERVYN PROWER hujus "Collegii olim Commensalis, qui vicesimo "ætatis anno, inter tumultum plebis A.D. "9th November 1867 læsus, A.D. Kal. Dec. "obdormivit. "Hoc desiderii sui virtutumque "ejus Monumentum ponendum curaverunt "æquales. Requiescat in pace."

He was buried at Purton, 4 December 1867.

II. JOHN ELTON PROWER, b. 11 Oct., bapt. at Purton, 14 Nov. 1852; *living* 1873.

III. NELSON PROWER, b. 7 Nov., bapt. at Purton, 14 Dec. 1856; *living* 1873.

1. MAUDE, b. 2 July, bapt. at Purton, 30 July 1854; *living* 1873.

2. MARION, b. 5 January, bapt. at Purton, 24 April 1859; *living* 1873.

3. BEATRICE, b. 3 Feb., bapt. at Purton, 3 July 1860; *living* 1873.

II. THOMAS PROWER, b. 27 April 1786; was in early life a Surgeon in the Royal Navy, and d. unm. 27 October 1823; he was buried at Purton,* 1 November 1823.

1. ANNE,† b. January 1779, bapt. at Purton on the 18th of the same month, d. 7th, and buried at Purton 12th April 1834, having married (30 Oct. 1810 at Purton,) Robert ISHERWOOD,† of Highgate co. Middlesex, and Doctors' Commons, who was b. about 1781, died 14th, and bur. at Purton 22nd July 1837, aged 56, leaving one child

ANNA, who was married at St. Michael's Church, Highgate 2 September 1837, to Harry CHESTER (son of Sir Robert Chester, Kn⁴ Master of the Ceremonies at S⁴ James's), Clerk of the Privy Council, and Chief Secretary of the Educational Department, who died 5 October 1868, aged 62; and was buried at S⁴ Margaret's, Westminster. Mrs. Chester died at the age of 40 years, and was buried 1 January 1855, at the cemetery of S⁴ James's, Highgate. The issue of the marriage were two sons and three daughters, viz. :

I. HARRY CHESTER.
II. MERVIN CHESTER. ⎫ All died under age
1. ANNA. ⎬ and unmarried.
2. DULCIBELLA. ⎭
3. CAROLINE, *living* 1873 unm.

1. FANNY, dau. of ROBERT PROWER and FRANCES MERVYN, mentioned in her father's will (1792), was b. (her age is not correctly stated in

---

* Mon. Insc. Vide note ante, p. 55.
† Mr. and Mrs. Isherwood were both buried in the Prower Vault in Purton Churchyard.

her burial certificate*) 10th Sept. 1746, and m. the Reverend Henry RIGBY, Vicar of Hockley and Prebendary of Salisbury, whom she survived. Mrs. RIGBY died at Salisbury, the 7th and was buried at Cranbourne,* 14th March 1827, aged 82, having had issue, one child HARRIET, who died unm. 13 August 1816, and was buried at Cranbourne,* aged 40.

2. BIDDY, dau. of ROBERT PROWER and FRANCES MERVYN, born at Cranbourne and baptized there 2nd October 1755,† is mentioned in her father's will (1792). She was married at Hinton Martell co. Dorset, 8 January 1788,‡ to the Reverend William STOREY§ Rector of that parish, and subsequently also (1793) Rector of West Purley in the same county, M.A. of Wadham College, Oxford, who died 1st October 1797, and was buried at Cranbourne,|| as was also his wife, who survived him, and was buried 26th May 1827. The issue of the marriage was an only son.

ANTHONY MERVIN REEVE STORY-MASKELYNE, (b. 8 May 1791, and bapt. at Hinton Martell on 16 July following,) of Basset Down House, Salthrope Lodge, and Lydiard Manor, co. Wilts; Horfield Court, co. Gloucester; and Glenusk, co. Brecon. He was educated at Wadham College, Oxford, where in 1811 he graduated with honors as double first in classics and mathematics, and was called to the bar in Michaelmas Term 1816. Mr. Story (who adopted the original spelling of his patronymic) assumed the name of MASKELYNE in 1845. He married at St. George's, Hanover Square on 22nd November 1819, MARGARET, the only child of the Revd. Nevil MASKELYNE, of Basset Down House and Purton, D.D., F.R.S., Astronomer Royal, Fellow of Trinity Coll. Cambridge, and Rector of North Runcton co. Norfolk.¶ Mrs. Story-Maskelyne

---

* *Inscriptions on Monument in the Chancel of Cranbourne Church:*—"Near this place, in the " vault of Robert Prower, M.D., are deposited the remains" "Of Harriet Rigby, grand-daughter of Robert " Prower, M.D. She died the 13th of August 1816." " Of Fanny, widow of Henry Rigby and daughter " of Robert Prower, M.D. She died 6th March 1827." The entry of Mrs. Rigby's burial in the parish Registers of Cranbourne states her age to have been 82. (She was in fact in her 81st year.)

† Cranbourne par. registers.

‡ Hinton Martell, par. registers.

§ Mr. William Storey [originally spelt Story], born 15 July 1734, and baptised at Holywell church Oxford, was the youngest, but only son who left issue, of Robert Story, of Oxford, formerly of Know, in the parishes of Arthuret and Kirkandrews on Esk, co. Cumberland, who was born 1 May 1681, and bapt. at Kirkandrews, where, on the 10 October 1713, he married Margaret Johnston, and dying on 13 April 1751, was buried, (as was subsequently his widow, Margaret,) at Holywell. This latter Robert Story was the son of another Robert Story of Know, and grandson of yet another Robert Story of the same place, who was the son of Herbert Story, also of Know, and Sybil his wife, who were respectively buried at Arthuret ; Herbert Story, on 8 Oct. 1627, and his widow Sybil, on 27 Dec. 1635. *Ex relatione*, Miss Charlotte Story-Maskelyne, 1873.

|| *Inscription on Monument in the Chancel of Cranbourne Church:*—"Near this place, in the vault " of Robert Prower, M.D., are deposited the remains" "Of the Revd. William Storey, A.M. He died " the 1st of Oct. 1797."

¶ Dr. Maskelyne was b. 16 October 1732, and d. 9 Feb. 1811 (bur. in the Maskelyne family vault at Purton), having married (21 August 1784, at St. Andrew's Holborn,) Sophia, one of the two daughters and co-heirs, (and, on the death without issue, 10 Sept. 1823, of her sister Lætitia, widow of Sir George Booth, Bart.,) the sole heir of John Pate Rose, of Cotterstock Hall, co. Northampton, who d. 3 Nov. 1758. Dr. Maskelyne was the youngest (but only son having issue), of Edmund Maskelyne of Purton, by his wife Elizabeth, only child of John Booth of Woodford, by Elizabeth his wife, daughter and co-heir of Edward Projer, of Hampton Court, of Westowe Hall, co. Norfolk, and of Gwernay, co. Monmouth, Equerry to King Charles II. [There are still existing at Basset Down many letters written and addressed by Charles I. and by Charles II., and the other children of Charles I., to this Edward Projer]. The before-

was born 20 June 1787, bapt. at the Old Church Greenwich; died, 15 February 1858, and was buried at Purton, leaving two sons and four daughters, all of whom are now (1873) *living*, viz. :—

I. MERVIN HERBERT NEVIL STORY-MASKELYNE, F.R.S., born 3 September 1823, baptized at Lydiard Tregoze, Honorary Fellow of Wadham College, Oxford, where he was educated. He graduated with honors, May 1845, and proceeded M.A. in 1849; Professor of Mineralogy to the University of Oxford, and Keeper of the Mineral Department of the British Museum; Deputy-Lieut. for the county of Brecon, was married on 29 June 1858, at Gorseinon church, Llangyvelach co. Glamorgan, to THEREZA MARY, eldest daughter of John Dillwyn LLEWELYN, of Penllergare co. Glamorgan, of which marriage there are issue, three daughters, all now (1873) *living*, viz. :—

    1. MARGARET EMMA, b. 1 April 1859, bapt. at St. James's, Paddington.
    2. MARY LUCY, b. 8 June 1861, bapt. at St. James's, Paddington.
    3. THEREZA CHARLOTTE, b. 3 June 1863, bapt. at St. James's, Paddington.

II. EDMUND MERVIN BOOTH STORY-MASKELYNE, b. 23 April 1829, bapt. at Lydiard Tregoze; graduated B.A. of Wadham College, Oxford, in March 1853; called to the Bar in March 1861; married 25 October 1860, at St James's Church Piccadilly, London, MARTHA BANGER, daughter of Thomas RUSSELL, of Beaminster co. Dorset, and has issue, a son and daughter, both now (1873) *living*, viz.:—

    I. ANTHONY St JOHN STORY-MASKELYNE, b. 31 July 1861, bapt. at Purton church, co. Wilts, September 1861.
    1. AGNES MARY, b. 22 March 1870, bapt. at St. Stephen's Paddington.

1. CHARLOTTE SOPHIA, b. 19 March 1822, bapt. at Purton church, *living* 1873.

2. MARGARET MERVINIA, b. 20 Dec. 1824, and bapt. at Lydiard Tregoze, where she married, on 25

---

named John Booth of Woodford was the grandson and lineal representative of Sir John Booth, Knt., (second son of Sir George Booth, created a Bart. 1611.) who married Dorothy St. John, the only child of Sir Anthony St. John fourth son of Oliver fourth Baron St. John of Bletshoe, created Earl of Bolingbroke 1644. The family of Maskelyne has long been settled in Purton, holding lands there and in Lydiard, co. Wilts. Dr. Maskelyne is the lineal male descendant of Robert Masklyn of Purton and Lydiard, through intermarriages (among others) with the following families, namely, Shackstaff of Lydiard; Stevens of Burderope; Richmond Webb of Lydiard Manor; Davys of Little Mitton co. Worcester; Norden of Roude co. Wilts; Houblon, of London; Bath of Purton, and Booth of Woodford. *Ex rele*, Edm. Mervyn Booth Story-Maskelyne, 1873. There was a Pedigree of the Maskelyne family registered at the Herald's Visitation of Wiltshire in 1623 when their Arms were recorded, viz.—*Sable a fess engrailed Or, between 3 Escalop Shells argent. Crest, A demy lyon sable holding between the paws an escalop shell argent.* (See Ms. Coll. Arm. 1 C 22 p. 106.)

April 1848, the Revd. THOMAS MASTERMAN, M.A. of Wadham College Oxford, Incumbent of Headington Quarry Oxford, (son of the late John Masterman, M.P. for the City of London.) He died 22 Sept. 1856, and was bur. in the cemetery at Torquay. The issue of the marriage were two sons and a daughter, all *living* in 1873, viz. :—

    I. JOHN STORY MASTERMAN, b. 14 July, bapt. at St. Leonard's Wallingford, 10 Sept. 1849; Fellow of Brasenose College Oxford, where he graduated B.A. with honors, first in classics in December 1872.

    II. NEVIL MASTERMAN, b. 13 July 1851, bapt. at Garsington church Oxford, 22 February 1852; Exhibitioner of Corpus College, Oxford.

    1. MARGARET ELIZA, b. 20 August, bapt. at Upton church Torquay, 21 Sept. 1855.

3. ANNA MARIA ANTONIA, b. 3 April 1827, bapt. at Lydiard Tregoze, married, 9 April 1864, at St. James's, Piccadilly, WARRINGTON WILKINSON SMYTH, F.R.S., M.A., of Trinity College Cambridge, Knight of the Italian Order of S.S. Maurizio and Lazzaro, and of the Portuguese Order of Jesus Christ; eldest son of the late Admiral William Henry Smyth, F.R.S., by his marriage with Anne, only child of Thomas Warrington, of Naples. There are issue of the marriage, *living* 1873, two sons, viz. :—

    I. HERBERT WARRINGTON SMYTH, b. 4 June 1867, bapt. at St. Andrew's church Pimlico.

    II. NEVILLE MASKELYNE SMYTH, b. 14 August 1868, bapt. at St. Andrew's Pimlico.

4. AGNES LUCY META, b. 3 November 1830, bapt. at Lydiard Tregoze, *living* 1873.

CORRIGENDA AND ADDENDA.

DEVONSHIRE BRANCH.

For ‘Bourchier’ read “Bouchier,” pp. 66, 67, 68.   Add following note at p. 66 :—

> “Dr. Thomas Bouchier, being then a Fellow of All Souls College, Oxford, was in 1678
> “elected Principal of St. Alban's Hall, an appointment he held until his death in 1723. He was
> “Commissary of the Archbishop of Canterbury and Archdeacon of Lewes, and died in May 1723,
> “aged 80, at Hanborow, co. Sussex, where he was buried. He was succeeded as Principal of
> “St. Alban's by his eldest son James Bouchier, Ll.D., of whom a portrait exists in the dining-room
> “of the Rev. William Charles Salter, the present (1873) Principal (See Anthony Wood's Ath. Ox.).”

Description of the Bouchier Arms, Appendix IV., p. iv should stand thus—

> “ MERVIN as above, impaling [Azure] a chev. [Ermine] between 3 [Leopards passant or] for
> “ BOUCHIER.”

The first connection of the name of MERVYN with the county of DEVON, of which I have
a note, dates from the 19th Henry VIII. (1527-8), when EDMUND or EDWARD MERVYN
held the office of Steward or Surveyor to the Lady of the Manor (Countess of Hastings)
of Stokenham.

I have not been able to trace who this EDMUND or EDWARD MERVYN was, or to
connect him with the Wiltshire family, the first member of which, who settled in Devonshire, was the Rev. RICHARD MERVYN, D.D., son of GEORGE MERVYN of Pertwood.*
Dr. Mervyn was a Church Dignitary, and appears to have had some Court influence, as he
held in 1639 the Crown living of Throwleigh, in the county of Devon, and the same
patronage obtained for him four years later, the appointment of Canon of Exeter Cathedral,
of which he subsequently became the Chancellor.

Dr. Mervyn acquired landed property in Devonshire which descended to his grand-
son Richard Mervyn, who in addition, purchased an estate in the parish of Marwood, near
Barnstaple, where he settled, and by whose lineal descendants it is now (1873) held.
The name of Mervyn in Devonshire became extinct, on the death in 1835 of the venerable
Mrs. Dorothy Mervyn, a memoir of whom will be found in the following pages.

RICHARD MERVYN, D.D., the third son of George Mervyn and his wife
Elizabeth Ryves, was born in 1600 at Upton in East Knoyle, where his father resided.
He was baptized in the parish church there† on the 18 Dec. 1600, and is recorded in the
Visitation of Wilts of 1623,‡ as being then twenty-three years old.   Dr. Mervyn's first
Church preferment would appear to have been in 1631, when he was nominated to the
Rectory of Pertwood by his uncle Thomas Mervyn (in whose will (1632) he is mentioned);§
he subsequently, in 1639 (15 Nov.) was inducted Rector of Throwleigh on the presentation of the King.   He occurs as Prebendary of the Cathedral Church of Exeter in the
year 1634 in the room of Thomas Clifford, and in the year 1643, being then B.D., was
elected Residentiary Canon of the Cathedral on the death of Archdeacon Helliar, under
a mandate from Charles I. (still preserved in the family,‖) from which it appears
that all or most of the houses belonging to the Cathedral had been leased out by the Dean
and Chapter, and in order that there might be no hindrance to the election of the
King's nominee on the plea of there not being any residence available for him, the
mandate made it a condition that “ the sayd Richard Mervine doe, att or before the

---

* See Ante, p. 47   † East Knoyle par. reg. APPENDIX III., p. ix.
‡ See APPENDIX III., p. iv.   § See Abstract of the Will, APPENDIX III., p. vii.
‖ See copy APPENDIX IV., p. xi.

" tyme of his Residence, provide himself of a convenient House wherein to keepe
" Hospitality and reside."

In 1644 Dr. Mervyn was (on the death of the Rev. John Hussey) admitted and
inducted Vicar of Okehampton,* of which living he was subsequently dispossessed under
the Ordinance against Pluralities ; and in the following year, 1645, he, being then still
Vicar of Okehampton, was summoned by the Prince of Wales (afterwards Charles II.) to
attend him at his Court at Launceston. The Summons† was in the following terms:—

> " After our hearty comendacons Whereas we sħall allwayes endeavoʳ and shall esteeme
> " it yᵉ greatest ornament and support of our Court and Campe to have about Us yᵉ most
> " Vertuous and able men of all Professions and Condicons, but especially of Divines, by
> " whose good examples and preaching yᵉ rest may be reformed and made better. These
> " are therefore (being informed that you are a Grave, Learned, and Orthodoxe Divine) to
> " desire & require you for yᵉ purpose aforesaid to give yoʳ attendance upon Vs for some
> " tyme, after which we shall dismisse you to yoʳ other occassions. And so we bid yoᵘ heartily
> " Farewell. Given at Our Court at Lanceston yᵉ 1ˢᵗ of February, 1645.
> " CHARLES P.

" To Mr. Richard Mervin,
  " Batcheloʳ in Divinity,
  " at Okehampton or elsewhere."

In June, 1660,‡ the Chancellorship of the Cathedral of Exeter being vacant,
Mr. Mervyn petitioned for the appointment, and his application, which was successful, was
backed by (amongst others) Dr. Lawrence Burnell and Dr. Sheldon, and in September of
that year he was installed Chancellor of the Cathedral, an office he held until his death.
In 1661 (May 6) Dr. Mervyn was (on the resignation of the Revd. Richard Newte)
admitted Rector of Heanton Punchardon, a living in the gift of Arthur Bassett, of
Heanton Court, which he also held up to the time of his death, and in which, as will after
be seen, he was succeeded by his fourth son, William Mervyn. In 1661 (July 3) he was
admitted D.D. of Exeter College, Oxford.

In January 166§ there appears to have been some recusancy on the part of the
Dean and Chapter of Exeter in not complying with a desire of the Crown " to accom-
" modate Dr. Cotton with the lease of Staverton," and Dr. Mervyn and Dr. Jonas Smith
attended in London to give explanations ; but apparently they were in no mind to remain
there longer than necessary, for I find that Secretary Burnet wrote complaining that they
did not stay "until the reports of their statements were made to His Majesty, whereby he
" might end the matter," and they were commanded to return, and the Dean and Chapter
were at the same time warned not to seal (which apparently they were about to do,) the
Agreement contrary to the wishes of the Crown, until the King had heard the whole
business. The learned Divines do not seem to have had any desire to return to the
Metropolis ; for in reply to the summons they, whilst professing their willingness to obey
the King's summons, pleaded that their attendance at the Church during the then approaching
Visitation was necessary, adding the expression of their hope that the weather and their
age might be accepted as their apology for their absence, and stating their willingness
to abide by and observe the report of the Referee.§ It does not appear that the
Chancellor was compelled to take the journey ; but it may be assumed that the Dean
and Chapter gave effect to the King's wishes, whatever they might have been.

Dr. Mervyn married URSULA TRUST ; and although settled in Devonshire, he
retained some of his family property in Wiltshire, viz.: a Mansion house, gardens and
orchard, as also the Barton and Manor of East Knoyle, which he purchased from his
eldest brother John Mervyn of Pertwood.

By a settlement he made in 1667, on the marriage of his eldest son George
Mervyn with his cousin Elizabeth Hayter, daughter of William Hayter, of Exeter, the

---

* *Ex rela.* Revd. C. W. H. Holley, Vicar of Okehampton, Oct. 1873.
† The original document is in my possession.
‡ Cal. State Papers, Dom. Series, Ch. II., Vol. vi., p. 8.
§ Cal. State Papers Dom. Series, Ch. II., Vols. 65 and 68.

Summons from Charles II when Prince of Wales to Richard Mervyn. B. D. to attend his Court at Launceston.

Photographed from the Original in the possession of Sir William Drake.

Chancellor charged his barton or farm of Upton, in the parish of East Knoyle, with an annual rentcharge of £60.*

Dr. Mervyn's Will† is dated 10th September 1668, whereby, after making provision for his wife Ursula, he disposed of his estates in Wiltshire, and the landed property which he had acquired in Devonshire, to his sons Richard, Bernard, William, Jonas and George.

The Chancellor died on 17th October 1669, aged 69 years, and was buried in Exeter Cathedral, where, on a gravestone in the North Choir Aisle, his death is recorded.‡ If his character is to be gathered from his epitaph, he was an honest, pious man, versed in business as well as books, and steady and unmoveable to his God, Church, and King.

His widow Ursula, survived her husband, and proved his will on the 29th November 1670, in conjunction with her son William Mervyn, with whom she resided at his Rectory of Heanton Punchardon. She also (in 1681) proved the will of her son Bernard (dat. 1675), of which she was the executrix. She died at Heanton on the 24th October 1687, at the age of 74, and was buried in the chancel of that parish church.§ Her will ‖ is dated 5th September 1687, and was proved in London 10th March 1688.

The surviving children of Dr. Mervyn and his wife Ursula, were six¶ in number:—

I. GEORGE MERVYN, of East Knoyle, who is described in his father's will (1668) as his eldest son, married, in 1667, his cousin** ELIZABETH HAYTER, the daughter of William Hayter of Exeter, who appears to have predeceased him, as in his will, dated 30th March 1675,‖ he does not refer to her, but mentions his daughter, Ursula, to whom he devises the Upton rentcharge settled by his father on his marriage. On his death, which occurred previous to 22nd June 1680 (when probate of his will was granted by the P. C. Cant. to Anna Hayter, widow), he left an only child:—

ULSULA,. mentioned in the will of her uncle Bernard (1675); she married John NEWELL of Barnstaple, and left issue a son and daughter:—

1. GEORGE NEWELL, of Barnstaple, who in 1772 resettled the Upton rentcharge of £60 per annum (created by Dr. Mervyn as above stated) on himself for life, remainder to his sister Elizabeth Newell, for life, with remainder to Dorothy and Margaret Mervyn the two daughters and co-heiresses of John Mervyn of Marwood.††

1. ELIZABETH NEWELL.

II. JOHN MERVYN, mentioned in both his father's (1668) and mother's (1687) wills. In the latter a direction is contained that his share under it should be laid out in the purchase of an annuity for his life. He is also mentioned in the wills of his brothers George (1675) and Bernard (1675.) He was buried at Heanton 21st May 1729,‡‡ having married (probably about 1690) JANE PRUST,§§ who was also buried at Heanton 5th Oct. 1742,‡‡ and by whom

---

* This rentcharge was created by Indenture dated 20 July, 19 Ch. II. (1667) and is still payable out of the Upton Farm. It is now (1873) the property of John Mervin Cutcliffe Drake, Major in the Royal Engineers, a lineal descendant of the Chancellor.

† See Abstract of the Will—APPENDIX IV., p. ix.

‡ See Mon. Inscrip., APPENDIX IV. p. iii.

§ See Mon. Inscrip., APPENDIX IV. p. iii, and Heanton Par. Registers, p. vi.

‖ See Abstract of the Will, APPENDIX IV, p. x.

¶ In the registers of the parish of Okehampton there appears an entry under date 18th May, 1646, of the baptism of a son, Richard, who would seem to have died young.

** Dr. Mervyn's sister Melior had married John Hayter of Little Langford, co. Wilts. See ante p. 47, and Visit. Wilts, 1623, Ms. Coll. Arms, " C 22," of. 23b. APPENDIX III., p. iv.

†† See post p. 70.

‡‡ Heanton par. reg. APPENDIX IV., pp. vi. and vii.

§§ The statements as to the marriage of John Mervyn and Jane Prust, and their issue, are made on

he had issue JOHN, b. and bapt. at Braunton, 1st July 1691,* who died unmarried, and two daughters, URSULA, b. 16th and bapt. at Braunton 26th May 1695,* who was wife of . . . KING of Hartland, and JANE, b. 18th Oct. and bapt. at Braunton 7th Nov. 1699,* who married Jeremiah LANGDON of Heanton Punchardon.

III. BERNARD MERVYN, mentioned in his father's will (1668).† His will‡ is dated 1 Jan. 1675; proved in London by his mother 25 Feb. 1681. In it he describes himself as a merchant, resident in the city of Lixa in Portugal.

IV. The Rev. WILLIAM MERVYN, M.A. (of whom hereafter).

V. The Rev. JONAS MERVYN, died 1st December 1693, and was buried at Heanton.§ He is mentioned in both his father's and his mother's wills; in the latter he is referred to as having at that time children. He is also mentioned in his brother Bernard's will (1675). He married MARGARET [BILLINGS of Cornwall], who survived him, and was party to a deed, dated 3rd Dec. 1722, in which she is described as "of Barnstaple, Widdow and Relict of Jonas Mervin, clerke, deceased." On his death he left two sons.

    I. The Reverend RICHARD MERVYN of Barnstaple, the elder son, was educated at Balliol Coll. Oxford, where he was admitted 7th March 1696,‖ and took his degree of B.A. 17th Oct. 1699.‖ He is described in the Barnstaple Register of the burial of his son Richard (1732) as Vicar of Buckland Brewer. He was party to the above mentioned deed of 3rd Dec. 1722 and was buried at Barnstaple, 1 April 1741,¶ having had issue by his wife MARGARET [HUNT], who was living in 1722 :—

        I. WILLIAM MERVYN, bapt. at Barnstaple,¶ 18 January 1709-10, bur. there 10 Nov. 1710.¶

        II. RICHARD MERVYN, bapt. at Barnstaple, 28 April 1710, bur. there 12 Nov. 1732.¶

        1. MARY MERVYN, bapt. at Barnstaple 1st November 1716,¶ bur. at Heanton 8th July 1747,** having married Charles MARSHALL of Barnstaple,†† who was b. 23 Nov. 1709, and had issue :—

            I. JOHN MARSHALL, bapt. at Barnstaple, 3rd July bur. there 19th Oct. 1735.¶

            II. CHARLES MARSHALL of Barnstaple, bapt. there

the authority of an old Ms. pedigree in my possession as executor of my aunt Frances Drake, confirmed however, in part, by entries in the parochial registers of Braunton and Heanton. The particulars are probably correct, as I find a memorandum in my aunt's handwriting stating that Jane Mervyn, daughter of a John Mervyn, married [Jeremiah] Langdon of Heanton, by whom she was mother of fifteen children, who all, except a son William Langdon, bapt. at Heanton, 22nd Feb. 1729, died young. This William married Agnes Crocker of Appledore, and died without issue. The memorandum from which I quote adds :—" Mrs. Langdon was always mentioned by the Mervyn family as ' Cousin Lang,' and I have " heard my mother and aunt often speak of her, and remember when a little child being taken to Heanton " that she might see me."

The representatives of the Langdon family appear about ten years since to have been under an impression that they were descendants of a Mervyn, which, however, was not the case, as my aunt's and Mrs. Dorothy Mervyn's notes very clearly show. The error seems to have arisen from the fact that Mrs. Jane Langdon, née Mervyn, after her husband's death resided at Heanton with her daughter-in-law Agnes [Crocker], who had, after HER husband's (William Langdon) death, married HIS cousin, George Langdon, from whom the present family of Langdon of Ashford descend.

  * Braunton par. reg., APPENDIX IV.₋ p. viii.
  † In the Ms. Pedigree mentioned in the first preceding note, this Bernard is described as "a Spanish Merchant."   ‡ See Abstract, APPENDIX IV., p. ix.
  § Heanton par. reg., APPENDIX IV., p. vi, and Braunton par. registers, p. viii.
  ‖ Ex rel. Robert Scott, Master of Balliol, in letter to Sir H. M. Vavasour, 12 Nov. 1864.
  ¶ Barnstaple par. reg., APPENDIX IV., pp. vii. and viii.
  ** Heanton par. reg., APPENDIX IV., p. vii.   †† See note p. 66.

6 Aug. 1741* (living 1776), who married SARAH, (daur. of William BOURCHIER of Minehead, by Mary his wife, eldest daughter of Philip Sydenham of Lee House and Binham, co. Somerset,) and had issue, an only daur.

    SARAH MARSHALL, bapt. at Barnstaple, 21 January 1784,* d. 23 May 1866, unmarried.

1. DOROTHY, bapt. at Barnstaple, 30 March 1737,* who married Lewis GREGORY.

2. MARGARET, bapt. at Barnstaple, 17 June 1739,* and married to Philip SYDENHAM of Barnstaple (eldest son of Philip Sydenham also of Barnstaple, by his wife Joan, only child and heir of Jacob Scott of Littcott and Highbray Devon, and grandson of Philip Sydenham of Lee House above mentioned) by whom she had issue.

3. MARY.

II. The Rev. WILLIAM MERVYN, who was born in 1682. He was educated at Exeter College, Oxford, and succeeded as Rector of the Clare portion of Tiverton 13th May 1721, and died without issue on 17th Dec. 1759, being then Rector of Atherington, co. Devon, and was buried in the chancel of that church.† He married in November 1736,‡ DOROTHY, only surviving child and heiress of the Rev. Gawen HAYMAN, of Southpool, co. Devon, who survived her husband.

VI. RICHARD MERVYN, the sixth son of Chancellor Mervyn, is described in his father's will as his "youngest son." Special provision was made for him by his mother's will, by which guardians were appointed, and he had only a life-estate in his share of her property. He is also mentioned in his brother Bernard's will (1675). He was born in 1652, and died (aged 37) on the 20th April 1689, at Heanton, where he was buried.§

    The Rev. WILLIAM MERVYN, M.A., the fourth son of Dr. Mervyn and Ursula his wife, was born in 1642, and is mentioned in both his father's (1668) and mother's

(1687) wills, and in will of his brother Bernard (1675). He was educated at Pembroke Hall, Oxford, and took Holy Orders; graduated B.A. at Christ's Coll. Oxford, and took his degree of M.A., 1 Feb. 1699, being then of Exeter College.| He succeeded his father as Rector of Heanton Punchardon, to which living he was admitted (on the presentation of John Bassett of Heanton Court) the 29th January 1669 (three months after his father's death), and he held the preferment for forty-nine years, until his death. On the death of his father-in-law Richard Newte (1678) he succeeded, 15th Feb. 1678-9, to the Rectory of the Clare portion of Tiverton. He died at Heanton (where he was buried) on 2nd Nov. 1719, at the age of seventy-seven years.¶

He married CHRISTIANA, the only surviving daughter of the Rev. Richard NEWTE,[*] of Tiverton, co. Devon (by Thomasine, only daughter and heir of Humphrey Trobridge) who died at Heanton, where she was buried, on 30th August 1695,[†] aged forty-six, leaving issue, two sons and three daughters, viz.:—

    I. RICHARD MERVYN (of whom hereafter).

    II. The Rev. WILLIAM MERVYN, A.M. who was born at Heanton, where he was baptized 6th June 1676.[‡] He was of Exeter Coll., Oxford, where he took his degree of B.A., 7 March 1704, and that of M.A., 10 July 1708, and proceeded B.D., 4 July, 1719.[§] He resided at Tawstock until he succeeded his father as Rector of Heanton Punchardon, to which living he was admitted 22nd March 1719, on the presentation of John Bassett of Heanton Court. He married LÆTITIA, daughter of Dr. Thomas BOURCHIER, Professor of Law, and Principal of St. Alban's Hall, Oxford, who died on the 13th, and was buried at Heanton on the 16th May 1730, aged forty-three years.[†] Mr. Mervyn survived his wife, and died 20th July 1744, aged sixty-seven, at Heanton, where he was buried on the 22nd of the same month,[†] having had two children; a son, Thomas Mervyn, and a daughter, Lætitia.

        I. THOMAS MERVYN, the son, was born at Heanton, where he was baptized on 10th Nov. 1723.[‡] He died unmarried 1st June, and was buried at Heanton, 3rd June 1742, aged 19.[†]

        1. LÆTITIA MERVYN, the daughter, and at her father's death his heiress, was married (2nd wife) 9th May 1752, in the church of St. Michael Bath, to the Rev. John MARSHALL,[||]

---

* A Biographical Notice of the Rev. RICHARD NEWTE appears in Prince's "Worthies of Devon" (*fo. ed*, 1701, *p.* 476); the narrative being founded upon the statement of his son, Mr. John Newte, who, at the time the old Devonshire chronicler wrote, was the Rector of Tiverton, and from it the following particulars are taken:—Richard Newte was born at Tiverton and baptized there on the 24th February 1612. He was the third son of Henry Newte, "a gentleman of good estate and reputation in that place." He married Thomasine, the only daughter and heir of Humphrey Trobridge, descended from the family of that name, of Trobridge, in the parish of Crediton. He was educated at the Tiverton Grammar School, and at 16 years of age was admitted member of Exeter College, Oxford, and proceeded M.A. 20th May 1636, when he became a Fellow and Tutor of his college, and was noted for his knowledge of Hebrew and Eastern languages, as well as of French and Italian. After a residence of 13 or 14 years at the University, Mr. Newte was, in 1641, promoted to two of the three Rectories at Tiverton, viz., the Clare and Tidcomb portions. On the breaking out of the Civil War, Mr. Newte appears to have gone abroad upon a travelling license from the King, visiting Holland, Flanders, Italy, and other parts of the Continent. In 1646 he returned to England, and during the Commonwealth was much persecuted, and, being ejected from his cure at Tiverton, retired to Ottery St. Mary, where he became Lecturer; but from that appointment he was also dismissed, when he was befriended by Colonel Bassett of Heanton Court, who, in 1656, presented him to the living of Heanton Punchardon, where he remained undisturbed until the Restoration in 1660, when he was again restored to his former preferments at Tiverton, and became Chaplain to Lord Delawar, and Chaplain in Ordinary to Charles II. He lived 18 years after the Restoration, and died at his Parsonage House at Tidcomb. He appears to have been a sound Divine, and a preacher of considerable power. His death occurred 10th August 1678, aged 65. He was buried in the chancel of the church at Tiverton, where his memory is recorded on a marble tablet, which notes that he left behind him his wife Thomasina, by whom he had ten children, of whom Henry, Catherine, and Susan died in his lifetime. Richard, John, Edward, Thomas, Peter, and Henry, and his daughter Christian, survived him; his son John being his successor in the living at Tiverton.

† See Mon. Insc., APPENDIX IV., p. iv., and Heanton par. registers, pp. vi. and vii.

‡ Heanton par. reg., APPENDIX IV., p. vi.

§ *Ex rel.*, Robert Scott, Master of Balliol, in letter to Sir H. M. Vavasour, 12 Nov. 1864.

|| The Reverend John Marshall was the elder brother of Charles Marshall, who married Mary, daughter of the Reverend Richard Mervyn (see *ante*, p. 64). They were the sons of John Marshall, who was Mayor of Barnstaple in 1711, by his second wife Dorcas Cook, which John was the only surviving son of Hugh Marshall (who died in 1701, having served the office of Mayor of Barnstaple in 1681) by his wife Joan, daughter of Alexander Hawkinge of Barnstaple, to whom he was married 14th June 1660. Hugh Marshall was the son of Alexander Marshall, of the parish of Loxbeare, co. Devon, who was probably connected with the family of the same surname, recorded by Westcote (View of Devon in 1630, p. 502) as settled at Exeter, and a member of which, John Marshall, was Mayor of that City in 1615; but the

who was born 8th, and baptised 27th December 1708, in the parish church of Barnstaple, and who succeeded his father-in-law as Rector of Heanton, to which living he was admitted 18th October 1744, on the presentation of John Bassett of Heanton Court. He was buried at Bath. Mrs. Lætitia Marshall survived her husband, and in 1775 resided as a widow in Barnstaple, but died at Heanton, where she was buried 22nd Feb. 1783,* having had eight children, of whom six survived her:—

I. The Reverend THOMAS MERVYN MARSHALL, M.A., baptized at Heanton, 6th August 1753.* He was Rector of Bow, co. Devon, where he died and was buried in 1794. He married 22nd April 1782, in the parish church of Barnstaple, SARAH, only daughter of Philip SYDENHAM of Barnstaple, by his wife Joan, only child and heiress of Jacob Scott, of Littcott co. Devon, who died in 1844, and was buried at Pilton, co. Devon. The issue of the marriage were two sons and three daughters, viz.:—

    I. JOHN MARSHALL of Barnstaple, Mayor of the Borough (1824), in the Commission of the Peace and Deputy-Lieutenant for the co. of Devon, was born 28th March 1785, and married in 1829 MARY, the daughter of Thomas DOCKER of Woodbury, co. Devon, by whom at his death in Barnstaple, 8th December 1866, he left issue:—

        I. THOMAS MERVYN BOURCHIER MARSHALL, born 15th June 1830, died 17th July 1859, unmarried.

        II. JOHN PHILIP SYDENHAM MARSHALL of Barnstaple, born 16th December 1831 (*living* unmarried 1873).

        III. JAMES CUTCLIFFE MARSHALL of Stoke-upon-Trent, born 1837, married at the parish church of Sutton, co. Surrey, 9th March 1872, MARY, daughter of J. J. COLE, of London, and Sutton, and has issue:—

            HUGH JOHN COLE MARSHALL, born 2nd June 1873, baptized at Barnstaple 9th September following.

family of Marshall was established in Barnstaple at an earlier date, as appears from the parochial registers of that town, in which the name appears in 1543.

* Heanton par. registers, APPENDIX IV., pp. vi. and vii.

1. AGNES MARSHALL, born 1833, *living* 1873.
2. LÆTITIA MARY MARSHALL (*living* 1873), born 1835, married 1stly, at Barnstaple, 1st November 1858, her cousin John Norris MARSHALL, (2nd son of the Rev. Bourchier Marshall and Eliza Norris, after mentioned,) and by whom she had issue EMILY FRANCES MARSHALL, after mentioned, and 2ndly Capt. Arthur George PAUL, of East Leigh Teignmouth, *living* 1873.
3. EMILY SOPHIA MARSHALL, born 1839, *living* 1873.

II. The Rev. BOURCHIER MARSHALL, M.A., who succeeded his father as Rector of Bow, and was Chaplain to the late Duke of Kent. He was born 24th April 1786, and married at the parish church of Barnstaple, 25th October 1820, ELIZA NORRIS, daughter of John Norris of Nonsuch, co. Wilts, and died at Pilton (where he was buried) in 1827, leaving issue at his death two sons, and two daughters, viz. :—

I. BOURCHIER MERVYN MARSHALL, born at Bow, 13th August 1821, educated at Christ Church, Oxford ; J.P. for co. Devon ; married ELIZABETH GEORGIANA BAKER, 9th June 1858, at the parish church of Bishops Tawton, and died 14th January 1870.

II. JOHN NORRIS MARSHALL, born at Bow, 1st November 1823 ; married (1st November 1858, at the parish church of Barnstaple), his cousin, LÆTITIA MARY MARSHALL, daughter of John Marshall and Mary Docker. He died 10th October 1867, having had issue.

> EMILY FRANCES MARSHALL, born 28th August 1860, died 11th July 1861.

1. ELLEN SUSANNA MARSHALL (*living* 1873), born at Bow, 1822, who married in 1843, Rev. Joshua Willoughby BRYAN, Rector of Cliddesden-cum-Farleigh, Hants, and has issue *living* 1873, four sons and five daughters.

2. EMILY FRANCES MARSHALL, born at Bow, 15th November 1824, and died December 1835, unmarried.

1. LÆTITIA, baptized at Barnstaple* 5th May 1783, married John Sherard CLAY of Barnstaple, and died 1849, s.p., leaving her husband (who remarried and is *living* 1873) surviving.

2. EMILY, born 27th January 1788, died unmarried.

3. SOPHIA, born 10th October 1792, died unmarried 14th September 1865.

II. JOHN WILLIAM MARSHALL, son of John Marshall and Lætitia Mervyn, born 5th, died 7th, and buried 9th July 1755, at Heanton Punchardon.†

III. WILLIAM MARSHALL, born at Heanton, 4th August and baptized there 15th Aug. 1756,† died unmarried at Barnstaple, where he was buried in .

1. LÆTITIA, born at Heanton, in June 1754, and baptized there 27th June 1754,† married William BARBOR of Fremington, where she died and was buried in 1816.

2. A daughter, born 2nd, and died 18th Augt. 1757.

3. FRANCES, born at Heanton, and baptized there 13th November 1758;† married Christopher HAMLYN, of Paschoe, in the Parish of Colebrook, co. Devon, and died in 1833, and was buried at Heanton.

4. ELIZABETH, born at Heanton, and baptized there 26th November 1759;† married Captain James CUTCLIFFE, R.N., and died and was buried at Torrington in 1818, s.p.

5. SARAH AMY, born 8th, and baptized at Heanton, 10th October 1761;† married the Rev. John ROWE, of Alverdiscott, co. Devon, and died there (where she is buried) in 1843.

1. SARA, the eldest daughter of William Mervyn and Christiana Newte, born and baptized at Heanton in 1677;† was married to the Rev. George BLAKE, Rector of Alwington, Devon. She died 27th May 1722, aged 45, and was buried at Heanton.‡

2. CHRISTIAN, was born in 1683. She died unmarried on the 17th, and was buried at Heanton on the 20th August 1748, aged 65 years.§

3. ELIZABETH, married at Heanton 18th February 1724,† James GAY, and was buried at Heanton 4th May 1765.†

* Barnstaple par. registers, APPENDIX IV., p. vii.
† Heanton par. registers, APPENDIX IV., pp. vi. and vii.
‡ See Mon. Insc., APPENDIX IV., p. iv.
§ See Mon. Insc., APPENDIX IV., p. iv., and Heanton par. registers, p. vii.

RICHARD MERVYN, the elder son and heir of the Rev. William Mervyn and Christiana Newte, was born at Heanton, and baptized there 11th February 1672.*

 He married at Tiverton† on 16th May 1707, MARGARET, eldest daughter of Robert BURRIDGE, of Tiverton.‡ She died on 18th June 1723,§ aged 41 years, and was buried in Marwood Church, where there is a tablet to her memory. Mr. Mervyn was a member of the Inner Temple, and Deputy Recorder of Barnstaple. and was commonly known in the family and amongst his friends as " Councillor Mervyn." He appears to have been a very general Trustee and adviser of families in the north of Devon. He purchased the Marwood Hill Estate (which is now held by his lineal descendants) and was buried in the church of that parish. He died 15th and was buried 19th November 1740,§ aged 67 years, having made his will ‖ dated 10th November 1740, which was proved by the sole executor, his son John Mervyn, at Exeter, 27th January 1740–1.

There were seven children of the marriage of " Councillor Mervyn" with Margaret Burridge, viz.:—

    I. JOHN MERVYN, who succeeded his father at Marwood, and of whom hereafter.

    II. & III. RICHARD and SAMUEL MERVYN, twin children, born and baptized¶ 21st Sept. 1717, and died and were buried the following day.¶

    IV. SAMUEL MERVYN, born and baptized at Marwood 7th Oct. 1719,¶ mentioned in his father's will (1740). He died unmarried 8th, and was buried at Marwood 11th January 1743,¶ aged 24 years.** Letters of administration to his effects were granted 9th Aug. 1744, by the Bishop's Court at Exeter, to John Mervyn, his brother and next of kin.

    1. MARGARET MERVYN, the eldest daughter, was born 8th, and baptized at Marwood 18th Feb. 1711.¶ She was married at Heanton on 26th January 1742-3* to the Rev. Nicholas GAY, of Newton St. Cyres, co. Devon, to whom she was third wife, and by him had issue eight children:—three sons, who all died unmarried, and five daughters, of whom three, viz., Penelope, Elizabeth, and Dorothy, also died unmarried ; Margaret married the Rev. John Bradford Coplestone, Rector of St. Thomas, Exeter, and Offwell, co. Devon, by whom she was mother of The Right Rev. Edward Coplestone, Bishop of Llandaff, b. 2 Feb. 1776, d. 14 Oct. 1849 ; and Frances, who married . . . . Roberts, and had issue.†† Mrs. Gay survived her husband, who died in 1775, and of whose will, dated 30th May 1765, she was executrix. She was party to a deed of 8th Feb. 1776, in which she is described as of Torrington, co. Devon, widow.

    2. ELIZABETH, who was born 15th March, and baptized at Marwood 8th April 1712,¶ married . . . . GRANT, of Bideford, co. Devon.

    3. CHRISTIAN, born 16th, and baptized at Marwood 27th Feb. 1715,¶ married at Braunton ‡‡ 7th Nov. 1741, Chichester INCLEDON (third son of John Incledon of Buckland, by Penelope, his second wife, daughter of Sir Arthur Chichester, Bt., of Youlston, co. Devon), by whom she had issue.

JOHN MERVYN, the elder son of "Councillor" Mervyn and Margaret Burridge, was of Marwood Hill. He was born 14th Jan., and baptized at Marwood 4th Feb. 1714.*

He died 21st,† and was buried at Marwood 24th June 1750,* at the age of 35, having made his will dated 20th May previous.‡ He married DOROTHY, daughter of Arthur CHICHESTER, of Hall and Pill, co. Devon (by Dorothy,§ daughter of the Rev. William Rowe,‖ of Otterton), who, after Mr. Mervyn's death, was married to the Rev. John Wright of Kenton, co. Devon, but by him had no issue. Mr. Mervyn was educated at Exeter College, Oxford, where, 14th October 1736, he took his degree of B.A., and proceeded to his Master's degree 3rd July 1739.¶

The only children of the marriage of John Mervyn and Dorothy Chichester were two daughters, DOROTHY MERVYN and MARGARET MERVYN, the latter being a posthumous child.**

DOROTHY MERVYN, the elder daughter and co-heiress, was born and baptized at Marwood, 1st July 1742,* and died unmarried on the 8th, and was buried at Marwood 16th May 1835,* at the advanced age of ninety-three.

---

* Marwood par. registers, APPENDIX IV., p. vii.
† See Mon. Insc., APPENDIX IV., p. iv.   ‡ See Abstract of the Will, APPENDIX IV., p. x.
§ Letters of Admin. to Mrs. Dorothy Chichester, described as then late of Barnstaple, widow deceased, were granted to her daughter, "Dorothy Mervin, wife of John Mervin," by the P. C. Cant., 18th July 1743.
‖ The Revᵈ William Rowe, Vicar of Otterton, co. Devon, who died in 1725, married Miss Musgrave, of Westmoreland, by whom he had twenty-two children, of whom sixteen grew up. One of the daughters married Dr. REYNOLDS, of Plympton, by whom she was mother of Sir Joshua Reynolds, P.R.A. Another daughter, DOROTHY, married Arthur CHICHESTER of Hall, as above, and another daughter was the wife of the Revᵈ William BRAND, of Kings' Brompton, co. Somerset, whose daughter, FEDERETA, married in 1750, the Reverend William CUTCLIFFE, of Colyton, co. Devon.—Ex. Ms. Notes of Dorothy Mervyn.
¶ Ex rel. Robert Scott, Master of Balliol, in letter to Sir H. M. Vavasour, 12 Nov. 1864.
** In connection with the death of Mr. John Mervyn, and the subsequent birth of his daughter "Margaret," I found amongst Mrs. Dorothy Mervyn's papers, the following Ms., being "The Account of my Mother's dream:"—"At the time of my Father's death, the 18th of June 1750, my Mother was expecting to "be confined, and was much distressed on account of my Father's dieing without a Will, knowing that in "case she had a son there could be no provision for me. I was then eight years old and sensible of knowing "my own situation, for nothing was kept from me. With a spirit of independence beyond my years (and "which has continued through a very long life) I told my friends that I was blessed with good health and "was strong, and that the labour of my hands would provide for me. My mother said she would run all "risks and take the guardianship of me, whether the child was a son or daughter. But what was to be done "for money? My father died at the early age of 35, and his affairs were left in much confusion. My mother "was fortunate in having three friendly advisers, the Revd. Mr. Gay, who had married my father's eldest sister; "the Revd. John Marshall, who was her dear friend; and an honest attorney, Mr. Philip Sydenham. They "were all doubtful whether anything could be sold; my grandfather, Councillor Mervin, left a parchment "book with an account of all his estates, showing what came by inheritance, and what had been purchased. "This book had been well looked over by all, but with no certainty that any estate could be sold. My poor "mother in great trouble went to bed, fell asleep, and, mark the goodness of Providence, she dreamed that "she and my Uncle Guy were walking in Munkley Wood, when he said, ' Why not sell this ?' ' It is "noted, at such a page in the Counsellor's book that he bought it, and it might be sold.' In the morning "she said she thought it was at such a page, the book was again examined, and was found to be paged "(which they had never before observed); but the pages my mother dreamed of were not to be found, two "pages were missing; but they were subsequently found stuck together. The wood was sold (but below its "value) to the Rector of the Parish of Marwood, the Revd. Richard Harding. My sister Margaret "Mervin, was born the 17th of Sept. 1750, to my mother and all her friends' great joy. As soon as she "attained the age of 21, she joined with me in paying all our father's debts, and what was left, has ever "prospered with us."

Mr. Mervyn did not in fact die without a Will, as stated by Mrs. Mervyn ; but altho' he made one, dated 20th May 1750 (Administration with will annexed.—no executor having been named in it—was granted by the Bishop of Exeter's Court on 11 August 1750, to Dorothy Mervyn, the Testator's widow and relict) it contained no provision for charging his debts on his real estate, consequently if the expected child had been a son, he would have succeeded not only to the estates included in the settlement made (26 and 27 August 1741) on Mr. Mervyn's marriage with Dorothy Chichester, but also to the unsettled real estate, leaving the personal property liable for debts, so that the money provision made for his then only daughter would have been entirely absorbed.

When I knew Mrs. (as in later life she was always styled) Dorothy Mervyn she resided in the parsonage-house at Ashford, near Barnstaple, where she went to reside in 1814, and it was one of the treats of my boyhood days to accompany her niece, my aunt Mrs. Frances Drake, in her daily visits to the old lady, who always cordially welcomed her young visitor. Great was my delight to listen to her never-failing Devonshire stories, told in their true dialect. Nor were the creature comforts forgotten; her narratives were seasoned with cakes and wine. What I might now think of her home-made beverages I know not, but then I thought them nectar. On Sundays, after church, there was always a family levée and lunch at the parsonage, at which my old friend, the late Revd. Mr. Bryan, of Westdown, who came to Ashford (there not being any resident clergyman there) to perform the service, generally assisted, and all the news of the preceding week was discussed, as well as the sermon.

Mrs. Mervyn's was a remarkable character, having for its foundation strong common sense, and a spirit of independence, which enabled her to hold her own against all comers. She was related to the Rolle family, being a first cousin to the late John, Lord Rolle, and his sisters, the Misses Rolle of Hudscot, and was, with the exception of my Aunt, the only connection of the Stevenstone family, over whom they did not attempt to tyrannize. "Cousin Dolly" held her own with the somewhat imperious Baron, who consequently always spoke of and treated her with marked respect, which he was not in the habit of bestowing on those who ventured to hold and express opinions in which he did not concur. Mrs. Mervyn held a strong belief in the hereditary transmission of "good" and "bad" blood, and many were the striking instances she gave in support of her theory. I recollect her once saying, when the probability of a marriage between a young couple was on the *tapis;* that she wished they would let the blood inherited by the lady, who was of an old Devonshire family, wear itself out, for no good would ever come of "*that* blood."

No less strong were the dear old lady's prejudices as to the line to be drawn between those of "gentle birth," and the "roturier." A few weeks before she died, my aunt was reading from a local newspaper the obituary notices, and amongst others, the record of the death of a very respectable tradesman, who having accumulated some money, was, in the notice dubbed "Esquire." At this her wrath was raised. "Fanny," said she to her neice, "bring me my desk;" from which she took a piece of paper on which she had written the terms in which she wished her death to be notified, and where she had described her father as "Esquire." "Give me a pen Fanny, it is time that a new distinction should be made, if tradesmen are now Esquires; my father was a Gentleman, and as the daughter of a Gentleman, I will be described," and forthwith she altered the memorandum; and, as altered, the notice was inserted in the newspapers when she passed to her rest in 1835, at the age of 93 years.

During the latter years of her life, when her bodily infirmities interfered with her active out-of-door occupations, Mrs. Mervyn amused herself by making notes of her recollections of the members of those Devonshire families in which she remembered five or six generations. These interesting manuscripts are in my possession, and have afforded me valuable and reliable information on many points connected with my genealogical researches.

The esteem in which Mrs. Mervyn was held was not confined to her immediate group of near relations. It was entertained by a numerous and wide-spread circle of friends. An interesting letter was addressed by her to Dr. Coplestone, on his being made Bishop of Llandaff, and is as follows:—

" My dear Lord, .

" As the oldest living member of your good mother's family, permit me to offer my " most sincere congratulations on your Lordship's justly merited preferment. May your " valuable life be long preserved a faithful follower of your blessed Master, and a firm " supporter of his holy Church. I hope all your family (to whom I beg my kindest regards) " are well, as, through great mercy, I am, at the advanced age of 85 years and six months, " and like your excellent aunt, my dear cousin Mrs. Gay, blessed with cheerful spirits. " None of my family are with me, or know of my writing to you, or I am certain they " would have offered their respectful regards and congratulations.

" I am, my dear Sir, with real esteem, your Lordship's sincerely obliged relation,
" DOROTHY MERVYN."

The Bishop's reply, dated " Oriel College, 6th January 1828," is in the following terms:—

" My dear Madam,

" There is not one among the many letters of congratulation I have received, which " has given me more pleasure, or for which I consider myself more obliged to the writer, " than yours. Having been always accustomed to associate feelings of respect and esteem " with the mention of your name, it is particularly gratifying to be so remembered by you. " My excellent and much valued aunt, Mrs. Gay,* has conveyed to me the same kind senti- " ments, although the use of the pen is, with her, nearly, I believe superseded. The " channel, however, which she chose for this communication was most acceptable; that of " a near relation. In return for your prayers, that I may be enabled adequately to discharge " the sacred duties involved in this appointment, in which I heartily join, I have only to " offer mine that the blessings of health and cheerfulness may continue to brighten your " days, and enable you, as you have hitherto done, to diffuse happiness amongst all your " friends. I am, my dear Madam, gratefully and sincerely yours,

E. Llandaff, Elect.

MARGARET MERVYN, a posthumous child and coheiress of John Mervyn by his wife Dorothy Chichester, was born and baptized at Marwood, 6th September

1750.† She died 24th April, and was buried at Marwood, 1st May 1792,† having married at Kenton.‡ 21st November 1776, CHARLES NEWELL CUTCLIFFE, of Damage, in the parish of Ilfracombe, and after his marriage of Marwood Hill, where he resided. Mr. Cutcliffe was the eldest son of Charles Cutcliffe of Weach, and Elizabeth Dene, and was born in 1746, and bapt. at Westleigh, 25 Feb. 1746.§ He was a Solicitor and Banker at Barnstaple; was appointed (20th March 1797) a Deputy-Lieutenant for the County of Devon, and in 1798 held a Com- mission as Captain-Lieutenant of the Fremington and West Down Volunteers, then commanded by Major Barbor. He survived his wife and died in December 1813, and was buried at West- leigh§ on the 22nd of that month. His will‖ is dated 25th November 1806, and was proved in London, 8th June 1814, by his son and sole executor John Mervyn Cutcliffe. The issue of the marriage were two sons and six daughters.

    I. JOHN MERVYN CUTCLIFFE, of Webbery, in the parish of Alverdiscott, co. Devon, born 12th October 1778. He was educated for the Army, which he entered in 1800, as Cornet or Ensign in the 23rd Light Dragoons: In the same year he became Lieutenant, and took part with his Regiment in the campaign of 1801, in Egypt: In 1809, having in 1804 obtained his Captaincy, he served in Portugal and Spain, and was present at the battle of Talavera: Promoted Major in 1813, he in that year accompanied his regiment in the campaign on the eastern coast of Spain, and subsequently took part in the operations in the Netherlands. Major Cutcliffe was present at the battle of Quatre Bras on the 16th, at the action at Genappe on the 17th, and on the 18th June he commanded the 23rd at the battle of Waterloo, where he was wounded, and was, on the recommendation of the Duke of Wellington, promoted to the rank of Lieutenant-Colonel. He received the medal of the Turkish Order of the Crescent, for services in Egypt, and on

* The Bishop's mother was Margaret Gay, the daughter of Margaret Mervyn and the Revd. Nicholas Gay. See Tabular Pedigree, APPENDIX IV., p. i. See also ante p. 70.
† Marwood par. registers, APPENDIX IV., p. vii. ‡ Kenton par. registers, APPENDIX IV., p. viii.
§ Westleigh par. registers, APPENDIX IV., p. viii. ‖ See Abstract of the Will, APPENDIX IV., p.x.

22nd June 1815, was made a Companion of the Order of the Bath: He was also Knight of the Royal Hanoverian Guelphic Order.

Colonel Cutcliffe married, in April 1808, the Honorable CHARLOTTE TALBOT, daughter of Baroness TALBOT DE MALAHIDE, but died without issue, and was buried at Westleigh* 16th July 1822. His will,† dated 8th July 1822, was proved in London 28th Nov. 1822. By it his widow became seized in fee of the ancient estates of the Cutcliffe family in the parish of Ilfracombe, which she re-settled by deed, dated 28th July 1827, on her husband's family. Mrs. Cutcliffe re-married Gerald FITZGERALD of Binfield, co. Berks, and died s.p. 9th Nov. 1863, and was buried at the Roman Catholic church at Reading.

II. HARRY LUPINCOTT CUTCLIFFE, died an infant.

1. FRANCES CUTCLIFFE, eldest daughter, married Zachary Hammett DRAKE, as after referred to.
2. ANNE CUTCLIFFE, born 27th October and bapt. at Pilton, 4th Nov. 1781,‡ died unmarried at Ashford on the 2nd,§ and was buried at Marwood on the 7th May 1859.‖
3. MARY CUTCLIFFE, died an infant.
4. MARY CUTCLIFFE, born 17th January 1784, died unmarried at Ilfracombe 13th, and was buried at Marwood 21st June 1831.‖
5. HARRIET ELIZABETH CUTCLIFFE, born 28th October 1786, died unmarried at Marwood Hill on the 12th, and was buried at Marwood¶ on the 17th April 1867, having by her will** dated 31st August 1863, devised her three-eighth shares in the Marwood property in trust for her two nieces the daughters of her nephew Charles Cutcliffe Drake, and their issue, and her like share in the Mervyn rentcharge on Upton, to her great nephew John Mervyn Cutcliffe Drake.
6. EMMA CUTCLIFFE, born 12th April 1788, died unmarried at Ilfracombe on the 14th, and was buried at Marwood on the 20th March 1865.¶

FRANCES CUTCLIFFE the eldest daughter, and (on the death of her brother Colonel Cutcliffe, without issue) coheiress of Charles Newell Cutcliffe and Margaret Mervyn, and on the death of her aunt Dorothy Mervyn  in 1835, coheiress of her grandfather, John Mervyn of Marwood Hill, which estate, under the terms of their father's and mother's marriage settlement, descended to Mrs. Drake and her sisters as tenants in common. Mrs. Drake was born 25th May and baptized at Pilton 6 June 1780.‡ She was married at Marwood on the 6th October 1803,†† to my father's brother, ZACHARY HAMMETT DRAKE, then of Chapel, in the parish of Moorwinstow, co. Cornwall, but subsequently of Springfield, near Barnstaple. He was born 5th Sept. 1777, and was the eldest son of Henry Drake of Barnstaple, by Anne his wife, daughter of Richard Hammett, of Clovelly, co. Devon, and sister of Sir James Hamlyn, Bart., of Clovelly Court.‡‡ Mr. Drake was a Deputy-Lieutenant and in the Commission of the Peace for the counties of Devon and Cornwall, and Major of the North Devon Yeomanry

---

* Westleigh par. registers, APPENDIX IV., p. viii.   † See Abstract of the Will, APPENDIX IV., p. x.
‡ Pilton par. registers, APPENDIX IV., p. viii.   § See Mon. Insc., APPENDIX IV., p. v.
‖ Marwood par. registers, APPENDIX IV., p. vii.
¶ Mon. Insc., APPENDIX IV., p. v., and Marwood par. registers, p. vii.
** See Abstract of the Will, APPENDIX IV., p. xi.
†† The marriage ceremony was performed by Mrs. Drake's uncle, the Revd. William Spurway, as appears by the following entry made by Mr. Drake in the family Bible. "6th Oct. 1803. I, Zachary "Hammett Drake, of Moorwenstow in the county of Cornwall, was this day married by the Revd. Wm. "Spurway, in the parish church of Marwood to Miss Frances Cutcliffe, eldest daughter of Charles Newell "Cutcliffe, Esq., of Marwood Hill, in the county of Devon."
‡‡ See Tabular Pedigree, APPENDIX IV., p. ii.

Dorothy Mervin (1776.)

Dorothy Mervin Aug.t 1834.
Aged 92 year.

From an Original Picture in the possession of Charles Henry Drake — Cutcliffe Esq.

Frances Drake. neé Cutcliffe

Cavalry, a corps with which he was connected for many years of his life, and in whose prosperity he took the greatest interest. He died at Springfield the 11th, and was buried at Marwood 17th March 1847.* His will was dated 10th March 1835, and was proved in London by his widow 27 August 1847.† His widow survived him twenty years, and during the latter portion of her life resided at Ashford, where, on the 5th of April 1867, she passed to her rest in the eighty-seventh year of her age, honored and respected by all who had the privilege of her acquaintance. She was buried at Marwood on the 11th . April 1867.* Her will‡ was dated 2nd June 1865, and was proved in London 6th May 1867.

I should not do justice to the affectionate respect I entertain for my aunt's memory, and to the love I bore her whilst living, if I were to content myself with the mere record of her birth and death; and yet I have a difficulty in writing of her as I should wish to do, because those instances which stand out prominently in my memory as best illustrating the beauty of her character are so intermixed with painful circumstances affecting others, which she would, I know, have wished buried in oblivion, that I dare not treat of them. Nor are they necessary to those of her belongings who knew her, and to those who had not that privilege, no description of which my pen is capable, could convey anything but a faint washed-out sketch, of the picture I would desire to paint of a true GENTLEWOMAN. It pleased God to visit her with more trials than often fall to a woman's lot; trials which she bore with fortitude, sustained by a firm reliance on the goodness of Providence, which never forsook her, and by a well-grounded faith in that future Refuge where " sorrow and sighing shall flee away." She was blessed with an elasticity of spirit which enabled her to bear up against her troubles, including the death of a husband to whom she was devotedly attached, and all her children, leaving her in her old age the last of her generation: an old age, however, green to the last, with all her sympathies young, to sympathise with the young. A mind well stored with the result of years of careful, but somewhat desultory reading, a memory replete with information on out-of-the-way subjects, and garnered with quaint information, made her a charming companion. With all the qualities of a good talker, she combined those of a good listener. She eagerly sought information connected with the topics and passing occurrences of the day, bringing to bear on them her vivid recollections of the public events of her younger years. Her comparisons of the " then " and " now," were full of combined naiveté and point. In the serious affairs of life, my aunt's great common sense, quick apprehension of relative positions, and the acceptance of facts as they existed, enabled her promptly to arrive at sound and practical conclusions.

I never knew anyone whose sense of JUSTICE was stronger, or whose discernment of character was quicker. She had her prejudices, and they were strong, but always directed against those in whom meanness, want of moral courage or truthfulness, were characteristics.

She inherited from her aunt Dorothy a love of genealogical research, and it is to her introduction in my boyhood to the pages of such works as Prince's Worthies, and Old Gwillim's Blazon, that I owe my love for a study which, though often (inconsiderately as I think) deemed trivial and useless, has at all events served as an agreeable relaxation from the arduous and serious pursuits of a busy professional life. To her inspiration is owing the present record of her mother's family, the collection of the materials for which commenced, as I have mentioned in the introductory note to these pages, more than a quarter of a century ago.

Mrs. Drake devised by her will§ her five-eighth share in the Marwood property, in trust for the two daughters of her second son Charles Cutcliffe Drake, and their

---

* Mon. Insc., APPENDIX IV., p. v., and Marwood par. registers, p. vii.
† See Abstract of the Will, APPENDIX IV., p. x.
‡ See Abstract of the Will, APPENDIX IV., p. xi.
§ See Abstract of the Will, APPENDIX IV., p. xi. Mrs. Drake's surviving sister, Harriett Elizabeth Cutcliffe, who was entitled to the remaining three-eighth parts of the Marwood Estate, settled them by her Will (APPENDIX IV., p. xi) in identically the same manner.

issue; whilst her similar interest in the Mervyn rentcharge she devised to her grandson John Mervyn Cutcliffe Drake.

The issue of the marriage of FRANCES CUTCLIFFE and ZACHARY HAMMETT DRAKE, were two sons and one daughter:—

I. THE REVEREND ZACHARY HAMMETT DRAKE, who was born 14th February 1805, and baptized at Moorwinstow.* He was educated at Exeter College Oxford, and was sometime Rector of Clovelly. He died at Erlangen in Bavaria, in June 1856, having married 1st January 1831, at Tamerton Foliott, co. Devon, ELEANOR PENROSE, the only daughter of Admiral Sir Samuel PYM, K.C.B., who survived her husband, and died 13th January 1868, and was buried at Gravesend. Letters of Administration were granted by the Principal Registry of H.M. Court of Probate, 22 April 1868, to her son, John Mervyn Cutcliffe Drake, the only surviving issue of her marriage.

    I. JOHN MERVYN CUTCLIFFE DRAKE, b. and bapt. at Heanton,† 9th, d. 10th, and bur. at Marwood 13th Sept. 1832.

    II. JOHN MERVYN CUTCLIFFE DRAKE, of whom hereafter.

    III. SAMUEL PYM DRAKE, b. at Clovelly Parsonage, 23rd Aug. 1838, and d. 15th Sept. following.

    1. MARGARET MARY, b. at Heanton Parsonage, 2nd and bapt. there 3rd July 1835,‡ d. at Looseleigh House, (the residence of her grandfather, Sir Samuel Pym), 24th Oct. 1836, and was bur. at Tamerton.

II. CHARLES CUTCLIFFE DRAKE, the second son, was born 29th September 1808, and baptized at Pilton.§ He married at Ilfracombe, 19th May 1836, MARY, the elder of the two daughters and on her sister's death the sole heiress of Henry CUSACK, of Girley, co. Meath, Ireland, by Ann, daughter of Richard Rothwell of Berfordstown in the same county. Mrs. C. C. Drake was born at Moyaugher House, co. Meath, 16th, and bapt. at Athboy, in the same county, on the 29th March 1808. She died on the 21st,‖ and was buried at Marwood on the 24th February 1870.¶ Mr. Charles Cutcliffe Drake, educated at Winchester College, was in the Commission of the Peace for the county of Devon, and a Captain in the North Devon Yeomanry Cavalry. After his father's death he resided at Springfield, where he died 18th,‖ and was buried at Marwood on the 23rd October 1858,¶ leaving his wife and the four children of his marriage surviving him. Letters of Administration with his will, dat. 11 July 1854,** annexed were granted by H.M. Court of Probate to his widow 23rd Sept. 1859.

    I. CHARLES HENRY DRAKE, the elder of the two sons of Charles Cutcliffe Drake and Mary Cusack, now of the Manor House Lee, in the parish of Ilfracombe, was born 4th June, and baptized 7th July 1840,†† at Ashford. On the death of his grandmother Frances Drake, he succeeded to the Cutcliffe Estates in the parish of Ilfracombe, and took by royal licence dated Whitehall, 18th May 1867,‡‡ the additional surname of "CUTCLIFFE." He married, at Braunton co. Devon, 6th October 1868,§§ HENRIETTA MARIA, daughter of the Revd. John Whittington Ready LANDON, Vicar of Braunton, (by his first wife Jane, daughter of Charles Chichester of Hall, co.

* Moorwinstow par. registers, APPENDIX IV., p viii.   † Heanton par. registers, APPENDIX IV., p. vi.
‡ Heanton par. registers, APPENDIX IV., p. vi.   § Pilton par. registers, APPENDIX IV., p. viii.
‖ See Mon. Insc., APPENDIX IV., p. v.   ¶ Marwood par. registers, APPENDIX IV., p. vii.
** See Abstract of the Will, APPENDIX IV., p. xi.   †† Ashford par. registers, APPENDIX IV., p. vii.
‡‡ See *London Gazette*, 24th May 1867.   §§ Braunton par. registers, APPENDIX IV., p. viii.

Devon,) who was born 7th January 1842, and baptized at Braunton. The issue of the marriage is one child :—

CHARLES BERNARD MERVYN DRAKE-CUTCLIFFE, born 17th July, and baptized 5th August 1869,* at Lee; *living* 1873.

II. JOHN ROTHWELL DRAKE, baptized 12th September 1842,† at Heanton, died 19th,‡ and was buried at Marwood 24th March 1859,§ unmarried.

1. DOROTHY MERVYN, born 18th February, baptized at Ashford, 27th March 1837,|| and died 31st March 1869, and was buried at Ashford,|| having married at Pilton, 30th April 1862,¶ the Revd. Charles Whittington LANDON, Rector of Ashford, who was born 3rd July 1830, and bapt. at Braunton, the only son (by his first wife Jane Chichester) of the Rev. John Whittington Ready Landon, before mentioned. The issue of the marriage were one son and a daughter:—

JOHN CHICHESTER CREWE LANDON, born 2nd April 1868, baptized at Ashford; *living* 1873.

FRANCES CHICHESTER MERVYN LANDON, born 25th February 1867, baptized at Ashford; *living* 1873.

2. ANNE FRANCES, born 13th December 1838, and baptized 14th January following at Ashford,| married 1stly, 27th April 1865, at the Cathedral Exeter, Thomas McGhie BRYDGES, who d. s.p. 30th April 1865, and was buried at St. David's, Exeter; and 2ndly, on 29th December 1868, at Pilton, Joseph Henry GOODBAN, (who was born 16th February 1838, and baptized at St. Margaret's, Westminster); by whom she has issue two children:—

I. MERVYN CHARLES CUSACK GOODBAN, born 11th July 1871, baptized at St. Mathew's church, Lee, co. Kent; *living* 1873.

II. JOHN ROTHWELL DRAKE GOODBAN, born 22nd December 1872, baptized 9th March 1873, at St. John's church, Blackheath, co. Kent; *living* 1873.

1. FRANCES MERVYN, baptized 29th September 1806, at Moorwinstow** co. Cornwall; married 3rd July 1838, at Heanton,† Colonel John GRAHAM of the E. I. C. S. She died without issue, at Dacca in the East Indies on the 19th October 1845.‡ Colonel Graham survived his wife and re-married. He died 21 Sept. 1861, leaving his widow and a daughter surviving.

JOHN MERVYN CUTCLIFFE DRAKE, a Major in the Royal Engineers, who on the death of his grandmother Frances Drake, and her sister Harriet Elizabeth Cutcliffe, became the heir-at-law of his grandfather Charles Newell Cutcliffe, and of his great grandfather John Mervyn, and the owner of the Upton rentcharge which Dr. Mervyn in 1667 settled, as before mentioned, on the marriage of his son George Mervyn with Elizabeth Hayter.

Major Drake was born at the Parsonage at Heanton Punchardon, where his father was then Curate, on the 6th and baptized on the 10th November 1833.† He was educated for the army, and joined the Royal Military Academy at Woolwich, as a gentleman cadet, in January 1848; and in December 1851, was appointed 2nd Lieutenant in the Royal Engineers. He was subsequently quartered at Guernsey, where, at the Church of St. Matthew Cobo, he on 4th March 1857, married LAURA AUGUSTA, daughter of Sausmarez CAREY of Guernsey.

---

* Lee par. registers, APPENDIX IV., p. viii.   † Heanton par. registers, APPENDIX IV., p. vi.
‡ See Mon. Insc., APPENDIX IV., p. v.   § Marwood par. registers, APPENDIX IV., p. vii.
| Ashford par. registers, APPENDIX IV., p. vii.   ¶ Pilton par registers, APPENDIX IV., p. viii.
** Moorwinstow par. registers, APPENDIX IV., p. viii.

In February 1854, he was promoted 1st Lieutenant, and embarked for Turkey, and landed at Gallipoli with the Light Division, under the command of Sir George Brown. Lieutenant Drake was employed in the construction of the Lines of Boulair, and in November of the same year he did duty in the trenches of the night attack before Sebastopol, after which he was moved to the Inkermann attack. It was at this time that he made, under circumstances of unusual difficulty and danger, a successful reconnaissance of the river Tchernaya, a service which elicited from the late Sir John Burgoyne, G.C.B., then the Commanding Royal Engineer in the Crimea, the following letter:—

" My dear Sir,   " Camp before Sevastopol, 25th January 1855.
" I have had great pleasure in laying before Lord Raglan the Report made by Major
" Gordon, Commanding Royal Engineer, of your spirited reconnaissance of the Tchernaya.
" Your report is very interesting and precise, although the observations for it were made
" under difficult circumstances: when overturned by the failure of your frail raft, you
" rescued the Corporal of Sappers who accompanied you, from being drowned ; and after
" getting out of the water, you had the firmness still to withdraw the materials that might
" have betrayed to the enemy, in whose neighbourhood the whole proceeding took place,
" what had been going on; and I am authorised by his Lordship to express his entire
" satisfaction at your conduct.

                         " My dear Sir,
                         " Yours very faithfully,
" Lieut. Drake,   " J. F. Burgoyne,
     " Royal Engineers."   " Lt.-Genl.

Lieutenant Drake returned to Sebastopol, and subsequently accompanied the expedition to Kertch, which was taken on 24th May 1855, and he remained there to complete some defence works at Ak Boroun ; and subsequently was appointed Joint Commandant de Place, with the duties of the Quartermaster-General's department, and acted as interpreter in French, Greek, and Turkish. At the conclusion of the Crimean War, he received the Crimean Medal, the Cross of the Legion of Honour, and the Turkish Order of the Medjidié. In 1858 he was sent as Adjutant to Malta, and during his service there, was, in April 1859, promoted 2nd Captain. On his return to England, Captain Drake was, in August 1864, appointed Instructor of Musketry to the Engineers, an office which he held until he obtained his Majority in July 1872, having for the preceding eleven years been employed in superintending the Range and Engineering work of the National Rifle Association at their Wimbledon Meetings.

The children of the marriage of John Mervyn Cutcliffe Drake with Laura Augusta Carey are 6 sons and 2 daughters, viz.:—

     I. Bernard Mervyn Drake, born at Malta 24th May 1858, and privately bapt. same day ; *living* 1873.
     II. Carey Pym Drake, born at Malta 12th August, and bapt. there 5th September 1860 ; *living* 1873.
     III. Edmund Cutcliffe Drake, born at Plymouth 11th January, and bapt. at St. Peter's church there, 9th February 1862 ; *living* 1873.
     IV. Hammett Drake, born at Plymouth 5th September, and bapt. at St. Peter's church there, 4th October 1863 ; *living* 1873.
     V. Mervyn George Drake, born at Gravesend 12th March, and bapt. 13th April 1871, at Holy Trinity church, Milton, near Gravesend ; *living* 1873.
     VI. William Hacche Drake, born at Gravesend 7th January 1873 ; bapt. at Holy Trinity church, Milton ; *living* 1873.
     1. Margaret Mervyn, born at Gravesend 16th March 1866, and bapt. at St. Mark's, Rosherville, near Gravesend ; *living* 1873.
     2. Eleanor Penrose, born at Gravesend 5th October, and bapt. 8th November 1868, at Holy Trinity church, Milton ; *living* 1873.

THE

IRISH BRANCH

OF THE

𝔐𝔢𝔯𝔳𝔶𝔫 𝔉𝔞𝔪𝔦𝔩𝔶.

The settlement in Ireland of a branch of the Mervyn family arose out of their connexion with the Touchet family.   George Lord Audley (afterwards created Earl of Castlehaven), who married Lucy Mervyn, the daughter and heiress of Sir James Mervyn of Fountel-Giffard, (*See ante, p.* 19), held military appointments, and served with distinction in that kingdom in the time of Elizabeth and James I.   After the death of his first wife Lucy, (who died between January 1608-9 and March 1611,) Lord Audley married Elizabeth, one of the daughters of Sir Andrew Noel of Dalby co. Leicester, Knight, and sister to Sir Edward Noel, Bart., who was created Baron Noel of Ridlington, and succeeded his father-in-law Sir Baptist Hicks as Viscount Campden.   In 1611 (12 March) a Grant, pursuant to the King's letter under Privy Seal, of large tracts of land in the counties of Tyrone and Armagh, was made to George Lord Audley and Elizabeth his wife, Sir Mervyn and Sir Ferdinando Touchet (two sons of the marriage of Lord Audley with Lucy Mervyn), and Edward Blount (husband of Anne, the eldest daughter of the same marriage): the lands granted to be held subject to the conditions of the Plantation of Ulster. See *Cal. Patent Rolls Ireland James I., p.* 222.

Elizabeth, Countess of Castlehaven, survived the Earl, and re-married "in the City of London "[*] Colonel Sir Piers Crosby, Knt., of Maryborough, in the Queen's County, Ireland, P.C. and a Gentleman of the King's Privy Chamber; but it appearing upon Inquisitions taken, that by leasing out portions of the granted lands to "*mere Irish*" in excess of the quantity which under the articles of the Ulster Plantation the Irish born were authorized to hold, "the conditions of the Ulster Plantation " had been broken and the estates had consequently become forfeited to the Crown, the King (Charles I.) under Privy Signet, dated 24 August 1628, directed a new grant of the lands in the county of Tyrone, and in the Barony of Orier co. Armagh, which had been held by Lord Audley and his wife, to be perfected to the Lady Elizabeth and her then husband, Sir Piers Crosby ; and this direction was carried out by Grant, dated 1 Sep. 1630, under the Commission to pass escheated lands in Ulster. See *Mss. Ulster's Office, Lodge's Absts. Chancery Rolls,* Charles I., *vol. i., p.* 230. It may here be noted that the Plantation in Ulster, was effected by James I. by disposal of the vast extent of land in that Province which had been

---

[*] *See Inq. Rot. Cancell. Hibernia, vol. ii., co. Tyrone Car. I.* (48).

forfeited and escheated to the Crown consequent upon the rebellion of the Earls of Tyrone and Tyrconnell. The scheme of Plantation was based upon a plan proposed by Sir Arthur Chichester, then Lord Deputy of Ireland, by which the persons to whom lands were to be assigned should be either the old Irish Chieftains and inhabitants, or Servitors of the Crown, or else English and Scotch "Undertakers." Great indulgence appears to have been accorded to the first class, as their under-tenants and servants were allowed to be of their own country and religion, whilst the British Undertakers could only make use of English or Scotch. The Servitors, though having the privilege of employing natives, were restricted to those who were Protestants. The lands to be planted were divided into estates of three sizes, viz., 2,000, 1,500, and 1,000 English acres. The grant of the largest estate involved on the Grantee's part an obligation to build a castle and bawn within four years, to plant on their land within three years 48 able men, 18 years of age or upwards, born in England or the inland parts of Scotland; to keep a demesne of 600 acres in their hands; to have 4 fee farmers on 120 acres each, 6 leaseholders on 100 acres each, and on the rest eight families of husbandmen, artificers, and cottagers. The grantees were also under obligation within five years to reside in person on some part of the estate, and to have a store of arms in their houses. They were unable to alienate any of their lands without a Royal licence, or to set them at uncertain rents, or for a less term than 21 years, or three lives; and their tenants were to live in houses, not in cabins, and to build their houses together in towns and villages. Proportionable obligations were imposed on the grantees of the second and third sized estates; the former being bound within two years to build a strong stone or brick house and bawn; and the latter to build a bawn. In this manner, and under these regulations, the escheated lands in Ulster were disposed of to 104 English and Scotch Undertakers, 56 servitors, and 286 natives.*

For information as to the genealogy of this branch of the Mervyn family, I was, in the first instance, dependent on two manuscript pedigrees; one compiled by the late Sir William Betham, *Ulster*, a copy of which I obtained from the Dublin Office of Arms; and the other by G. F. Beltz, *Lancaster Herald*, preserved in the College of Arms in London (A ix., *Miscell. Ped. J. P.* 9). The statements contained in these pedigrees I compared with the information to be found scattered through the pages of Lodge and Archdall's "Peerage of Ireland"; with the Irish Funeral Certificates (a collection made by Sir William Betham), preserved in the Library of the College of Arms, and with some copies which I obtained from Ulster's Office. These sources of information satisfied me that neither Betham's nor Beltz's pedigree could be absolutely relied on; in fact, in both there were evident imperfections and inaccuracies. Under these circumstances, I sought the aid of my friend Sir Bernard Burke, who, although precluded by the reasons stated in my Introductory Note from affording it in his *official* character, nevertheless applied himself to the verification of the pedigree I had prepared, and he furnished me with valuable information and documentary evidence, which enabled me to establish the genealogical descent from Sir Audley Mervyn in a satisfactory manner. Subsequently, however, I discovered a means of verifying, in an undeniable manner, the greater portion of the pedigree, and of making additions to it, from the proceedings in the litigation which arose in reference to the Will of Sir Audley's grandson (Audley Mervyn, who died in 1717), and a note of the evidence in which, will be found in APPENDIX V., p. iv.

I am, therefore, now enabled to print the pedigree of the Irish Mervyns with the same confidence in its accuracy, as I have done the genealogies of the other branches of the family.

---

* The King's Commission, with Articles of Instructions, for the Plantation of Ulster, addressed to Sir Arthur Chichester and others, to enquire into lands escheated to the Crown, and to set out such lands in order to their being "planted with Colonies of Civill Men, and well affected in religion," will be found in the Appendix to the 2nd vol. of "*Inq. Ret. Cancell. Hib.*;" pub. by Record Com. Dub. 1829. See also Carte's *Life of Ormonde, fo.*, Lond. 1736, vol. i., p. 151, et seq.

SIR AUDLEY MERVYN* was, as I have shown (*ante pp.* 36-37), the second son, but on the death without issue of his brother Captain James Mervyn,† he became the heir of Sir Henry Mervyn‡ and Christian Touchet. He settled in Ireland, and allied himself prominently to the Puritan party. In 1640 the Earl of Strafford had collected an army of 8,000 men by the King's orders, for the invasion of Scotland, under the command of the Earl of Ormonde, which was encamped near Carrickfergus. In the muster roll of this army, Audley Mervyn appears in the list of the Captains of Sir Henry Tichbourne's regiment raised in Ulster.

This army was disbanded without entering on its purpose, for the Scots having entered England by the invitation of the popular leaders in the English Parliament, and the English soldiers and officers being ill-affected to Charles I., a treaty was made at Ripon that the war should end and the Scotch be paid the cost of their invasion. The purpose of the Puritan party was the calling a Parliament to raise funds to pay the Scots, in which they had secretly resolved to impeach Strafford. But they looked to Ireland for aid in preventing evidence in his favor being forthcoming from that country, and accordingly, whilst the impeachment of the Earl was proceeding in England, the House of Commons of Ireland impeached before the Irish House of Peers, the Lord Chancellor (Sir Richard Bolton), Dr. John Bramhall, Bishop of Derry, and Sir Gerard Lowther, Chief Justice of the Commom Pleas, who were charged with being his counsellors and assistants in the High Treason which was alleged against the Earl during the period he had filled the office of Lord Lieutenant. Audley Mervyn was employed to conduct the impeachment, and the following is a specimen of the characteristic speech which he made on that occasion to the Irish House of Peers :—

" My Lords,
" I am commanded by the Knights, Citizens and Burgesses of the Commons' House
" to present unto you Ireland's tragedy—the gray-headed Common Lawes Funerall and
" the active Statutes' death and obsequies. This dejected spectacle answers but the
" prefiguring type of Cæsar's murther, wounded to death in the Senate—and by Brutus,
" his bosom friend. Our Cæsar's image by reflection, even the fundamentall Lawes and
" Statutes of this Kingdome, the sole meanes by which our estates are confirmed, our
" liberties preserved, our lives secured, are wounded to death in the Senate—I mean in the
" Courts of Justice, and by Brutus too, even those persons that have received their beings
" and subsistence from them. So that here enters first those inseparable twinnes—Treason
" and Ingratitude. In a plaine phrase (my Lords) I tender unto you Treason, High
" Treason, such a Treason that wants nothing but words to express it. To counterfeit the
" King's Seale, to counterfeit the King's money, it is treason; but this dyes with the
" individuall party. To betray a Fort is treason, but it dyes with a few men. To betray an

---

* In the National Portrait Gallery of the Dublin Exhibition, 1872, there was a portrait of Sir Audley Mervyn, lent by Captain Archdall, M.P., a descendant of one of Sir Audley's granddaughters.

† James Mervyn was a considerable "Undertaker" of lands in the Barony of Omagh co. Tyrone. (See *Inq. Rot. Canc. Hib. Car.* I, No. 35). I have previously stated (page 36) that this James Mervyn settled in Ireland, and I now find that he did so in respect of property (including Trelick) in the co. of Tyrone which had been settled by Lord Audley upon the marriage of his daughter Christian with Sir Henry Mervyn, and which property was by Deed dated 29 August 1626 conveyed by Sir Henry and his wife Christian to their son and heir James, who in 1634 obtained a new Grant of the Estates from the Crown. (*Abst. Chancery Rolls, Ulster's Office, Ch.* I, *vol.* i., *pp.* 230-45.)

‡ Since the preceding pages were in print I have met with a notice of Sir Henry Mervyn which gives the precise date of his death and place of burial. It is in "Luttrell Collection of Eulogies and Elegies," *Vol.* i., *p.* 81. (*Brit. Mus., C.* 20 *f.*), and is a broad sheet printed in London 1646, entitled " An " Elegie in memorie, and at the Interring of the body of the most famous and truely Noble Knight, Sir " Henrie Mervyn. Paterne of all true valour, worth, and arts, who departed this life the 30 of May and " lyes interred at Westminster, Anno Do : 1646," " By W. Mercer." The Elegie is full of inflated nonsense in which Sir Henry is styled—"The quickest Wit, the rarest mind, the best. Dame Nature's " darling, singular in skill of all the arts and sciences," &c., &c.—and closes with an Anagram on his name —" Henrie Mervyn "—"Merry in He'ven."

" Army is treason, but it dies with a limited number, which may bee reinforced againe by
" politique Industry. To blow up both Houses of Parliament is Treason ; but succeeding
" ages may replant Branches by a fruitful Posterity. But this High Treason which I doe
" now againe in the name of the House of Commons charge and impeach Sir Richard
" Bolton, Knight, Lord Chancellor of Ireland, and Sir Gerrard Louther, Knight, Lord
" Chiefe Justice of the Common Pleas, John, Lord Bishop of Derry, Sir George Ratcliff,
" Knight, in its nature so farre transcends any of the former, that the rest seeme to be but
" Petty Larcenies in respect of this.
" . . . . . .
" " What is it to subvert the fundamentall Lawes of this Kingdom ? High Treason.

" My Lords, having such a full and rushing Gale to drive me into the depth of these
" occasions, I can hardly steere and confine my course within the compasse of Patience,
" since I read in the first volume of their browes, the least of these to be the certaine
" ruine of the subject : and if proved, a most favourable Prologue to usher in the Tragedy
" of the Actors, Counsellors, and Abettors herein. What was then the first and maine
" question ? It was the subversion of the fundamentall lawes of this Kingdom. Let then
" Magna Charta, that lies prostrated, besmeared, and grovelling in her owne goare,
" discount her wounds, as so many pregnant and undenyable proofes.
" . . . Yet, my Lords, though Magna Charta be so sacred for antiquity ; though
" its confirmation be strengthened by oath ; though it be the proper Dictionary that
" expounds meum and tuum, and assigns every subject his birthright ; it onely survives
" in the Rolls, but is miserably rent and torne in the Practice.
" These words ' Salvo Contenemento ' live in the Rolls, but these are dead in the
" Castle Chamber. These words ' Nullus liber hujus ejicitur è libero suo tenemento in
" præjudicium parium ' live in the Rolls, but they are dead where property and freehold are
" determined by paper petitions. These words ' Nulli Vendemus, nulli differemus justitiam '
" live in the Rolls, but they are dead when the suites, judgements, and execution of the
" Subject are wittingly and illegally suspended, retarded, and avoyded.
" Shall we desire to search the mortall wounds inflicted upon the Statute Laws ; who
" sees them not lying upon their death-beds, stab'd by Proclamations ; their primitive
" and genuine Tenures escheated by Acts of State, and strangled by Monopolies ? Will
" you survey the liberties of the subject ? every prison spews out illegal attachments and
" commitments,—every pillory is dyed with the forced blood of the Subjects, and hath ears
" though not to ear, yet to witnesse this complaint. . . . . Inquire of the Nether
" Lands why their fields are growne fertile by the inundations of blood,—why the pensive
" matrons solemnize too too frequent funerals of their husbands and issue,—and they will
" answer that it was for the preservation of their Lawes, which tyranny would have
" innovated. This Kingdom personated in the sable habit of a widow, with dishevelled
" haires, seems to petition your Lordships, that since she is a mother to most of us, yet
" certainly a nurse unto us all, that you would take some order for a redress of her
" tyrannicall oppressions.
" The most vehement and trayterous encounter of Satan, is lively deciphered in the
" true example of Job, where first I observe the disanalogy ;—he overthrows not Job's
" Magna Charta, he disseizes him not of his inheritance, nor dispossesses him of his
" leases, but only disrobes him of some part of his personall estate : when he proceeds to
" infringe Job's liberty, he doth not pillory him, nor cut off his eares, nor boore him through
" the tongue, He only spots him with some ulcers : Here Satan staies, when these persons
" by their trayterous combinations envie the very blood that runnes unspilt in our veines,
" and by obtruding bloody Acts, damn'd in the last Parliament, will give Satan Size-Ace
" and the Dice, at Irish, in inthralling the lives of the Subjects, by their arbitrary
" judicature." *

In 1641 Mervyn, again as the organ of the Puritan party in the Irish House of
Commons, was deputed to convey a message to the House of Lords, which gave him an
opportunity of making another of those pompous declamatory speeches in which
throughout his public life he loved to indulge. Carte refers to his oratorical displays in

* " A Speech made before the Lords in the Upper House of Parliament in Ireland, by Captain
Audley Mervyn, March 4th 1640, together with certain Articles of High Treason against Sir Richd. Bolton,
Lord Chancellor ; John Lord, Bishop of Derry ; Sir Gerard Lowther, Lord Chief Justice of the Common
Pleas ; and Sir George Radcliff, Knt." 4to, Printed, A.D. 1641.

language far from complimentary, he terms him "the most tiresome and continual speech-
"maker of the Puritan party in the House."

During the Irish Rebellion, which commenced in October 1641, and did not cease
until September 1643, Audley Mervyn appears to have abandoned his civil career for a
military one, and, although prominently connected with the Puritans, he kept up
communication with the Catholic party, which included members of his own family.

The Irish Rebellion was, according to Carte and other writers, brought about by
the Roman Catholic priests, who, not content with being allowed to exercise their religion
in a private manner, desired to have a public recognition of their right to celebrate their
offices with the same pomp as in those Catholic countries, in which the large majority of
them had been educated, and from whence they had returned to Ireland imbued with
principles of unlimited obedience to the Pope independent of their allegiance to their
King. The priests were seconded by the chiefs of the old Irish septs, who were discon-
tented with the dispossession of those tracts of land which their ancestors had forfeited
by their rebellion under the Earls of Tyrone and Tyrconnel in James the First's time,
and which had been granted to British undertakers, who had planted them to the great
civilisation and improvement of the county.*

Of the old chiefs who took an active part in the Rebellion, one of the first in
point of rank was Connor Macguire, Baron of Enniskilling, the chief of the clan of that
name in the county of Fermanagh; his brother Rory Macguire, to whom is attributed
many of the cruelties which marked the conduct of the rebels towards the English settlers,
had married Sir Audley Mervyn's sister Deborah. From the statement subsequently (1643)
made by Sir Audley to a Committee of the House of Commons appointed to inquire as
to the outbreak of the Rebellion, it seems that Rory Macguire communicated with his
brother-in-law on the designs of the rebels as early as October 1641, when, to use
Mervyn's own words, he "came unto Castle Trelich, in the county of Tyrone, being this
"examinate's then house, who, amongst other discourse, told this examinate it was resolved
"amongst themselves to employ him into England to represent unto His Majesty upon
"what grounds they had taken up arms, and what desires being granted, they would lay
"them down. The reasons, Rory Macguire acquainted this examinate, withal for the
"present were that the Parliament of England was fully bent to the extirpation of the
"Catholique religion, as was apparent in the execution of some of their priests, and that
"they (the Parliament) invaded the King's prerogative, in which their greatest security
"reposed."

To the reasons adduced Mervyn states that he opposed the following argument:—
"To the first I answered him, the power of the Parliament in England extended only to
"that kingdom, their statutes obliged not us until confirmed, it being found agreeable to
"the constitution of this kingdom, by our own Parliament. As to the second, we were no
"competent judges of the Parliament's proceedings, &c., and further desired to know in what
"high point those poor Protestant souls already murdered had offended His Majesty's pre-
"rogative. He replied that when he came next with the heads of their remonstrance unto
"me, he would satisfy me in every scruple. Upon his departure, this examinate called
"him aside, advising him (in respect the said Rory Macguire had married his sister, and
"by her got £900 per annum inheritance) that he would desist from further prosecuting
"so barbarous and treasonable a design, and that it were feasible to procure his pardon,
"if he would bestow his endeavours in appeasing the rebellion."

Failing in persuading Macguire to abandon his connection with the outbreak,
Mervyn urged that he would "repress the fury of the fire and sword," in which appeal
he partially succeeded, and was enabled to give notice to the Protestants about him
"to dispose themselves towards Derry;" "and so, by the blessing of God, many were
"saved, and this examinate, his wife, two sisters, and children escaped in the night,

---

* This is the view taken of the origin of the Rebellion by Carte and other writers; but the Roman
Catholic Priests are not without their defenders, and amongst them Dr. Curry (*Review of the Civil Wars of
Ireland, Dublin*, 1786), who stoutly asserts their innocence, and endeavours to show that the English
Protestants were by their conduct responsible for the outbreak.

" saving nothing but their lives. Such as remained (being deluded by the rebels' promises
" and wedded to their own habitations) were massacred."*

Sir Audley, then Captain Mervyn, retired to Londonderry, where he principally
resided during the war, and became Colonel of one of the six regiments formed out of
the forces at the disposal of the Government in the province of Ulster, called the Laggan
Forces. The Civil War in Ireland ended, Mervyn again appears taking part in politics;
and in 1643 he promoted, in his place in Parliament, the Declaration against the
Covenant, the taking of which the Scotch were then endeavouring to enforce in Ireland.
Ormonde, confiding in his loyalty, and considering him as a man of voluble tongue,
popular in the country, and capable of doing service to the Government, made him
Governor of Derry, in which character he forbad the preaching ministers from Scotland
to bring the Covenant into the city; but after a time, the Covenanters gained so powerful
a footing there, that Sir Audley finding the stream too strong, yielded and took it himself.
The fact is, that Mervyn was essentially a temporizer, and an able one; he went with the
current, but always with an eye to the necessity that might arise for a change of course;
accordingly he concurred with Sir Charles Coote and Lord Broghill in forwarding the
Restoration, and as a reward was made King's Sergeant by Privy Seal on 20 Sept. 1660,
and by patent 21 March 1661. He was one of the Commissioners for executing the
King's Declaration of 3 Nov. 1660, for the settlement in Ireland, and in 1661 he was
elected Speaker of the House of Commons in that kingdom. This latter position gave
him further opportunities for speech making, and when the Duke of Ormonde was
appointed Lord Lieutenant, Sir Audley as Speaker, had audience with his Grace, at
which he delivered, "in his quaint, tropical, unintelligible manner of haranguing," a
speech of thanks at his Majesty's selection,† which was followed by an oration of similar
character, when he was presented as Speaker to the Lords Justices.‡

A further opportunity for a display by the Speaker of his oratorical powers occurred
on the occasion of the House of Commons attending in 1662 the Lord Lieutenant, for
the purpose of urging that stricter rules and directions than those imposed by the King's
instructions should be laid down for the ordering of the proceedings of the Commissioners appointed for executing the Act of Settlement in Ireland. The House of Commons
was at that period composed principally of "adventurers" and soldiers, who, guided by
self-interest, desired that facilities should be afforded to the Cromwellian grantees, and
obstacles, practically insurmountable, should be interposed to prevent the Irish claimants
from recovering the lands of which they had been deprived. One of the rules which the
House desired should be imposed upon the Commissioners, was that when an Irish
claimant was dismissed, he should leave the deeds and charters on which he grounded his
claim in the Court. In addressing the Lord Lieutenant upon this part of the proposal of
the House, Sir Audley said : " As to that part that desires the writings of nocent Papists
" to be left in the Court, it cannot work a prejudice for them; for the Lands being adjudged
" against them, to what purpose will the writings operate in their hands ? But, Sir, I
" correct myself. They will have an operation. And this puts me in mind of an apposite
" similitude. Sir, in the North of Ireland the Irish have a custom in the winter when
" milk is scarce, to kill the calf and reserve the skin, and stuffing it with straw they set it
" upon four wooden feet, which they call a Puckan, and the cow will be as fond of this
" as she was of the living calf. She will low after it, and lick it, and give her milk down,
" so it stand but by her. Sir, these writings will have the operation of the Puckan ; for,
" wanting the lands to which they relate they are but skins stuffed with straw. Yet, Sir,
" they will low after them, lick them over and over in their thoughts, and teach their

---

* See " A Collection of all the Public Orders, Ordinances, and Declarations, of both Houses of
" Parliament from 9 March 1642-3 until December 1646, pp. 256-259. Folio, London, Edward Husband,
" Printer to the House of Commons, 1646."
† Carte's Life of Ormonde, vol. ii., p. 237.
‡ " A speech made by Sir Audley Mervyn, his Majesty's Prime Serjeant-at-Law in Ireland, the 11th
" day of May in the House of Lords when he was presented Speaker by the Commons, before the Right
" Honorable Sir Maurice Eustace, Knight, Lord Chancellour of Ireland, Roger Earl of Orrery, and Charles
" Earl of Mountrath, his Majesty's Lords Justices of his Kingdome of Ireland." Ordered (on 11 May 1661)
to be printed and published by the House of Commons. Dublin, 1661, 4to.

" children to read by them instead of Hornbooks, and if any venom be left, they will give
" it down on the sight of the Puckan, and entail the memory of revenge though the estate
" tail be cut off."

From the simile thus used the speech was known as "The Speaker's 'Puckan'
Speech."*

The reply which the Lord Lieutenant and his Council returned to the proposals
made by the House of Commons not being satisfactory to the majority of the Members,
it was ordered by resolution of the House, that the Speaker's speech should be printed in
Dublin, which was done, and it was reprinted in London, and distributed with great
industry by those who desired to stir up the Protestant cry against the Catholics. The
speech contained many offensive passages, and the Duke of Ormonde wrote to the
House complaining of their having printed the speech with " inconsequent inferences
and offensive passages." The English printer of the speech was taken up at the instance
of the Crown, and the Dublin printer prosecuted ; but Sir Audley, protected by his official
position, appears to have escaped any personal ill-consequences, although the imprudence
he had committed in advocating, in the violent terms he did, the views of the House of
Commons, lost for him all Court favour, and apparently terminated his public career,
although he survived some fourteen years. He died 24 Oct. 1675,† having made his
will dated the 18th of the same month,‡ and was buried on 26th of the same month at
St. Werburgh's Church, Dublin.**

At the time of his death there appears to have been a debt due from the Crown to
Sir Audley, or as it is expressed in the Address from the Irish House of Parliament to the
Lord-Lieutenant Lord Capel, " a debt of £6,000, due to the children of Sir Audley
Mervin, Knight, formerly Speaker of the House of Commons in this kingdom, for his
long and faithful service to the Protestant interest of this kingdom."† This Address was
forwarded with a letter dated 5th Nov. 1695, from Lord Capel to the Lords of the
Treasury (*Cal. Treasury Papers, vol. xxxv.,* 1695), and in the Treasury Minute Book
(*vol. vi., p.* 103), mention is made of an order that the Address is to be laid before the
King, and again (*p.* 114) the Address was minuted as " read and respited ;" but I have
not been able to trace the allowance of the payment.

About two months previous to his death, Sir Audley executed a deed "for
" the better settling his estates in his family name and blood," by which he conveyed
his estates to trustees, to the use of himself for life, and after his death (subject to
provisions for Dame Martha, his wife, and his younger children) to the use of Henry
Mervyn his eldest son, in tail male, remainder to Hugh his second son, remainder to
George his third son, with ultimate remainder to his own right heirs.‡

Sir Audley Mervyn married twice. His first wife was MARY DILLON,§ by whom
he had issue :—

    I. HENRY MERVYN, his eldest son,‖ of whom hereafter.
      1. LUCY, died unm., 1 Jan. 1671, and was buried, as appears by her funeral
        certificate, at St. Werburgh's church, Dublin.¶

Sir Audley's second wife was MARTHA, daughter of Sir Hugh CLOTT-
WORTHY, of Antrim, Knight, who survived her husband, and died 24th, and was
buried on the 27th August 1685, at St. Werburgh's, Dublin.** By her he left issue :—

    I. HUGH MERVYN,†† who was of the Naul, in the barony of Duleek, co. Meath,
      and subsequently of Baldwinstown, in the same county. He certified

---

* " The speech of Sir Audley Mervyn, Knight, His Majesty's Prime Serjeant-at-Law, and Speaker of
" the House of Commons in Ireland ; Delivered to his Grace James Duke of Ormonde, Lord Lieutenant of
" Ireland, the 13 day of February 1662 in the Presence Chamber in the Castle of Dublin. Containing the
" sum of affairs in Ireland ; But more especially the interest of Adventurers and souldiers."—*Dublin and
London* 1662 4to.
  † See APPENDIX V., p. ii.   ‡ See APPENDIX V., p. iv.   § Betham's Pedigree.
  ‖ See also the Commons' Address to the Lord-Lieutenant, which will be found to contain some
particulars of Sir Audley's family. APPENDIX V., p. iii.
  ¶ See APPENDIX V., p. ii.   ** See Funeral Certificate, APPENDIX V., p. ii.
  †† See the Commons' Address to the Lord Lieutenant. APPENDIX V., p. iii.

the accuracy of the Funeral Certificate of his mother in 1685.* He married FRANCES, daughter of . . . . TALBOT. By his Will, dated 20 September 1723,† (made when he was about 79 years of age), he, after giving a life estate in Baldwinstown to his widow, bequeathed to his eldest son Arthur Mervyn all his real estates, subject to annuities to his two daughters Martha and Frances. Hugh Mervyn died in 1727, leaving his widow surviving, as also three children, as under:—

I. ARTHUR MERVYN of Baldwinstown and the Naul, the only son, whose will was dated the 28th March, and proved 23rd May 1776.† He was twice married, first to ELIZABETH, daughter of . . . . . . HAMPSON and sister of Charles Hampson of Nonsuch, and widow of . . . . MACAULY, who died in 1767 (having made her will dated 17 April, and proved 15 September 1767,†) by whom he had issue two daughters, viz.:—

1. FRANCES, who is mentioned in her mother's will (1767), as also in her father's will (1776).

2. LETITIA, who appears to have made "an imprudent marriage" with . . . HOGAN, was cut off by her mother's will with "one shilling;" a treatment also adopted by her father in his will (1776), whereby it was also declared that "neither she nor her issue shall ever inherit any of "my fortune real or personal."

After his first wife's death, Arthur Mervyn appears to have married, in 1768,‡ JANE CUNNINGHAM, the widow of the Rev. Caleb CARTWRIGHT, whose will is dated 12th March 1769,† between which year and 1771 she died, not having had any issue by ARTHUR MERVYN, who however left, as appears by his will, an illegitimate son called ARTHUR RUSSELL, *alias* MERVYN. On the testator's death in 1776, the male issue in the legitimate line of Sir Audley Mervyn became, so far as I can ascertain, extinct.

1. MARTHA, mentioned in her father's will (1723), and was living in 1731,§ at which time she was the wife of Thomas Bamfield RUSSELL of Curragh, co. Dublin.

2. FRANCES, also mentioned in her father's will (1723).

II. GEORGE MERVYN,‖ the second son of Sir Audley Mervyn, (by his second wife, Martha Clottworthy), was married in 1680 to ELIZABETH, eldest daughter of Sir Walter BURROWES of Gilltown, co. Kildare, Bart., and widow of William JONES, son of Henry Jones, Bishop of Meath. He is mentioned in the Address presented by the Irish House of Commons in 1695 to the Lord Lieutenant, in reference to the claims of the then late Sir Audley Mervyn. His issue were two children, viz.:—

I. AUDLEY MERVYN, who is mentioned in the Funeral Certificate of his grandmother Martha Lady Mervyn (1685).*

1. ELEANOR, also mentioned in that Certificate.*

1. CHRISTIAN, who married Robert CECIL of Tewin, co. Herts, son of William Cecil of Tewin, and grandson of William Cecil, 3rd Earl of Salisbury, K.G.¶

---

* See Funeral Certificate, APPENDIX V., p. ii.
† See Abstract of the Will, APPENDIX V., p. v.
‡ Betham's Pedigree.   § See Abstract Deed, APPENDIX V., p. vi.
‖ See the Commons' Address to the Lord Lieutenant, APPENDIX V., p. ii.
¶ See "*Clutterbuck's History of Herts,*" vol. ii., p. 341, and Funeral Certificate of Martha Lady Mervyn, which also mentions two children of the marriage, vizt., William and Robert Cecil, APPENDIX V., p. ii.

HENRY MERVYN, the eldest son and heir of Sir Audley Mervyn, (by his first wife,) was of Trelich, co. Tyrone, and appears to have succeeded to the extensive estates in that county, which were possessed by his father, and by his uncle Captain James Mervyn. He was twice married, his first wife being HANNAH, the daughter of Sir John KNOX, of Dublin, Knight, by whom he had issue an only son and three daughters.

In 1684 Henry Mervyn was party to a post-nuptial settlement on the marriage of his son Audley with Olivia Coote, whereby he settled his estates upon the issue of that marriage, with remainder to the heirs male of his stepbrother Hugh Mervyn, with remainder to Hugh's brother George, in tail male. His desire, as set forth in the settlement, being that the estate should continue in the name, blood, and family of Mervyn.* After the death of his first wife, Henry Mervyn married SUSANNA, the youngest daughter of Sir William BALFOUR, Knight, of Pitcullo, Fifeshire, N.B., and widow of Hugh Lord HAMILTON, Baron of Glenawly, co. Fermanagh, Ireland. She died on the 11th, and was buried on the 14th December 1687, in St. Werburgh's church, Dublin, without having, as appears by her Funeral Certificate,† had any issue by her second husband.

Henry Mervyn died in 1699, having made his will, dated 10 December 1696 ; pr. 21 August 1701,‡ leaving issue by his first wife:—

 I. AUDLEY MERVYN of the Naul, of whom hereafter.
 1. ELIZABETH, married William ARCHDALL, of Castle Archdall, co. Fermanagh, by whom she had issue two sons and one daughter.
  ·I. MERVYN ARCHDALL, mentioned in the will of his uncle Audley Mervyn (1717), and who died 1727 unmarried.
  II. EDWARD ARCHDALL, who married, but died without issue, before 1730.
  1. ANGEL ARCHDALL, who eventually, on the death of her brothers, became the heiress of her father, married Nicholas MONTGOMERY, of Derry Gonnelly, co. Fermanagh, who assumed the surname of Archdall,§ and was the great-grandfather of Captain Mervyn Edward Archdall, M.P. for Tyrone (*living* 1873).
 2. MARTHA, who married Edward CAREY, of Dungiven,‖ by whom she had issue a son.
  HENRY CAREY, mentioned in the will of his uncle Audley Mervyn (1717), and who died in September 1756 ; ¶ who appears to have married Anne HAMILTON, and to have had issue, of whom Letitia, eventually sole heiress, married 8th August 1738, William Blacker of Castle Blacker, in Ireland, and had issue.**
 3. DEBORAH, the wife of James MOUTRAY, of Aghamoyles, otherwise Favour-Royal, co. Tyrone, whose will, dated 10 March 1718-19, was proved 26 January 1719, and by whom she had issue a son and daughters.‖
  JAMES MOUTRAY, of Favour-Royal, the son, married (1698) REBECCA, eldest daughter of James CORRY, of Castlecoote, co. Fermanagh, the great great-grandfather of the Rev. John James Moutray, of Favour-Royal (*living* 1873).‖

AUDLEY MERVYN, of Trelich, co. Tyrone, and also of the Naul, co. Meath, only son of Henry Mervyn and Hannah Knox, and grandson and heir of Sir Audley Mervyn, married about 1683-4 OLIVIA, one of the five daughters of Richard COOTE,

---

* See Abstract of the Deed, APPENDIX V., p. iv.
† See "*Lodge and Archdall's Peerage, Ireland*," vol. ii., p. 300, and Funeral Certificate, APPENDIX V., p. ii.
‡ Betham's Pedigree.
§ See "*Lodge and Archdall's Peerage, Ireland*," vol. iii., p. 280.
‖ Ex rele, Sir Bernard Burke, Ulster.   ¶ See APPENDIX V., p. v.
** See "*Burke's Landed Gentry*," ed. 1863, article "Blacker."

Baron Coloony,* who died in 1720,† having survived her husband,‡ who was buried in Christ Church, Dublin, 18 June 1717,§ leaving a will dated 15th and proved 27 June 1717,‖ as to the construction of which, in connection with the limitations of the settlement made in 1711 by Audley Mervyn on the marriage of his son Henry with Mary Tichborne, considerable litigation arose. Audley Mervyn, of Trelich, on his death, left four sons and two daughters, viz.:—

    I. HENRY MERVYN of Trelich, who was born before the 18th Dec. 1684 (the date of the post-nuptial settlement on his father and mother's marriage, in the limitations of which he is mentioned), was married in 1711 to MARY, the widow of . . . TICHBORNE, who appears to have died in 1735. It would seem that the large estates which had been acquired by Sir Audley Mervyn and by his brother James, had descended to Henry Mervyn, who sold the principal portion of them; and it was in reference to one of the sales, that the litigation to which I have referred, took place.¶ Henry Mervyn by his will in 1747** devised in strict settlement such of his estates as he had not sold, to the use of his brother-in-law James Richardson, who had married his sister Anne, with remainder to their daughter Letitia, with remainder to his kinsman Mervyn Archdall, with remainder to his nephew Wesley Harman, with remainder to his nephew William Irvine. Henry Mervyn died without any issue, and with him terminated the eldest male line of the descendants of Sir Audley Mervyn.

    II. AUDLEY MERVYN of the Naul, mentioned in his father's will (1717), died 1st February 1747, unmarried.††

    III. JAMES MERVYN, also mentioned in his father's will (1717), died either in 1721 or 1726 unmarried, and was buried in the church of Clonmarden.‡‡

    IV. THEOPHILUS MERVYN, also named in his father's will (1717), died unmarried in 1736.††

    i. LUCY, eldest daughter of Audley Mervyn and Olivia Coote, married in the lifetime of her father to Wentworth HARMAN of Moyle, co. Longford, the son of Wentworth Harman of the same place, Captain of the "Battle Axe Guards," by his first wife Margaret, daughter of Garrett Wesley of Dangan, co. Meath, by Anne daughter of . . . . Cusack, and relict of Christopher Nugent.§§ Lucy Mervyn at her death in 1737 left issue by her husband Wentworth Harman two sons:—

        I. WESLEY HARMAN, mentioned in the will of his uncle Henry Mervyn (1747), died 6 April 1758, having married MARY, daughter of the Rev. Nicholas MILLEY, D.D., of Carlow, by whom he had issue‖‖ one son and one daughter:—

            I. WENTWORTH HARMAN.

            i. LUCY, mentioned in the deed of 19th August 1747, as then living.

        II. THOMAS HARMAN, Cornet of a Regiment of Horse; bapt. 16 January 1728, d. 9 May 1765.

---

* See Funeral Certificate of Richard Coote, Baron Coloony (APPENDIX V., p. ii.), which mentions the marriage of his daughter Olivia with Audley Mervyn.
  † Betham in his pedigree states that Mrs. Olivia Mervyn made a will, dated 5th and proved 10th April 1720.
  ‡ See "*Lodge and Archdall's Peerage, Ireland,*" vol. iii., p. 208.
  § See Fun. Cert., APPENDIX V., p. iii.   ‖ See Abstract of the Will, APPENDIX V., p. iv.
  ¶ See APPENDIX V., p. iv.   ** See Abstract of the Will, APPENDIX V., p. v.
  †† See APPENDIX V., p. v.
  ‡‡ See Funeral Certificate, APPENDIX V., p. iii.
  §§ See "*Lodge and Archdall's Peerage, Ireland,*" vol. iii., p. 237.
  ‖‖ Ex. aucte. Sir Bernard Burke, Ulster, in correction of Lodge and Archdall, who state erroneously that Wesley Harman died s.p. See also APPENDIX V., p. vi., Abstract of deed of 19th August 1747.

2. ELEANOR, who was mentioned in her father's will (1717), married (2nd wife) Christopher IRVINE, of Castle Irvine, co. Fermanagh, High Sheriff of that county (1725), named in the will of his brother-in-law Henry Mervyn (1747), and party to deed of 31 July 1752.* Mrs. Irvine survived her husband, and was living a widow in 1760, (when she was party to the Appeal, "Teatt v. Strong," APPENDIX V., p. iv.,) having had issue two sons and three daughters, viz. :—

    I. WILLIAM IRVINE, of Castle Irvine, M.P. for Ratoath ; b. 1734; mentioned in will of his uncle Henry Mervyn (1747).
    This William Irvine was the great-grandfather of Henry Mervyn-D'Arcy-Irvine, of Castle Irvine, who died in July 1870, leaving issue by his wife Huntly-Mary Prittie, a son Henry-Huntly. b. 14 Aug. 1863.

    II. HENRY IRVINE, mentioned in will of his uncle Henry Mervyn (1747).

    1. OLIVIA, mentioned in will of her great uncle Arthur Mervyn (1776).

    2. MARY.

    3. ELEANOR.

3. ANNE, mentioned in her father's will (1717), and also in the will of her brother Henry (1747), was party to a deed in 1752,† and was living a widow in 1760.‡ She married twice, her first husband being Hugh EDWARDS, of Castlegore, co. Tyrone, by whom she had three children, viz. :—

    I. JAMES EDWARDS.

    1. ELIZABETH, eldest daughter, party to deed of 7 January 1752.†

    2. OLIVIA.

After the death of Hugh Edwards, Anne married James RICHARDSON of Castlehill, co. Tyrone, who on his marriage took the surname of Mervyn, and by whom she had issue an only child—

    LETITIA, who is mentioned in the will of her uncle Henry Mervyn (1747), and who married in 1764 Richard ROCHFORT (son of Robert Rochfort, Earl of Belvidere and Lieut.-Col. of the 39th Regiment), who also on his marriage assumed the surname of Mervyn, but died in 1776 without issue.§

4. JANE, mentioned in her father's will (1717) ; died in 1725 s.p.

5. EUPHALIA, buried 15 January 1714, unmarried.‖

A

CHAPTER

ON THE

𝕳𝖊𝖗𝖆𝖑𝖉𝖗𝖞 of the 𝕸𝖊𝖗𝖛𝖞𝖓𝖘,

AND THE

ARMORIAL BEARINGS

OF SOME OF THE FAMILIES WITH WHOM THEY ALLIED BY INTERMARRIAGES.

"*First Coat.*"　　　"*Second Coat.*"　　　"*Third Coat.*"

HE MERVYNS have borne three coats, each distinct from the other. That which I have above designated the "First Coat," was borne by Sir John Mervyn (1566), of Fountel-Giffard, and in the absence of a Grant, of which I find no trace, may be assumed to have belonged to him by descent from his great-grandfather John Mervyn (1476); if so. it equally attaches to the Durford, Pertwood, Devonshire, and Irish branches, and may be used by persons entitled to bear the arms of either of those families. The "Second Coat" seems to have belonged specially* to the Pertwood branch and thence by descent to the Devonshire Mervyns. The "Third Coat" was exclusively that of the Irish branch, unless indeed, it was theirs by descent from the MERFYNS by whom it was borne (*See* APPENDIX I., *p.* xv.) ; but as I have failed to establish any connection with that family, it will be safer to assume that Sir Henry Mervyn (1636), adopted it in substitution for his paternal coat, an act recognised by the Irish Heralds, as proved by the Arms given by them, in his, and his descendants' funeral certificates. (See

---

* There is, however, evidence that one member of the Fountel-Giffard family bore this coat. (Vide ante, p. 9, footnote ‡ and post p. 92.)

APPENDIX II., p. iv., and APPENDIX V., p. ii.) Hence it would follow that all the members of the Fountel-Giffard, Durford, Pertwood, Devonshire, and Irish branches were entitled to use the " First Coat ;" that the Pertwood and Devonshire branches were also entitled to bear the " Second Coat ;" and that in addition to the " First Coat," the Irish Mervyns were entitled to quarter the " Third Coat."

I. MERVYN. The earliest authority for the coat of Mervyn as here given, viz.:—" *Sable, 3 lyons pass⁴· guard⁴·· per pale or and argent*," is, so far as I can ascertain, the Funeral Certificate of Sir JOHN MERVYN who died 19th June 1566, (Ms. Coll. Arm. "*I.* 13," *p.* 75. See APPENDIX I., p. xii). It should however, be remarked that another coat is attributed to Sir John in the Ms. now in the Cottonian Collection of the British Museum, "*Claudius C. iii.*," *p.* 169, being, "The names " and arms of those that were advanced to the honorable ordre of " Knighthode in the happy reign of Kinge Edward the Sixt." In this Ms. appears the name of " Sir John Mervyn," as having been knighted at the camp at Roxburgh by the Protector Duke of Somerset, I Edw. VI.; and in connection with that entry, the following arms are given, viz.:—"*Argent, a demi-lyon rampant sable.*" There is corroborative evidence that about that date a member of the Fountel branch of the family, bore the last-mentioned coat; for in the Visitation of Wilts in 1565, (Ms. Coll. Arm. " *G.* 8," *p.* 48⁴) there is a record of the marriage of Elizabeth Mervyn, (sister of Sir John above-mentioned,) with Thomas Hall of Bradford, co. Wilts, and her arms, in impalement with her husband's, are there tricked thus:—Quarterly 1st and 4th, *Argent, a demi-lyon rampant sable* ; 2nd and 3rd, *Ermine, a Squirrel sejeant gules, cracking a nut or.* Sir James Mervyn, the eldest son of Sir John, used the arms given in his father's funeral certificate, as appears from the remains of his seal affixed to two original letters written by him to Lord Burghley, *(Lansd. Ms. Nᵒ· 70, Arts. 66 & 70).* The coat attributed to Sir James in the list of Knights in the Brit. Mus. *(Add. Ms. 5482 fo. 14⁴·)* is " *Sable, 3 lyons pass. guard⁴· argent.*"

Almost contemporary with Sir John Mervyn's funeral certificate (1566) there is a record of the second coat of arms borne by the Mervyn family, viz.:—"*Argent, a demi-lyon rampant sable, charged on the shoulder with a fleur-de-lis or,*" which occurs (Mervyn of Pertwood,) in the Visitations of Wilts, 1565 and 1623. (Mss. Coll. Arm. " *G.* 8," *p.* 54, and " *1, C.* 22," *p.* 23⁴) THAT coat, *excepting* the charge of the fleur-de-lis, is identical with the arms attributed to Sir John Mervyn and his sister Elizabeth Hall, as before mentioned.

The arms borne by the IRISH branch of the family appear to have been, uniformly, "*Or, a chevron sable,*" being the coat adopted by Sir Henry Mervyn, Admiral of the Narrow Seas, as shown by his seal attached to an original letter from him to the Admiralty Commissioners. (*See ante, pp. 29 and 35.*) This bearing was similar to that used by the family of MERFYN of Kent and London; as to which see APPENDIX I., p. xv.

II. SQUERIE. This coat, "*Ermine, a squirrel sejeant gules, cracking a nut or,*" is given in Philipott's "Survey of Kent" as borne by SQUERIE, of Squerie's Court in the parish of Westerham, in that county; one of the co-heiresses of which family married Richard Mervyn, of Fountel. (*See ante, pp.* 3, 4.) It first appears in connection with the Mervyn coat, in Sir John's funeral certificate, to which reference has been made.

III. MOMPESSON of Bathampton, co. Wilts. MARY MOMPESSON, the wife of WALTER MERVYN, whose paternal coat "*Argent, a lyon rampant sable,*" is here impaled with the arms of her husband, was entitled to the two quarterings of GODWYN "*Gules, a chevron ermine between 3 leopards' faces or,*" and DREWE "*Ermine, a lyon passant gules.*" Vide Visit. of Wilts, 1623, Ms. Coll. Arms. ("1, *C.* 22," *p.* 9.)

IV. GREEN. The coat of John "GREEN" or "GRENE," of Stotfold, co. Beds, whose daughter and co-heiress, ELIZABETH (by a co-heiress of Latimer) married JOHN MERVYN, of Fountel, as given by Philipott in his collections for Bedfordshire, Ms. Coll. Arms. ("*Philipott's Beds* 49," *p.* 16), was "*Azure, 3 stags trippant or,*" as shown in the illustration. Elizabeth Green, altho' the daughter of a co-heiress, was NOT (as has been supposed) entitled to quarter the arms of her mother; that lady having remarried Sir John Mordaunt, and by him had male issue.

V. BASKERVILLE. The arms, "*Argent, a chevron between 3 hurts, the chevron charged with a crescent or,*" here given as those of JANE, daughter of Philip BASKERVILLE, of Erdesley, co. Hereford, are from the funeral certificate of Sir John MERVYN, of Fountel, whose first wife she was. It should, however, be remarked that in the Ms. in the College of Arms, in which I find the marriage reeorded, ("*Vin.* 155," *p.* 65*[b]*) the arms given for Baskerville vary in the respect that instead of *azure*, the chevron is *gules*; a colouring apparently followed by all modern authorities.

VI. MOMPESSON. The coat of ELIZABETH, the daughter of John MOMPESSON, of Bathampton, who was the second wife of Sir JOHN MERVYN, is here given, with the quarterings to which she was entitled, viz., 1st MOMPESSON, as before described; 2nd GODWYN; 3rd DREWE, as described under No. III.; 4th WATKIN, "*Azure, a fesse between 3 leopards' faces jessant-de-lis or.*" Mss. Coll. Arm. ("1, *C.* 22," *p.* 9*[b]*, "*Vin.* 147," *p.* 45*[b]*.)

VII. CATESBY. The arms of JANE CATESBY, who first married Robert Gaynesford, and secondly EDMUND MERVYN, were "*Argent, 2 lyons passant sable, crowned or.*" Ms. Coll. Arm. ("*Vincent's Northamptonshire,* 114," *p.* 157.)

VIII. CLARKE. The coat belonging to AMYE CLARKE, the wife of Sir JAMES MERVYN, " *Or, 2 bars azure; in chief 3 escallops; in fesse a mullet gules.*"* Bodleian Library. (*Let's Mss. "Wood's Coll.* 14 *D.*")

IX. PILKINGTON. The arms given by Philipott, in his collections for Berks and Bedford, Ms. Coll. Arms, (*Philipott* 3, 2, 1, *fo.* 21.) as those to which DEBORA, daughter and co-heir of James PILKINGTON, Bishop of Durham, who (having first married Walter Dunch, and after his death, 4th June 1594,) married Sir JAMES MERVYN, was entitled, were, Quarterly, 1 and 4 *Argent a cross patonce gules, voided of the field,* for PILKINGTON ; 2 and 3 *Paly of six argent and gules, on a bend sable 3 mullets or* for . . . .; the whole charged with a crescent for difference. But it should be noted that another coat, being a variance of the coat of Pilkington, was confirmed to the Bishop, by Dethick, *Garter,* 10th Feb. 1560, viz.:—" *Argent a cross* " *patonce gules voided of the field, on a chief vert 3 suns in* " *their splendour or.*" Ms. Coll. Arm. ("*Vincent*" 169, " *Gifts of Arms,*" *fo.* 21.)

X. AUDLEY. The arms borne by George BARON AUDLEY, (subsequently created Earl of Castlehaven,) who married for his first wife LUCY, the only child and heiress of Sir James MERVYN, of Fountel-Giffard, Knight, were :— Quarterly 1 and 4, *Ermine, a chevron gules* for TOUCHET, 2 and 3 *Gules a frette or,* for AUDLEY.

---

* These arms are similar (except the colour of the field and the escallops) to the coat given to Erington, of Walwick Grange, co. Northumberland, viz.:—Argent, 2 bars az. in fesse a mullet and in chief 3 escallops of the second. (*See Harl Ms. 1565, p. 3b, being copy Visit. Wilts in 1565.*)

XI. PAKENHAM. The coat here impaled with Mervyn is that of ELIZABETH the 3rd daughter and co-heir of Sir Edmund PAKENHAM of Sussex, viz. :—*Quarterly or and gules, in the first quarter an eagle displayed vert;* to which she was entitled to add the four following quarterings, viz.:—DE VALONIJS (*Paly wavy of six argent and gules*) CREKE (*Sable, a hand ppr, in a maunche, (arg. or or.) grasping a fleur de lis or*). GLANVILLE, (*Argent, a chief indented azure*), and BLUNDUS (*Lozengy or and sable*). See Mss. Coll. Arm. ("*Vincent's Baronage* 20," *pp.* 26*b*, 27, and "*Vinc. Sussex* 121," *p.* 373.)

XII. WINDSOR. The following is the description of the full coat of arms to which EDITH, daughter of Sir Anthony WINDSOR, (who married HENRY MERVYN of Durford,) was entitled according to the records of the College of Arms, viz:—Quarterly of eight. 1st and 8th, WINDSOR, *Gules, a saltire argent between* 12 *cross crosslets or.* 2nd, MOLYNES, *Azure, a cross flory argent pierced of the field.* 3rd, BINTWORTH, *Gules,* 5 *lyoncels rampt.* (1, 3, *and* 1) *or.* 4th, ANDREWS, *Argent, on a bend cotised sable,* 3 *mullets of the field.* 5th, WEYLAND, *Argent, on a cross gules,* 5 *escallops or.* 6th, BURNAVILLE, *Gules, a rose barbed and seeded or.* 7th, STRATTON, *Argent, on a cross sable five besants.* Mss. Coll. Arm. ("*Vincent* 20," *p.* 237; "*Philipott's Mullett,*" *p.* 175, where a full pedigree of the Windsor family will be found).

XIII. JEPHSON. The arms of ANNA JEPHSON, who married EDMUND MERVYN of Durford, are recorded with the family pedigree of Jephson in the Visitation of Hants, 1622-34, Ms. Coll. Arms, ("C. 19," p. 82), as "Azure, a fesse embattled or, between 3 cocks' heads of the last, combed and whattled gules."

XIV. RYVES. The arms of RYVES of Damory Court. and Ranston co. Dorset, are recorded with the pedigree (which gives the double marriage of that family with Mervyn of Fountel and Mervyn of Knoyle), in the Visitation of Wilts, 1623. Ms. Coll. Arm. ("1. C. 22," p. 192), thus "Argent, on a bend cotised sable, three lozenges ermine."

XV. SHELDON. The arms here given "Sable, a fesse argent between 3 sheldrakes ppr." are recorded in the College of Arms as the coat of SHELDON in the Visitation of Worcester 1634 Ms. Coll. Arms ("C 30," p. 98). The authority for its introduction as the arms borne by Sheldon, of Manston co. Dorset, is the monumental stone still existing in the chancel of Pertwood Church, erected about 1734, under the directions in the will of Sheldon Mervyn (APPENDIX III., p. viii.) "and my Coat of Arms fairly cut."

XVI. VAVASOUR and YATES Or, on a fesse indented sable a fleur de lis argent, being the Arms exemplified and confirmed in 1791 to Henry NOOTH on taking the surname and arms of VAVASOUR (of Spaldington). Ms. Coll. Arms (Grants 17, p. 326) . impaling YATES:—Per fesse sable and ermine, on a fesse embattled counter embattled between 3 gates, as many goats' heads erased, all counter changed, which was the coat granted in 1791 to ANNE ASSHETON NOOTH, eldest daughter and co-heir of MAIL YATES, then late of Maghull in co. Lancaster, and wife of HENRY NOOTH of Sturminster co. Dorset. Ms. Coll. Arms. (Grants 17, p. 318.)

XVII. NEWTE. "*Gules, a chevron between three human hearts argent, each pierced through with a sword in bend sinister ppr, hilt and pommel or.*" This coat is registered (with the addition of *a bordure wavy or*) in the College of Arms *("Grants,*[*] *24," p. 25),* and is engraved on the monumental stone in the church at Heanton Punchardon, co. Devon, recording the death of CHRISTIAN, the daughter of the Revd. Richard NEWTE, of Tiverton, and wife of the Revd. WILLIAM MERVYN, of Heanton. See also "Prince's Worthies of Devon" *(fo. ed. 1701, p. 476).*

XVIII. BURRIDGE, of Tiverton, co. Devon. "*Azure, three dolphins naient embowed argent; on a chief or, three rudders sable.*" This coat was granted 8th March 1700, by Sir Thomas St. George (*Garter*), and Sir Henry St. George, *Clarencieux,* (Ms. Coll. Arm. "*Regr. Nob: & Gent: V." fo.* 42) to Robert Burridge the father of MARGARET BURRIDGE, who married RICHARD MERVYN, of Marwood, co. Devon.

XIX. CHICHESTER, of Hall, co. Devon. With the Chichester coat, which is here impaled with Mervyn, viz.: "*Chequy or and gules, a chief vair,*" DOROTHY CHICHESTER was, according to the entries in the College of Arms, entitled to quarter the following four coats:—1. RALEIGH; *Gules, a bend vair, between 6 cross crosslets or.* 2. GRAAS; *Ermine, a fesse between 3 cinquefoils gules.* 3. HALL; *Azure, a chevron ermine between 3 chaplets or.* 4. GOUGH; *Sable, a chevron between 3 mermaids argent, each holding a mirror in the hand.*—Visit. Devon, 1620, Ms. Coll. Arms, ("1.C.1," p. 23ᵇ). The foregoing were not, however, the only quarterings to which Dorothy Chichester, as daughter of Arthur Chichester of Hall, was entitled. The full coat would appear to be as follows:—1. CHICHESTER; *as above.* 2. RALEIGH; *as above.* 3. STOCKAY; *Azure, six martlets 3, 2, and 1 or; on a canton of the last, a mullet gules.* 4. PEVERELL; *Azure, three garbs argent banded gules, a chief or.* 5. GRAAS; *as above.* 6. WATTON or WOTTON; *Gules, three garbs argent.* 7. MOELLS; *Argent, two bars gules, in chief three torteaux.* 8. PROUZ; *Sable, three lyons rampant argent.* 9. PROUZ (2nd Coat); *Argent, three blackamoors' heads in profile sable.* 10. . . . . . .; *Sable, a fesse between three mullets or.* 11. DYMOKE; *Sable, two lyons passant argent ducally crowned or.* 12. HALL; *as above.* 13. GOUGH; *as above.* See Ms. Coll. Arms, ("*Norfolk* 7," p. 87.)

---

* Being a Grant and Exemplification to Thomas Mountford, the illegitimate son of Thomas Newte of Tiverton, co. Devon, on his taking the surname of Newte, under the will of his father 1806. So far as I can ascertain, the legitimate descendants of the Revd. Richard Newte are extinct; if so, the descendants of Christian Newte and William Mervyn would be entitled to quarter the above coat.

XX. CUTCLIFFE, of Damage, in the parish of Ilfracombe, co. Devon. *"Gules, three pruning knives argent."* In the Visitation of Devonshire, in 1620, (Ms. Coll. Arm. *" 1.C.1," p. 217*) the pedigree of this family was recorded ; but the arms were omitted to be described or tricked. This omission was afterwards supplied on a special application, in 1673, to the Earl Marshall, by John Cutcliffe, of Ilfracombe.

XXI. DRAKE, Quarterly, 1 & 4, DRAKE. *Argent, a wyvern with tail nowed gules,* 2nd & 3rd, HACCHE, *Gules, two demi-lyons passant guardiant or.* Visit. Devon, 1620 (Ms. Coll. Arms. *" 1 C. 1," pp. 187 and 218*[b].) impaling quarterly 1st, CUTCLIFFE, as above, 2nd, MERVYN (Pertwood), 3rd, MERVYN (Fountel) and 4th, SQUERIE.

XXII. PHILIPOT, of Hampshire. *Sable, a bend ermine,* borne by ELIZABETH, daughter of Sir John PHILIPOT, Knight, of Thruxton, co. Southampton, who married Captain JAMES MERVYN, eldest son and heir of Sir Henry Mervyn, Knight, of the Durford Branch. *(Funeral Certificate, Ulster's Office, vol. ix., p. 42.)*

XXIII. CLOTWORTHY, of Antrim, Ireland. *Azure, a chevron erm. between three chaplets or,* being the arms of MARTHA, the daughter of Sir Hugh CLOTWORTHY, of Antrim, and second wife of Sir AUDLEY MERVYN, Knight. *(Funeral Certificate, Ulster's Office, vol. xi., p. 73.)*

APPENDICES.

TABULAR PEDIGREE

OF THE

FOUNTEL-GIFFARD Branch

OF THE

Mervyn Family.

Richard Mervyn, of Fonn = Dorothy, younger dau. of Thomas Squerie, of Squeris Court, co. tayne, alias Fountel, co. Kent, and coh. of her brother John Squerie. (*Philpott's Surv. Kent.* Wilts.) — *Inq. p.m., 17, Hen. vi., 1439, No. 25.*

Ralph Mervyn, of Fountel. = . . . daughter of . . . . Parre. (" *Vinc. Ped.*" *See Mis. Coll. Arm.* " *Vincent's Sussex* 121," *p.* 392 ; and " *J. F. ix.*")

John Mervyn, acquired the Manor and Estate of = Joan, daughter of Lord Hungerford, Fountel-Giffard from the Hungerford family. Living of Heytesbury. (" *Vinc. Ped.*") 1476.

HughMervyn, 2nd son.

1st wife. Joan, who died = Walter Mervyn, eldest son, succeeded to the = Mary, daughter of John Mompesson, of Bath- s.p., (*Inq. p.m.* Fountel Giffard estates. Will dated 20th Nov., sampton, co. Wilts (by Isabel, dau. and coh. of 4 *Hen. viii.*, Allen. viii. (1510,) died 12th July, 1512. (*Inq. p.m.,* Thomas Drewe) who was Sheriff of his county, No. 74.) 4 *Hen. viii., No. 74.* 18 Edw. iv.

Daughter and coh.

m. . . . . . . Brighton of Corsham, co. Wilts. (*Vinc. Ped.*)

Elizabeth, daughter and coh. of John Green, of Scotfold, co. Beds. (by Edith, dau. and coh. of S Nicholas Latimer, who remarried S John Mordaunt, K by whom she was mother of John, 1st Lord Mordaunt, and after his death, mar., thirdly, S John Carew, K) Elizabeth Mervyn survived her hus- band, and was mentioned in Inq. p. m., 4 Hen. viii. (1512), No. 74, and also in her mother's (Edith Lady Carew) will 1517.

John Mervyn, elder son, living 1502, died vit. pat. (*Inq. p. m., 4 Hen. viii. No. 74.*)

S Edmund Mervyn, K of Durford Abbey, co. Sussex.

See Pedigree of the **Durford Abbey** *branch of the* MERVYN family.

Edward Burley, of Writtle, co. Wilts.

3 Jane Mervyn.

See Vint., Wilts, 1565.

1st wife. Eleanor = Ambrose Mervyn. Daunteasey, of West Lavington, co. Wilts.

2 Daughter m. . . Fitz- james, of Redlinch, co. Somerset. (" *Vinc. Ped.*")

William Mervyn, = Margaret, of Pertwood, dau. of co. Wilts ; William Sheriff for Wilts Fletcher. and Dorset, 5 Hen. vii. (1489-90.)

See Pedigree of the **Pertwood** *branch of the* MERVYN family.

See Vint., Wilts, 1623.

1st wife. S John Mervyn, K of Fountel-Giffard, = Jane, daughter of Philip Basker- = Elizabeth, dau., and eventually one of succeeded his grandfather Walter Mervyn ; ville, of Sherborne, co. Dorset. the four co-heirs of John Mompesson, of was M.P. for Wilts, 1554 ; died 19th (afterwards of Erdesley, co. Here- Bathampton, and widow of S June, 1566. (*Inq. p.m., 12 Eliz., No. 116,* ford,) and widow of William Richard Perkins, of Ufton, co. Berks, also *Funeral Cert., Mis. Coll. Arm. "J. 13,"* Peverell, of Bradford Peverell, K ; died 25 Sept., 1581, s.p. (*Inq. p. 75.*) Will dat. 8 June, pr. 20 June, 1566. co. Somerset. Buried at Fountel. p.m., 24 Eliz., No. 92.) Will dat. 24 July, 1581; pr. 27 Sept. 1581-2.

Elizabeth = Thomas Hall, Mervyn of Bradford, co. Wilts. (*Visit. Wilts,* 1565.)

See Visit. Wilts, 1623.

William Mervyn.

George Mervyn, died s.p. (" *Vinc. Ped.*")

2nd | son. Edmund Mervyn, mar. at Carshalton, co. Surrey, 19th Feb., 1588-9. Living 1578.=Jane, dau. of Sir Richd. Catesby, Knt., and widow of Robert Gaynesford, of Carshalton, co. Surrey, (*Mt. Coll. Arm.,* "*Visit. Northumb.* 114," *p. 275.*)

3rd | son. John Mervyn, living 1578; died s.p. ("*Visit. Ped.*")

4th | son. Philip Mervyn, living 1578; exor. of his father's will; died s.p. ("*Visit. Ped.*")

5th | son. Ambrose Mervyn, exor. of his father's will; living 1610.=Susan, dau. of Geoffry Upton of Warminster, co. Som. (*Visit. Somerset, 1591.*)

—Deborah, daughter of James Pilkington, Bishop of Durham, and widow of Walter Dunche, of Little Wynam, co. Berks; died s.p.

2nd wife.
—Sr. James. Mervyn, Knt., of Fountel Giffard, "Esquire for the body of the Queen's Majesty," born 1529; succeeded his father in 1568; was M.P. for Wilts 1572. He settled the Fountel estates on the marriage of his granddaughter, Christian, with Sr. Henry Mervyn; died 1 May, 1611 (*Inq. p.m., 13. Jac. I. No. 190*); will dated 1 April, 1610, proved 21 Nov. 1611.

1st wife.
—Amy, daughter of Valentine Clarke (by Elizabeth, dau. and h. of Roland Bridges) and widow of E. Horne, of Sarsden, co. Oxon. (*Lee's "Gatherings of Oxon, Am. 1574," Bod. Lib., Wood's Coll. 14 D.*)

—Lucy Mervyn, only child and heiress, living 20th January, 1608-9, but died in her father's lifetime (*Inq. p.m., 13 James I., No. 190*).

—George, Lord Audley of Heleigh, born 1551, created Earl of Castlehaven in 1617, in which year he died.

—Sr. Henry Mervyn, Knt, (of the Durford Abbey branch of the family) succeeded to the Fountel estates on the death of Sir James Mervyn in 1611 (*Inq. p.m. 13 Jac. I. No. 190*) created by patent (*1677-8*), Admiral and Captain-General of the Narrow Seas. Will dated 20 May 1646, in which year he died. He sold the Fountel estates to his brother-in-law, Mervyn Lord Audley and second Earl of Castlehaven; on whose attainder in 1631, they became forfeited to the Crown.

—Christian, sixth child, and fourth daughter, married previously to Trinity Term 1607 (*Inq. p.m., 13 Jac. I, No. 130*). (Living 1631).

See Pedigree of the **Durford Abbey** branch of the MERVYN family.

1st | son. John Mervyn, mentioned in his grandfather's (Sir Jno. Mervyn) will (1566) living 1578.=Edmund Mervyn, mentioned in his grandfather's (Sir John Mervyn's) will (1566) living 1578.=Ann Huddleston ("*Visit. Ped.*")

James Mervyn, ("*Visit. Ped.*")

3rd | son. Richard Mervyn, also mentioned in his grandfather's, (Sir John Mervyn) will (1566), living 1578.

Philip Mervyn living 1610. Legatee under his uncle's (Sir James Mervyn) will.

Eleanor Mervyn, eldest daughter of Sir John Mervyn, in whose will (1566) she is mentioned.

(*See Visit. Somerset, 1643.*)

2nd wife. Robert Hill, of Yarde, co. Somerset.

2nd | dau. Edith Mervyn, died unm.

3rd | dau. Margaret Mervyn, living 1566.=John Cook, of Underbridge, Isle of Wight.

4th | dau. Elizabeth Mervyn.=John Ryves, of Damory Court, co. Dorset, mentioned in Sir John Mervyn's will (1566).

(*See Visit. Wilts, 1643.*)

5th | dau. Margaret Mervyn, "the younger," (second daughter of this name).=Francis Perkins, of Ufton, co. Berks, nephew of Dame Elizabeth Mervyn. (*See will of Dame Elizabeth Mervyn, 1581.*)

(*See Mt. Coll. Arm., "I.13," p. 75.*)

6th | dau. Anne Mervyn.=Edward Corbury, of Shute, co. Soton.

(*See Mt. Coll. Arm., "I.13," p. 75.*)

Two other daughters are mentioned in Sir John Mervyn's Funeral Certificate as having died s.p. (*Mt. Coll. Arm. "I.13."*)

Abstracts OF " Inquisitiones Post Mortem."

Inquisition taken at Devises, in the county of Wilts, after the death of WALTER MERVYN :—   14th October, 4 Hen. VIII. (1512) No. 74.

The jurors found that Walter Mervyn was seised of the Manors of Fontel Gyfford and Farnehyll, in co. Wilts, in his demesne as of fee, and that on 9th April, 1 Hen. VIII. [1510] he enfeoffed Henry Bodenham, Ambrose Dauntsey, William Dauntsey, and others, of the same Manors for the fulfilment of his last will, which he afterwards made on 20th November, 2 Hen. VIII. [1510]; whereby he willed that Elizabeth Marvyn, widow of John Marvyn deceased, should receive the issues and profits of the said Manors as long as she remained sole, and after her death, or if she married, the said issues and profits were to go to John Mervyn, kinsman and heir of the said Walter (to wit), son of John, son of the said Walter, and his heirs. And the jurors found that said Elizabeth was then still living, and unmarried. And that the said Manors are held of the Abbess of Shaftesbury, by fealty.

The jurors also found that said Walter was also seized of the Manor of Hardenhewyssh, &c., in Stopp, in the parish of Fontel Giffard, in the said county; and that by his charter indented dated 30th July, 14 Henry VII. [1499], he granted the same to William Frost and others, to the use of John Mervyn, then deceased (son and heir apparent of the said Walter), and Elizabeth then wife of the said John, and the heirs of the body of the said John, and in default thereof to the use of the right heirs of Walter Mervyn. And the jurors found that said John Mervyn afterwards had issue one John, and died.

And the jurors further found that said John, son of Walter Mervyn, John Jenour and Thomas Sprott were seised of two messuages, two gardens, 200ª land, 30ª meadow, 300ª pasture, and 10ª wood, in Samberley and West Knoyle, otherwise Knoyle-Odyern in the said county. And that they being so seized John Mordaunt, William Mordaunt, Wistan Brown, William Gascoign, John Vynter, and Thomas Chaffyn recovered the same tenements against the said John Mervyn, John Jenour, and Thomas Sprott, by writ of entry sur disseisin in le post (to wit) in Michaelmas term 18 Henry VII. [1502]; which recovery was to the use of the said Elizabeth and the heirs of her body, and in default thereof to the use of Cecily Clifford, widow, and the heirs of her body; and in default thereof to the use of the said John Mordaunt, William Mordaunt, and the other recoverers aforesaid, and their heirs, to sell the same and fulfil therewith the last will of John Grene, late of Stoffold.

And the jurors also found that said Walter Mervyn was also seized of the Manor, &c., of Wydecombe, in the parish of Helmerton, and of lands in Crokerton, both in the county of Wilts, in his demesne as of fee, and that by charter dated 14th September, 3 Hen. VIII. [1511] he had enfeoffed thereof Richard, Bishop of Winchester, Thomas Welle, Esquire, Henry Bodenham, Esquire, William Hawles, Tristram Fauntleroy, Ambrose Dauntsey, Thomas Mompesson, and William Pyrke, and their heirs, to the use of the said Walter Mervyn during his life, without impeachment of waste, and after his death, to the use of Edmund Mervyn (son of the said Walter) and Eleanor Fauconer, and the heirs of the body of the said Edmund, and in default thereof to the use of the right heirs of the said Walter, as appeared by a charter of covenants indented, made between the said Bishop and Thomas Welle of the one part, and the aforesaid Walter and Edmund of the other part, dated 8th September, 3 Henry VIII. [1511].

And the jurors further found that Thomas Browne, chaplain, and William Hendelowe, being seized of lands and hereditaments in Lavyngton Episcopi, Worton, Mershton, Hurst, Stert, Fedyngton, and Southbrome, in said county of Wilts; as also of lands in Erylstoke and Potern, in their demesne as of fee; of 1 messuage, 1 toft, 100ª land, and 200ª pasture in Gore; did, by charter tripartite indented, dated 7th Sept., 6 Edw. IV. [1466], grant the same property to the said Walter Mervyn and Joan his wife, and the heirs of the body of the same Joan, and that if the said Walter and Joan died without such heir, the premises in Potern were to remain to Thomas Roger, of Bradford, in the county of Wilts, his heirs and assigns, and the premises in Lavyngton and the other places were to remain to Nicholas Hall, his heirs and assigns. And the jurors found that said Joan died without heir of her body, and that Walter Mervyn died on the 12th day of July then last [1512], so that the premises in Lavyngton, &c., remained to Thomas Hall, as son and heir of the said Nicholas Hall, the same Thomas being 50 years of age and upwards. And that the premises in Potern remained to William Roger, as son and heir of the said Thomas Roger, the same William Roger being 50 years of age and upwards.

And the jurors further found that John Mervyn was "consanguineus" and heir of the said Walter Mervyn, viz., son of John Mervyn the son of said Walter, and that he was then of the age of 9 years and upwards.

G

Inquisition taken at New Sarum, in the county of Wilts, after the death of Sir JOHN MERVYN, Knt:—

The jurors found that Sir John Mervyn was seized in his demesne as of fee tail (to wit, to him and the heirs of his body, with remainder to his right heirs,) of the Manor of Wydcombe, in county Wilts, and of lands, &c., in Helmerton and Crokerton, and of one water-mill in Tisburye next Fountill Gifforde. And that said John Mervyn was also seised in fee tail as above, with remainder to the right heirs of Walter Mervyn deceased, his grandfather, whose heir he was, of the Manor of Hardenhuishe, with the advowson of the church there, and of hereditaments in Stoppe within the parish of Fowntell Gifforde, And that said John Mervyn was also seised to him and his heirs male (with remainder to the right heirs of John Mervin deceased, his great-grandfather, whose right heir he was), of the Manors of Fontel-Giffard and Farnehull, with the advowson of the church of F. G. &c., and also of hereditaments in Tisbury Overffountell and Swallowcliffe. And further that said John Mervin was also seised in his demesne as of fee simple of the Manors of Hatch, Swallow-cliffe, and Compton Bassett, and of divers pastures, woods, and woodlands, in the parish of Tisburie, called Rowcombparke and Wike. And also of hereditaments in Fontel-Giffard (formerly parcel of the late Monastery of Charterhouse Wittam in county Somerset.) And of meadow and in pasture in Busshopes Knoell and West Hatche in county Wilts. And further that said John Mervyn was seised in his demesne as of fee tail of hereditaments in Semble. And the jurors found that the said before-mentioned premises descended to James Mervin, Esquire for the Queen's body, as son and heir of said John Mervyn.

And the jurors also found that said Sir John Mervyn had died on the 18th June, 8 Elizabeth [1566], and that since his death Elizabeth Mervine, widow of the said John, had received the issues of the manor or farm of Compton Bassett. And that John Rives had received the issues of the Manors of Hatche and Swallowclife; except certain sums which said James Mervyn had received, he having also received the issues of all the other premises.

Inquisition taken at Devizes, in the county of Wilts, after the death of Lady ELIZABETH MERVYN :—

The jurors found that Lady Elizabeth Mervyn was a widow, and late the wife of John Mervyn, Knight, deceased. That she died seized in her demesne as of fee of the Manor of Bathampton, &c., which on her death, on the 25th of September then last (1581), descended to Susanna Mompesson, her sister, and to the issue of Anne Wayte, another sister (then deceased), and to the son of Mary Wells, another sister (then also deceased), as the co-heirs of said Lady Elizabeth Mervyn.

Inquisition taken at Devizes, in the county of Wilts, after the death of Sir JAMES MERVYN, Knt. :—

The jurors found that Sir James Mervyn had died seized in his demesne as of free tenement for term of his life, of the chief messuage and Manors of Fontel-Giffard and Fernehull, and of certain messuages, lands, and tenements called Founthill Charterhouse, late parcel of the possessions of the Monastery of Charterhouse Witham, in co. Somerset, and afterwards parcel of the possessions of Thomas Arundell, Knight, attainted of felony, and which afterwards King Edward VI. by his letters patent dated 24th February, in his 7th year, had granted to John Mervin, Knight, father of the said James. And the jurors also found that said Sir James Mervyn had also died seized of the Manors of Hatch and Swallowcliffe; and of one messuage and tenement in Over Founthill; and of divers lands, woods, &c., called Rowcombe Parke in the parish of Tisburie, and of two messuages in Sembly; and of a messuage in East Knoyle; and of certain lands, woods, &c., called Ashell's Wood, in the parish of Tisburie; the remainder pertaining to one Henry Mervin, Esquire, and his heirs male begotten of Christiana, " then and now his wife," with further remainder to other persons [not named] in fee tail, and with further remainder to the right heirs of the said James. And the jurors further found that in Trinity term 5 James I. a fine had been levied between Thomas Thynne, Knight, and Hugh Hill, Esq., plaintiffs, and said James Mervin, Henry Mervin, and Christiana, deforciants, concerning the premises (by a somewhat different description, Fountel Episcopi, Berwick St. Leonard's, and Hindon being mentioned in addition to the foregoing places) whereby the deforciants quit-claimed to the plaintiffs and the heirs of Thomas; which fine was levied to the use of the said James during his life, and after his decease (with regard to all the premises except those known by the name of Week), to the use of Henry and Christiana and the heirs male of the said Henry, begotten of the said Christiana, with remainder to " divers other persons" in fee tail, and then to the right heirs of said James; and with regard to the premises called Week, after decease of James Mervyn, to the use of the said Henry Mervyn and his heirs male, &c., as above, as appeared by a quadripartite indenture dated 7th May, 6 James I. (1609), between the said James, Henry and Christiana 1st part, Thomas Thynne and Hugh Hill 2nd part, Edward Blount and William Goddard 3rd part, and Richard Warman and William Weeksteed 4th part; by virtue whereof, and of the Statute of Uses, the said Sir James Mervyn was seized of the premises.

And the jurors also found that said Sir James Mervyn was also seized in his demesne as of fee of the Manors of Compton Bassett and Widcombe, and of a messuage, lands, &c., in Crokerton; and that he being so seized a fine was levied between Hugh Hill and John Greene. plaintiffs, and the said James Mervyn, deforciant, the latter quit-claiming the said Manor of Compton Bassett and the advowson of the church there to the plaintiffs, to the intent that they should permit Sir Mervyn Audelay, Knight, to recover the said manor and advowson, which he did in Hilary Term, 6 James I., being seized to the use of the said James Mervyn during his life, and after his decease to the use of Lucy, Lady Audelay, mother of the said Mervyn Audelay for the term of her life, and then to the use of the said Mervyn Audelay and his heirs male, and then to the use of the right heirs of the said Lady Lucy and Mervyn Audelay, as by an indenture tripartite, dated 20th January, 6 James I., appeared. And the jurors further found that by another indenture of the same date, the said S* James Mervin had bargained and sold the said manor of Widcombe to the said Hugh Hill and John Greene and their heirs, to the intent that they should permit said Mervyn Audelay to recover same, which he did in the same term, to the use of said S* James Mervyn for term of his life, remainder to the use of George Lord Audelay for life, remainder to the use of the said Lady Lucy, wife of the said George, for life, remainder to the use of the said Mervin Audelay and his heirs male, then to the heirs of his body, then to the right heirs of the said Lucy and Mervin, as appeared by an indenture of 20th January, 6 James I. [1609.]

And the jurors found that said Sir James Mervin died on the 1st of May, 9 James I. [1611], at Fountel aforesaid.

And the jurors also found that said Mervin Audelay, Knight, was the grandson (*nepos*) and next heir of the said James, (to wit) son and heir of Lucy Lady Audelay, daughter and heir of the said James, the said Lady Lucy having died in the lifetime of her father, and that the said Mervin Audelay was of the age of 23 (?) years.

And the jurors further found that said Mervyn Audelay had received the profits of the manors of Compton Basset and Widcombe from the death of S* James Mervin, and that Henry Mervin had received the profits of the remainder of the premises since the same time.

Abstracts AND Copies OF Wills.

JOHN MIRFYN, of London, Gentleman. To be buried in the crypt of the chapel of Jesus, in the cathedral of St. Paul's, or in the church of the Holy Trinity, at the discretion of executors. To George Myrfyn my father £20. To Katerine Myrfyn my aunt (by my father's side) "amite," £10. To 2 Katerine my sister, on her marriage, 20 marks. To the said George Myrfyn my father his heirs and assigns all my lands and tenements in Hantram, Elsenham, Stanstede, and in the hamlet of Blechenden, in county of Essex. Residue of all and singular goods and chattels absolutely to my wife Cicely, and my executors to be distributed "pro salute anime mee" in works of charity, as they shall be prepared to answer in the dreadful day of judgment. Executors: my aforesaid wife Cicely, William Hampton, Knight, and John Myddelton, Mercer, citizens of London. Proved at Maidstone, 6 May, 1473, by Cecily the relict. (Register P.C.C., 9 *Wattis*.)

Margin: 20th Oct., 1471, A°. reg. Edw. iv. Abstract.

JOHN MERVYN. To be buried in the chancel of St. Peter of Lawford, betwixt the sepulcher and the lecture there, and the gravestone that I bought at Coventry, &c., to be laid there; to the moder church of Litchfield, to the churches of Dynley, Wolston, Newbold-upon-Avon, Rokeley, Browneston, Clyfton, and the Chauntrie of Swynford, &c., &c., a vestment each price xx° and upon these vestments to be sett a scrowe wrytyng these words: Pray for the sowles of John Mervyn and Margaret his wyfe, oon of the executors of the testament of Nich* Cowley, late of Swynford, and the sowle of Nich* Cowley and Maude his wyfe, and the sowle of William Newnham and Margery his wife; a priest at Church Lawford to pray for my soul and Johan my moder, and my son Lawrons, with the soule of Nich* Cowley and Maude his wife, and all his brothers and sustern, and the soule of William Newnham and Margary and Margarete his wyfes, and Thomas his fadyr, and Alys his moder, with all his children, brethren, and susters. I bequeath to my fader John Merven 2 of my best side gownes and 2 of my best short gownes, and C* in money to fynde him, to be delyvered to him at tymes as it can be founde most necessary; to Margarete M., my wife, house, &c., in Lawford; to Hugh Merven, not to be so wasteful as he hath been; to my son William M. land in Aston; to Hugh M., aforesaid, all lands in Westcote, Rokeby, Lilborne, Brackley, and Isham, &c., and heirs male; rem. to said William M. and his heirs; rem. to Eliz. Cave, Agnes Knyghte, and Jane Lane, and their heirs for ever; to my daughter, Elizabeth Cave; to my daughter, Agnes Knyghte; my daughter, Jane Lane; to Margaret M., the daughter of Lawrons M.; my executors not to be vexed by Elizabeth Clerke, her moder; to Edward Cave and Margaret Cave, children of Richard Cave; to Jane, the daughter of Hugh Merven, and if Hugh hir fader die, &c.; to William Lane and Jane, my daughter; Richard Cave and Elizabeth my daughter; John Knight and Agnes my daughter; and to William Nerven, my youngest son, equally; they executors. Proved in London, 20 November, 1492. by executors. (*Regr.* 10 *Doggett.*)

Margin: 22 Oct. 1492. Abstract.

MARGARET MARVYN, widow. To be buried in St. Peter's, nigh my husband; my son, Hugh M., my best bowl and cover; my daughter, Jane Lane, my silver salts, &c.; my daughter, Agnes Knight, 6 spoons, &c.; my daughter, Margaret Mervyn, part of my cattle, when married, to be kept by my son-in-law, William Lane, till then; to Edward and Margaret Cave, children of my daughter Elizabeth Cave, 5 ewes each; to Thomas and Margaret Knight, children of my said daughter, Agnes Knight 5 ewes, in the keeping of her father, John K.; my granddaubter Cecilia Lane, 5 ewes; to John Knight, son of said John K., a cow; to Johan Mervyn, the daughter of Hugh M., 40* at marriage. All the rest to my sons Hugh M., and William Lane, my executors. Proved in London, 24 November, 1496. (*Regr.* 25 *Vox.*)

Margin: 23 July, 1494 Abstract.

CICELY MYRFYN, of London, widow. To be bur⁴ in the church of the Holy Trinity the little, in London, with John Myrfyn, my husband; said church, £4; Church of St. John Zachary, where I am a parishioner, ij torches; our Lady of Stanyng Church, 10s.; Church of Longesden, in Derbyshire, £4; a priest to pray for my soul and the souls of Richard and John, sometime my husbands; Brotherhood of Pappey, where I am Sister, 10s.; Robert Merfyn, my husband's brother, 20s.; Thomas Merfyn skinner, cup and cover; Agnes, his sister, 20s.; my sister Dame Margaret Shaa, widow, a ring; prisons, each, 3/4; cousin Thomas Ilom, £6 13s. 4d.; my cousin Cecily Kynwallmersah, my brother John Knyveton'ad aughter, £3 6s. 8d.; residue to Sir John Shawe, Knight, Alderman of London. To Lucy Knifton, £6 13s. 4d. To aforesaid sister Dame Margaret Shaw, widow, dwelling in Ripton; cousin John Blunt, and Elyn his wife, and John his son; kinsman Richard Griston; Rauf Bagot, my sister's son, debts he oweth me. Proved in London, 5 Dec. 1502, by Sir John Shawe, Knight (*Reg.* 19 *Blamyre.*)

WALTER MERVYN of Fountel-Giffard. That Elizabeth Mervyn, widow of John Mervyn, deceased, should receive the issues and profits of his Manors of Fontel-Giffard and Farnehull, co. Wilts, as long as she remained sole, and after her death or marriage, said issues and profits to go to John Mervyn, testator's kinsman and heir, (to wit) son of John the son of testator, and his heirs.

  N.B. This will cannot be found. The above note of it is taken from the Inquisition held after the death of the above-mentioned Walter Mervyn. (*Inq. p. m.*, 4 *Henry viii. No.* 74.)

Will of SIR THOMAS MERFYN, Knight.

In the Name of God Amen The secunde day of the moneth of Septembre in the yere of our Lorde God a thousande fyve hundred and xxiij And in the xv yere of the reigne of our souersigne Lorde King Henry the viij^th by the grace of God of Inglonde and of Fraunce Kynge defender of the feith and lorde of Irlonde I THOMAS MIRFYN Citizein and Alderman of the Citie of London being of hole and parfite mynde (&c.), for the welth of my soule and the proufit of my wife my childern and other my lovers and frendes make ordeyn and declare my testament and last will. My body to be buried in the Charnel house in Paulis Churchyarde in London where the body of Dame Alice late my wife lieth buried and there where my tombe is made. And I will that I be honestly buried after and according to my degre. AND WHERE for mariage to be had betweene me and Dame Elizabeth my wife doughter of Aungell Donne late Citezein and Alderman of London and Anne his wife decessed wiche Anne sir Robert Dymmok knyght after the deth of the said Aungell Donne hir first husbonde was maried vnto, a writing was made remaynyng with the said sir Robert subscribed as well by the said sir Robert as by me the said Thomas Myrfyn; the tenour wherof ensuyth in these wordes. , The xv^th day of Octobr the xj^th yere of the Reigne of Kynge Henry the viij^th It is covenanted and agreed betwene Thomas Mirfyn maire of the Citie of London of the one partie and Robert Dymmok knyght on the other partie That the said Thomas shall w⁴ the grace of God mary and take to wife Elizabeth Donne doughter and heire to Aungell Donne late Alderman of London and the said Thomas Mirfyn on thisside the fest of the natiuitie of our lorde that shalbe in the yere of our lord god M^lV^cxxij^li shall cause a sure and a laufull astate to be made after the sure fo^rme of the lawe vnto the said Elizabeth Donne of londes rentes and tenementes to the yerely value of xl^li clere ouer and aboue all charges for terme of lyfe of the said Elizabeth; ffurder the said Thomas promyseth that he shal leve vnto the said Elizabeth his wife y^f God fortune hir to lyve after him the doble that she brought to him which sume of hir porcion amounteth M^cccl^xxxiiij^li iiij^s viij^d and x^li gevyn to hir by hir grandam which doble shall amount M^lM^cCxlviij^li ix^s iiij^d And also the said Thomas hath promysed that the said Elizabeth shalbe at hir choise to chose to haue the thirde parte after the custume of the Citie or the some abouewriten. Also the said Thomas promyseth that if the said Elizabeth decease afore him that she shalhaue C^li to distribute and make her will of beside all hir apparell and Juelles And the said sir Robert promiseth that he shalbe bounde to paye in three yeres next and immediatly folowing to the said Thomas M^l^lxxiiij^li iiij^s viij^d by evyn porcons Also the said Thomas promyseth that the said sir Robert shalhaue in his house at saint Margaret patens parishe the lodging that Alice Stamford did lye in with free entre and yssue and at all tymes to haue licence to cary awaye suche stuffe as apperteyneth to the said sir Robert w⁴out contradiction of the said Thomas and Elizabeth y^f there be any thinge that wantes from in the premisses it to be amended by maister Broke Sergeaunt at the lawe accordinge to the true entent AND after this I the said Thomas and the said Elizabeth were maried togider AND WHERE the said sir Robert and other persones at his request were and yet stonden bounden to the Chambreleyn of London and his successours by recognisaunce vpon condicion for the payment of the sume of M^l^lxxiij^li iiij^s viij^d to Edward Donne and Frances Donne the childern of the said Aungell, then orphanes of the said Citie, which childern ben all decessed except my said wife at the day of the said writing made and mariage betwene me and my said wife soo that all the said hole sume of M^l^lxxiiij^li iiij^s viij^d was then to thuse of my said wife by the survivor of hir said brethern accordinge to the lawe and custume of the said Citie of London by whiche mariage the said bonde made to the said Chamberleyn of London was and is to the vse of me and my said wife AND HOWBEYT I haue ben alwey redy to haue made a sure astate of londes and tenementes of the yerely value of xl^li ouer and aboue all charges and reprises to the same dame Elizabeth my wife for terme of hir lyfe and all the residue in the said bill specified on my parte to be executed; I was content y^f the said sir Robert wolde haue made payment to me and my said wife of the said sume of M^l^lxxiij^li iiij^s viij^d or wolde haue ben bounden for the payment therof at daies reasonable in the said writing conteyned by vs to haue ben appoynated or at reasonable other daies sith the said thre yeres expressed in the said writing by the said sir Robert and me to haue ben appoynted ; And therupon I and my said wife of the same recognisaunce wolde haue discharged the said sir Robert and thother persones named and bounden by the same recognisaunce for the payment of the said M^lxxiiij^li iiij^s viij^d and wolde haue caused the said recognisaunce to haue ben made frustrate voide and cancelled, which premisses to do the said sir Robert on his part and behalf hath refused not only contrary to his said promyse in the said writing specified but also contr'y to the condicion of the said Recognisaunce. WHERFOR my will and mynde is yf the said sir Robert or his executours by thassent and agrement of my said wife by her wri,ing make payment to myn executo'^s w^in six monethes next after my death of the said sume of M^llxxiiij^li iiij^s viij^d, that then I will that my said wife for terme of hir lyfe shalhaue all my houses landes and ten'tes of Merditche and Wrayttes w^t thappurten'nces in the parishe of Hornechurch in the countie of Essex my mano^r of Downe w^t thapp'ten'nces in the countie of Kent and those my londes and ten'tes lying in the parishes of Fanchurch and Aldermary and of saint Petyr in Cornehill w^t thappurten'nces whiche ben of the clere yerely value of fourty poundes over and aboue all charges and reprises and better as the thirde parte as well of all my goodes catalles and dettes and of the said sume of M^llxxiiij^li iiij^s viij^d after my debtes paide funeralles and ordynary charges born and allowed after and according to the lawe and custume of the said Citie orelles at the libertie of my said wife to haue of myn executours the said some of M^lM^cCxlviij^li ix^s iiij^d the doble that she brought w^t her, and that I shulde haue had of the said somes to hir belonging and to haue ben paide vpon hir mariage according to the true meanyng of the said writing, she than making a Relees to myn executo'^s of all accions suyttes and demaundes which in any wise she myght haue demaunde or clayme ayenst myn executours by the custume and lawe of the said Citie as shalbe reasonably aduised by myn executo'^s. And yf she refuse to haue the said some of M^lM^cCxlviij^li ix^s iiij^d And will holde hir to the said thirde part of my goodes catalles and debts in fourme beforsaid according to the lawe and custume of the said Citie then she to make a Release to myn executours of all accions suyttes and demaundes which in any wise she myght or then may haue ayenst them by reason of any promyse agreament or graunt conteyned in the forsaid writinge the said promyse and graunt of the said Mano'^s londes and tentes that she shuld haue for terme of hir lyfe oonly except And yf the said sir Robert and his executours pay not nor content ne paye to myn executours or their executo'^s the said M^llxxiiij^li iiij^s viij^d w^in vj monethes next after my decesse but refusith the same to doo, then my mynde and will is that my said gifte and bequest to my said wife as well of the said Mano'^s landes and ten'tes be vtterly voide and noon effect as of the said some of M^lM^cCxlviij^li ix^s iiij^d the doble that she brought with her when I toke hir to my wife And if the sajd sir Robert or his executo'^s content and paye within vi monethes next after my decese the said some of M^llxxiiij^li iiij^s viij^d, then I will and my mynde is that all the premisses be doon and executed in suche wise and fourme as before it is expressed AND then also I will and my mynde is that my sonne Edward Mirfyn immediately after the death of my said wife shall haue all my howses or ten'tes of Merdith or Wraittes with thappurten'nces in the parishe of Hornechurch in the Lordship of Havering at Bowre in the Countie of Essex my houses londes and tenementes in the parishe of saint Mary Fanchurch, those two newe houses in Bogerrowe lying in the parishe of saint Antonyne and of saint Johns in Walbroke whiche I late buylded, to haue to him and to his heires of his body laufully begotten. And for default of suche issue to be and remayn to Mary my doughter and to the heires of her bodye laufully begotten. And for default of suche issue to be and remayn to Fraunces my doughter and to the heires of hir body. And for default of suche issue to remayn to my right heires foreuer. ALSO I geve and bequeth to Mary my doughter my Mano'^r londes and ten'tes w^t thappurten'nces of Down in the countie of Kent; to haue and to holde immediatly after the deathe of my said wife, to my said doughter and to the heires of hir body laufully begotten. And for default of suche issue to be and remayn to my said sonne Edward and to the heires of his body laufully begotten. And for default of suche yssue to remayne to my said doughter Fraunces and to the heires of her body laufullye begoffen. And for default of suche yssue to be and remayn to my right heires for euer. ALSO I geve and bequeth vnto the said Fraunces my doughter that my ten't lying in the parishe of Aldermary in London, and that my ten't lying in the parishe of saint Petir in Cornehill, to haue and to holde immediatly after the death of my said wife to my said doughter ffraunces and to the heires of hir body laufully begotten. And for default of suche Issue to be and remain to my said daughter Mary and to the heires of hir body laufully begotten. And for default of suche Issue to be and remayn to my said sonne Edwarde and to the heires of his body laufully begotten. And for default of suche Issue to be and remayn to my right heires foreuer. AND in caas yf the said sir Robert nor his executours pay not nor doo not to be paid to thexecutours of me the said Thomas Myrfyn nor their executours the said M^llxxiiij^li iiij^s viij^d w^in vi monethes next after my death, that than my will is as before is saide, that my said wife shall not haue the said meas'es londes and ten'tes therof, nor any parcell therof, but then I will my said childern shall immediately after my death and the vi moneths expired and past have the said meas'es londes and ten'tes to theym in suche wise and w^t like remaynders as I before haue declared and willed theym to haue after the death of my said wife yf the said sir Robert or his executours had paide the said M^llxxiiij^li iiij^s viij^d to myn executo'^s w^in vj monethes next after my deth ; and my said wife then to haue noon of my said landes nor of my goodes catalles and dettes but oonly after my dettes paid my funeralles and ordynary charges and expenses concernyng the same contented and paide She to haue the thirde parte of that shall then remayn And my said childern a nother thirde parte of the same Remaynder And the other thirde parte, all the residue, to be myn executours for the performaunce of my last wille after and according to the lawes and custumes of the said Citie ALSO I geve and bequeth to the high awter in the parishe Churche of saint

B

Antonyne (&c. &c. &c.) Item I bequeth vnto my sonne dane George Mirfyn Monk at Westm, xx^{li} to be paide
him euery yere iiij^{li} by thandes of myn executours. I bequeth vnto Margaret Pargetour the wife of Thomas
Pargetour a blak gown and to hir husbonde a nother and in money to theym x$^{li.}$. Also I bequeth vnto
euery child that she in lyve whan they shall come to lauffull age xl^s a pece. I bequeth vnto Gilbert Hardegrave
v^{li} and vnto euerych of his childern xl^s to be paid w^{t}in a yere after my decesse. Item, I bequeth vnto
my suster Agnes Loke the wife of Mighel Loke x^{li}. I bequeth vnto Elizabeth the wife of Elyot v$^{li.}$ and
vnto euery Childe that she hath xl^s. Also I bequeth vnto John Story the sonne of Robert Story xx$^{li.}$. Item,
I bequeth to Mighel Loke my suster's sonne xl^{li} and vnto euery childe that he hath a lyve v$^{li.}$. Item, I
bequeth vnto John Bande beddill of the Crafte of Skynners to pray for my soule a blak gowne and in
money xl^s. Also I bequeth vnto John Broun Clerk of our Lady Company of the said Crafte of Skynners a
blak gowne and in money xl^s. Also I bequeth vnto the Chapel of Barwey in the Countie of Cambrige
where I was born and cristened in the honor of God and of saint Nich'as a vestment and an aube w^t all
thapparell thereunto belonging for a prest to synge in of the value of xl^s (&c., &c.) Also I geve and bequeth
towardes the rep'acions and mayntenyng and supporting of the said Chapell to pray for my soule my fader
and moder soules my wife soule and all my childern soules xl^s. Also I bequeth vnto saint Mary Church of
Yely where my fader lieth buried on whose soule Jhus haue mercy, a vestment w^t an awbe with all thinges
belonging vnto a prest of the value of xl^s, ij awter clothes price iiij^s a corporas and a caase of the price of
iiij^s iiij^d a masse boke price x^s, ij newe torches price xij^s, ij awter clothes of red and yelowe silk one for
aboue the other for byneth and ij curteyns sutable of the value of xl^s which forsaid auter clothes and curteyns
I will shalbe orderid and hangid in the North Ile of the same Church by the quyre door to thentent the
prestes may synge and sey masse there and to pray for my soule the soules of George and Kateryn my fader
and moder my wife soule my childern soules and all x'pen soules   Also I bequeth to the maister and
wardeyns of the guylde of corpus Cristi of the Crafte of Skynners of London and to their successo^{r}s a Cope
(&c., &c.)   I bequeth vnto the parishe church of saint Antonyne in Bygierrowe in London an hole sute of
vestments (&c., &c.)   And I will that the churchyarde on the south side of saint Agnes chapell of the said
Church of saint Antonyne shalbe pavid w^t Brabant stone that is to sey from the Est ende vnto the
West ende of the said chapell and a faire stone of marble to be laide in the myddes of the said
churchyarde with all my Childerns names to be graven and sett on the same stone of marble that is
to seyd Thomas, John, George, Thomas, John, Fraunces, Richard, John, Robert, Edward, and
Bartilmewe, Margaret, Mary, and Fraunces, and that this be doon within one yere after my decesse.
I bequeth vnto Fraunces Poulter the sonne of Richard Poulter Esquire dwelling in the countie of Northt' so
that he by his sufficient dede release all his right and title which he shalhaue to the maner of Downe
w^t thappurten'nces in the countie of Kent as his fader hath doon before him in such wise as it shall be
advised by the counceill lerned of myn executours and to suche persones as my said sonne Edwarde, Mary
and Fraunces my doughters shall name lxvj^{li} xiij^s iiij^d. Also I bequeth vnto Elizabeth my wife two of my
best saltes w^t couer, my best standing Cup gilt with a couer, also a nother standing Cup gilt w^t a couer
with chekers in the botom, xiiij gilt spones, and all hangings in my house, reseruyng suche hanginges as
hangen in the parlo^r ou^r the strete w^t the fore chambers ou^r strete which said hanginges I will Edward
my sonne haue and ij fetherbeddes and a matrasse. Also I bequeth to Mary my doughter ij gilt saltes with
a couer which were maister Martyns and a doseyn of siluer sponys a standing Cup w^t a pellican. Also I
bequeth vnto dane George my son being monk in Westm^r a salt with sonbemes w^t a couer and half a doseyn
spones knopped w^{t}h lions and a gilt Cup. Also I bequeth vnto Edward my sonne two square saltes
parcell gilt with a couer and a standing cup w^t an akorne on the knop and a doseyn spones. Also I
bequeth vnto Fraunces my doughter a standing Cup w^t a maydens hede which^{d}I will shall be kepte to her vse
And yf she fortune to dye I will that it shall goo remayn and be to the said Crafte of Skynners And I will
that it shalbe in the custodye and keeping of the same crafte till she come to lawfull age orelles to be
maried. Also I bequeth vnto John Judde gentilman iij^l vj viij^d and to his wyfe a Ryng of golde price
xx^s and to either of theym a blak gowne. THE RESIDUE of all and singuler my goodes I will shalbe equally
deuided in two partes and porcions, wherof I will the one moytie shalbe truely deuided to and amonges the
forsaid Edward, Mary, and Franceis my childern ; and the other moytie therof to be disposed in charitable
dedes for the weale of my soule and all the soules abouesaid at the discrecions of myn executours. AND I
ordeyn and make Edward Myrfyn my sonne and Andrew Judde my sonne in lawe myn Executours, and
Oueeseers of the same my present testament and last wille I ordeyn and make the right reurende fader in
God Cutbert, Bishop, of London, and sir Richard Broke knyght. And I bequeth vnto either of theym for his
labour aide and good counceill to be gevyn in the execucion of this my present testament and last wille
twenty poundes sterlinges. Proved in London 15 Oct. 1523 by the executors named in the will, (*Reg.* 13
Bodfelde.)

3 Mar. 1527.   EDWARD MYRFYN, Citizen and Skinner of London. To be buried at the charnel house in Paul's
Abstract.   churchyard, where lye the bodies of Thomas and Alice my father and mother, and £5 to go to repairs of
the chapel. Bequests to churches of St. Andrew-Undershaft London, and Hornchurch in parish of Havering,
co. Essex. Legacies to divers servants. To Alice Brygandyn my wife's daughter, £20 at full age or marriage,
and to Agnes, another of my said wife's daughters, £6 13. 4. to her marriage, and to John Brygandyn,
my wife's son, 5 marks. To Pargeter and his wife and child, money and wearing apparel. To Richard
Southwood, wearing apparel, bedding, &c To my wife Alice my manor of Burtyns, in the town of
Frecknam, co. Suffolk, for life ; remainder to the child she now goeth with ; but if said child die before

coming to full age, then the said manor to go to Alice Brygandyn, my wife's daughter. To my brother in law, Andrew Judde, a furred gown and 5 marks, and to my sister his wife a ring of 40s. To Richard Bury my jackett of black velvet. Residue to my wife and the child she now goeth with, and my wife to be Executrix. My brother in law Andrew Judde, and Richard Bury, gentleman, to be overseers. Proved in London, 11 May, 1528, by the Executrix. (*Regr.* 31 *Porch.*)

Will of SIR JOHN MERVIN, Knt, 1566 :—

IN THE NAME OF GOD. AMEN, I, JOHN MERVIN, of Fowntell Gifforde, in the county of 8th June, 1566. Wiltess, Knighte, doo make my last will and testamente in manner and forme followinge, that is to saye, I Copy. gyve my soull vnto allmightie God, my boddie to be buried in the Churche of Saincte Nicholas at Fowntell, by the Ladie Jane Marvin, my late wief. And that my executours doo see my boddie, and my ladie Elizabethe's boddie, my wief that now ys, to be buried after a worshipfull sorte there, accordinge to our estate. Allso I, give to my parrishe Churche of Saincte Nicholas, twenty shillinges. Item, vnto oᵉ Ladie Churche of Sarum, tenne shillinges. Item, first I give and beqᵗʰ vnto Elizabeth my ladie and wief, my wholl enteere Mannoᵉ of ffowntelstoppe and Stopfountell, lyinge and beinge of the parrish of Stopfountell and in Fowntell, also withe all the errable landes, meddowes, pastures, wooddes, vnderwooddes, feadinges, leasures, and comens vnto the same belonging, or in any wise apperteyninge. Allso I give my Mannoᵉ of Compton Bassett, my entier mannoᵉ there, vnto my wief for terme of her lief withoute impechement of waste. (All the tenauntries there to be resᵉᵤid to be bestowed hereafter in my will and testame't.) Item, I geve vnto my wief all the stockes of Vston, Bapthamᵗᵒⁿ, Langford, Apshill, Wiley, and Deplorde. I geve vnto my wief all suche thinges as she broughte wᵗʰ her and her warde also. Item, I give vnto John Mervin, Phillipp Marvin, and Ambrose Marvin my sonnes my wholle intier lease of Chesster-in-le-strate, that I boughte of my sonne James Mervin, equallie to be devided betwixte them three. Item, I give the lease of Compton Bassett vnto Ambrose my sonne, after the deathe of my wief, wᵗʰ all the tenᵉntries there for terme of his lief. Item, I give vnto John Mervin, Edmuᵈde Mervin, and Richard Mervin, my sonne Edmondes sonnes, the lease of Boyton, and the stock vppon the same. Item, I give vnto John Mervin, sonne of Edmonde, all my purchaced landes to him and his heires males, and for lack of heires males of his boddie laufullie begotten vnto Edmond his brother; and for lack of heires males of his boddie laufullie begotten, vnto Richard there brother ; and for lack of heires males lefullie begotten of his boddie, vnto my righte heires. Item, I comitt the govᵉⁿance of these three children with landes, and lease, and stock vnto my sonne in lawe Mr. John Ryves, vntill they coom to twentie and one yeres. Item, I will and give vnto my daughtᵉ Margarett the yonger twentie poundes by the yere oute of my purchaced landes, that John Mervin shall have, vntil John Marvin be of the age of twentie and one yeres ; afterwardes, to remeyne vnto him and to his heires males as before written. The residewe of my gooddes not bequethed, my dettes and dewes tuulie paide, I give and bequeth vnto Phillipp Mervin and Ambrose Mervin, my sonnes, whom I make my executours, they to dispose my gooddes to the plesuer of God, and helthe of my soule. Wittnesses vnto this my last will and testamente, Mr. Thomas Glanfilde, Richarde Boughton, William Bingham, Thomas Byer, and William Gill, pᵉson there. Proved in London, 20ᵗʰ June, 1566, by Executors. (*Regr.* "16 *Crymes.*")

Will of SIR JAMES MERVIN, Knight :—

IN THE NAME OF GOD, AMEN, the ffirst daye of Aprill, in the yere of oure Lord God, 1 April, according to the Englishe computacon, one thowsand sixe hundred and tenne, and in the yeres of the 1610. Raigne of oure Soueraigne Lord JAMES, by the grace of God, Kynge of England, Scotland, Fraunce, and Copy. Ireland, Defender of the Faith, &c., that is to say, of England, Fraunce, and Ireland the Eighte, and of Scotland the three and fortith, I, Sᵗ JAMES MERVIN, of Fountell, in the countie of Wiltess, Knight, considering the certentie of deathe, and that all fleshe must dye, and the vncertentye of the tyme, Do therfore, in the tyme of my good healthe and sound memorye, wherein I nowe am (thankes be given to Almighty God) make this, my last will and testament, touching the disposing of all my worldlie gooldes and thinges, in manner and forme folowing, viz.: FFIRST, I bequeath my soule to Almightie God and my bodye to be buryed within my parishe churche of Fountell aforesayed, nere vnto AMYE my first wife that deade is, and in the tombe wherein she was buryed, in a modest and decent manner, at the good discretion of my Executors, whome I do praye and require hereby, to make a comelie and decent tombe ouer my ffather and mother, whoe ar buryed on the right hand, at the vpper end of the chauncell, of the churche of Fountell aforesayed : ITEM—I giue and bequeath vnto my loving graundchilde, Sᵉ MERVIN AWDLEY, Knight, sonne and heire apparant of the Righte Honorable George Lorde Awdley, and Dame Lucie his wife, my only daughter, all and singular wrytinges obligatorye, statutes, recognizaunces, and bondes whatsoeuer, wherein my twoe neiphues John Mervin, Esquire, deceased, and his brother Edmond Mervin, nowe allso deceased, or either of them, stand bounde to me, in any somme or sommes whatsoeuer ; And all and singular debtes, sommes of money, and penalties whatsoeuer, in the sayed wrytinges obligatory conteyned. ITEM, I bequeathe allso to the saied Sᵉ Mervin Awdley my greate guilte bason and ewer that is ymbost, weighing one hundred and twentie ounces, or theraboutes, as I remembᵉ ; And I do allso giue and bequeathe vnto hym all suche householdstuffe as, at the houre of my death, shalbe in and aboute my house at Compton Basset, in the saied countie of Wiltess, as bedding, and all furnitures therunto apperteyning, hangings of tapistrie or otherwise, carpettes, cushions, tables, stooles, pewter vessell, and all other ymplementes of and for the saied house; And further, I do allso giue vnto hym, the saied Sr Mervin Awdley, my stocke and store of thirtie milche kyne and a bull, depasturing and beying at my house and mannor of Compton Bassett aforesayed; And my stocke of ewes, that shall, at the hower of my deathe, be depasturing in and vppon my sayed matnor of Compton Bassett aforesayed; And allso my best horse that I shalbe maister of at my deathe; And one of my best foaling mares to breede on, as he shall make choyse of; And my longe silke grogoran cloake, furred with sables; And my buffe jerkyn, laced with parchment lace of gould; And my wroughte veluet gowne. ITEM: Whereas, for the greate and mutuall loue and naturall affection which I haue and do beare to my name and familye of MERVYN, and for the better supporting therof: And to continewe my chiefe house of Fountell, and the greatest parte of my mannors, landes, and tenementes, in my name and bloud of Mervyn, so longe as yt shall please Almightie God; I have, therfore, for some yeres latelie past, agreed and concluded with my cozin EDMOND MERVYN, late of Durford, in the countie of Sussex, Esquire, deceased, for a marriage betwene HENRY, his eldest sonne, and XPISTIAN MERVIN my graundchilde, one of the daughters of the sayed Lorde Awdley, and Dame Lucie his wife, which mariage, hath ben synce had and solemnized accordinglie; and for my parte, I haue accordinglie assured and established my saied house, and the greatest parte of my mannors, landes and tenementes, in remaynder after my decease vnto the sayed Henry Mervin and his heires males of his bodye lawfullie begotten.   At the tyme of the concluding of which marriage, yt was agreed and coven'nted by and of the parte of the saied Edmond Mervin that he should likewise assure and conveye, vnto the saied Henry Mervyn and the heires males of his bodye all his mannors, landes, and tenementes called or knowne by the name or names of Durford and Bramshott in the sayed countie of Sussex, or by any other name or names whatsoeuer.   And all other his landes, tenementes and hereditamentes, in the saied countie of Sussex, and in the countie of Sowthampton, or in either of them, by what name or names soeuer, the same or any parte therof, were called or knowne, wherof he had any estate of inheritance, (as by certayne Indentures in that behalfe amongest divers other thinges conteyned in them dothe appeare); which ye saied Edmond Mervyn did not perform, allthoughe I often required the same, and did expect performance therof.   But nowe, for that the saied Henry Mervin hath of late, and to good purpose, as I hope, aliened the saied landes, late his saied ffathers, and hath, by that meanes procured and purchased the fferme of Knoyle for many yeres yet to come; And allso the fferme of vpper Fountell, for the lives of Mr. William Grove, and Robert and Hughe Grove, brothers of the sayed William, my will and meaninge ys, and I do desire that the sayed twoe ffermes for and during the saied seuerall estates and interestes in them, or either of them, may be, by the sayed Henry Mervyn, graunted, assigned, sett, conveyed, and setled, in suche sorte, as that the same ffermes, and eyther of them, may be and continewe vnto the sayed Henry Mervyn, and the heires males of his bodie, in lieu of the saied landes, so by him aliened; and with, and accordinge to, suche limitacons for the continewance therof in my name, as the sayed landes so by him aliened, should or oughte, by the purporte and true intent, and meaninge of the sayed couenante of the saied Edmond Mervyn: in which behalfe I referre my selfe to the sayed indenture, which, as I take yt, is tripartite, betwene me, and the saied Edmond, and some other p'sons named therein as parties therunto: And to the end the same shalbe the better and rather done and performed by the saied Henry Mervin, according to this my will, meaninge, and intent hereinbefore declared, wherof I haue an earnest care, desire, and expectacon for the good of my name and familie, I do therfore, by this my last will and testament, vppon condition that, and soe as the saied Henry Mervin do, within one yere after my decease, graunte, settle, and establishe the sayed leases as aforesayed, will, bequeathe, and devise that he, the saied Henry Mervin and Christian, his wife, during their liues, shall haue the vse and occupation of all my household stuffe, ymplementes, and furniture, of and in my sayed house of Fountell; as namely, all the hanginges, beddes, and bedsteades. with all the ffurnitures of them; tablebourdes, stooles, fourmes, chairs, carpettes, quiltes, quishions, lynnen of all sortes, all my pewter vessell, pottes, pannes, brewing vessells, andyrons, and other necessaryes and thinges of my saied house whatsoeuer expressed, and mentioned, in my great ledger booke, as well in the chardge of William Weekested, my servaunte, as otherwise; and all my flockes, stockes, and stoares of sheepe, and other cattell, as rother beastes, and horse-beastes, goynge, depasturing, or beyng at Fountell, or in any of my groundes thereto belonging, or elswhere; other then suche horses, mares, sheepe, and other cattell, as I do by this my will otherwise dispose, or bequeathe to any person or persons; And all theise parcells of plate, hereafter mentioned, viz., my second best gilded bason and ewer, which is not ymbossed, with my armes engraved in yt, my payer of guilded flaggons, my three deepe guilded bolls with their covers, my three great guilded flatt bolles, with chasseworke, without any covers to them; my three highe guilded bolles, my three lesser guilded bolls, and twoe standing guilded cupps, called sacke cuppes; my twoe greate guilded saltes, with a couer; and my trencher salte, without the couer; my paire of siluer livery pottes, which ar vnguilded; my three white deepe frenche bolles, with a cover; my three ymbossed white bolles, with theire covers; my sugar boxe and chafing dishe; twoe dosen of siluer spoones, and all my siluer vessell, and siluer plates, aswell all guilte, and parcell guilte, as vngylt, and all other my white siluer plate, as candlestickes, colledge jugges of siluer, and suche like; they, the saied Henry Marvyn and Xpistian his wife to haue all the saied plate herein before bequeathed to them; And the sayed ymplementes and ffurnitures of my said house at Fountell, as heireloomes; And after theire decease, the same to be to James Mervyn, theire sonne, my godsonne and graundchilde, as heireloomes, to goe, and be enioyed in and wth my saied house of Fountell; (except suche parcells of plate as I do herein otherwise dispose of.) And, because I will that all my saied plate, and siluer vessell, ymplements, furniture, and household stuffe of my sayed house shall for euer be preserved and maynteyned, to contynewe and be in and with my saied house, as heireloomes, and not to be aliened, or consumed, my will and mynde ys, and I do hereby streightlie will and desire my executors that they take suche sufficient assuraunce of the saied Henry Mervyn, as in the discretion of them shalbe thoughte fitt, for the preservacon and good vsuage of the same, without waste or spoyle ; and to leaue the same, or as good, in valewe, to theire saied sonne James, or to suche theire sonne and heire maļe of the bodye of the saied Henry Mervyn, to whome my saied house of Fountell and landes aforesaied shall discend, or come, after the deathe of the saied Henry Mervyn ; And yf the saied Henry Mervyn shall not, according to this my will, graunte, assigne, and settle the saied twoe ffermes, and the saied estates and interestes in them, or shall not giue suche sufficient assuraunce, for the preservacon, well vsing, and contynewance, of my saied plate, fyne lynnen, househould stuffe, ymplementes, and furnitures of my saied house of Fountell aforesayed, as by this my present will is appoynted, but make defaulte ; That then, my will is, that all my saied plate, fyne lynnen, househould stuffe, and furnitures of my saied howse of Fountell, so by me willed and lymited, to be secured and preserved, shall whollie be to the saied Sr Mervyn Awdley ; he first giving suche sufficient assuraunce as aforesaied to my saied executors, or the greater nomber of them, to pɾserve, well vse, and leaue the same, or as good in valewe, to the saied James Mervyn after the deathe of his sayed father and mother, and to the heires males of the bodye of the saied Henry Mervyn, inheritable of my said howse of Fountell. ITEM, I do giue vnto my brother Ambrose Mervyn one whole suite of my apparrell, and a guelding, suche as my executors shall assigne vnto hym. ITEM, I giue vnto Sr Thomas Thynne, Knighte, my best foalinge mare, such as he shall make choise of. ITEM, I giue and bequeathe vnto my graundchilde, Sr Ferdinando Awdley, twentie poundes in money, and a good gueldinge. ITEM, I do allso giue and bequeathe to my neiphue, Philipp Mervyn, twentie poundes in money. ITEM, I giue to my neiphue, Hughe Hill Esquire, one good gueldinge such as he shall make choise of, and to my good neice, his wife, a ringe of gould worthe twentie shillinges, and to her daughter, Winifride, a rynge of gould worthe tenne shillinges, and to James Hill, my god-sonne, theire sonne, one of my deepe silver basons, with the ewer. ITEM, I giue vnto John Exall, my olde servaunte, sixe poundes thirteene shillinges fower pence, and vnto my servaunt, Walter Thomas, sixe poundes thirteene shillinges fower pence. ITEM, I allso giue and bequeathe vnto my servaunte William Wigsted, sixe poundes thirteene shillinges fower pence. ITEM, I giue and bequeathe vnto William Pennye, Richard Rogers, and John Moore, fortie shillinges a peece. ITEM, I will and bequeathe vnto Mathewe Gatterell, William Jones, Roger Dowdinge, and Francys Knighte, twentie shillinges a peece. ITEM, I giue and bequeathe vnto Nicholas Barter, Alexander Knighte, Nich'as Pennye, George Skevington, and to Roger Norman, tenne shillinges a peece. ITEM, I giue towardes the mayntenance of my parishe churche of Fountell, three poundes sixe shillinges eighte pence ; and to the parishe churche of Tisburye, twentie shillinges ; and to the parishe churche of East Knoyle, twentie shillinges ; and to the parishe churche of Bishops Fountell, and of Barwicke Saint Leonard, tenne shillinges, to eache of them. ITEM, I do further giue and bequeathe tenne poundes in money, to be distributed and giuen to the poore at the tyme of my deathe, or buryall. AND LASTLY, I do giue vnto my servaunte Thomas Huyde, the Baylie of my Mannor of Compton Bassett, three poundes sixe shillinges and eighte pence. PROUIDED allwayes that yf the saied Sr Mervyn Awdley, or the Lord Awdley, or any of the heires or assignes of the sayed Sr Mervyn Awdley, or any other, occupying my Mannor of Compton Basset, or the cheife mansion house and demeasnes of my sayed Mannor of Compton Bassett, or vnder his estate right or title therein, shall wittinglie and advisedly refuse to allowe and ratifie suche leases and estates as I haue made to any of my servauntes or tenⁿntes, or to performe this my last will and testam¹ That then, and from thencefourthe, all the sayed legaceys to them, herein bequeathed, shall surcease and be voyde ; And that then, and from thencefourthe, I do will and devise, that all the saied goodes and chattells to them hereinbefore devised, shalbe and goe to the satisfaction of suche my leasees and tenⁿtes, as shalbe molested, disturbed, put out, or indammaged, by the sayed Henry and Christian, and the heires males of the bodye of the sayed Henry. PROUIDED allso, that yf the saied Sr Mervyn Awdley, or the Lord Awdley, or any of the heires or assignes of the sayed Sr Mervyn Awdley, or any other, occupying my Mannor of Compton Basset, or the cheife mansion house and demeasnes of my sayed Mannor of Compton Bassett, or vnder his estate right or title therein, shall wittinglie and advisedly refuse to allowe and ratifie such estate or estates as I haue made within my Mannor of Compton vnto my servⁿntes William Wigsteed, Thomas Huyde, Richard Rogers, or any of them, or any other of my tenauntes of the saied mannor, or shall seeke or goe abowte to ympeache, or avoyde, theire or any of theire saied estates, yealding, doyng, and performing the rentes, customes, and services due ; That, I will and devise, that all the saied goodes and chattells herein-before to hym devised, shall be, and goe, to the satisfaction of suche of my saied leasees, and tenⁿntes, as shalbe so disturbed, or evicted, by the saied Sr Mervyn Awdley, Lorde Awdley, or either of them, or by the heires or assignes of the saied Sr Mervyn Awdley : AND finallie of this my last will and testament I do name and appoynte my honorable and welbeloued graundchilde Sr Mervin Awdley, and Sr Thomas Thynne, Knightes, my good freind William Gibbes, of Parrat, Esquire, Henry Mervyn aforesaied, and my Neiphue Hughe Hill, Esquires, to be myne Executors, vppon the speciall truste and confidence which I repose in them, to be carefull for the performance of this my will, and to the vse of the saied Henry Mervyn, so as he performe or procure suche assurⁿnce as aforesaied, to be dulie performed ; And then I will, that he shall haue all the residue of my goodes and chattells whatsoeuer, as chaynes of pearle, jewells, money, plate not herein formerlie by me bequeathed ; And for his defaulte of suche assuraunce, Then I giue the same residue to my saied graundchilde Sr Mervyn Awdley, vppon suche condition as aforesayd. IN WITNESSE wherof I haue hereunto subscribed my name, and put to my seale, the daye and yere first aboue written.

JAMES MERVYN.

Subscribed, sealed, and deliuered in the presence of vs Francis Ducket, John Chafye, Walter Thomas, John Willoughbie, Luke Sympson.

ITEM, I do allso giue and bequeathe vnto Mr. Person Duckett one of my cloathe nightgownes and

I

three poundes sixe shillinges eight pence in money. This legacey is written with my owne hande, this thirteenth of November, one thowsand sixe hundred and tenne.

JAMES MERVYN.

MEMORAND, that this will was eftsoones declared and affirmed, by the withinnamed S^R JAMES MERVIN, to be his last will and testament, with these additions as foloweth; ITEM, I do further giue and bequeathe vnto my brother AMBROSE MERVYN, tenne poundes in money; ITEM, I do allso further giue and bequeathe vnto his sonne, PHILIPP MERVYN, fowerscore poundes in money, ouer and besides the twende poundes which aboue in my will I haue given hym; Altwayes prouided, that yt is not my will or meaninge, that he shall fynger, or haue yt deliured vnto hym, but that the saied hundred poundes shalbe ymployed to rayse tenne poundes yerelie towards his mayntenⁿnce, so longe as he, the sayed Philipp Mervyn, shall live; And that my adopted sonne, Henry Mervyn, shall, with this hundred poundes, see the saied Philipp dulie payed quarterlie, fiftie shillinges in money so longe as the sayed Henry Mervyn shall or will keepe the saied hundred poundes in his owne possession, and after to be disposed to y⁰ vse aforesaied, by the ouerseers of this my last will. ITEM, I do allso giue and bequeathe vnto Mr. Francys Duckett, parson of Fountle, sixe poundes thirteene shillinges fower pence in money, and one of my cloathe nighte gownes. LASTLIE, I do desire Henry Mervyn and his wife, in respect of the love and bountye that I haue bestowed on them, that they would bestowe meate, drincke, and lodging vppon my brother Ambrose Mervyn during his life, as I haue heretofore done: And this was so declared and affirmed by the sayed Sr James Mervin, the thirtith daye of Marche, in the yere of oure Lord god one thowsand sixe hundred and eleaven, in the presence of vs, viz., JAMES MERVYN, JO. WILLUGHBIE, LUKE SYMPSON, JOHN CHAFY.

PROBATUM fuit Testamentum suprascriptum, apud London, vna cum codicillo predicto, coram venerabili viro domino Johanne Benet, milite, legum doctore, curie prerogatiue Cantuarienss Magistro custode siue commisario legitime constituto, vicesimo primo die mensiss Novembris, Anno Domini millesimo sexcentesimo vndecimo, Juramento HENRICI MERVIN, vnius Executorum in evdem testamento nominat. Cui commissa fuit administracio, bonor, Jurium, et creditorum dicti defuncti, de bene et fideliter administrand, &c., ad sancta dei Evangelia Jurat. Reservata potestate similem Commissionem faciend Dno. Mervino Awdley, et Dno. Thome Thynne militibus, necnon Willm's. Gibbes et Hugoni Hill Armigeris, Executoribus etam in eodem testamento nominatis, eam cum venerint petituri in debita juris forma admissuri. (*Regr.* "*89 Wood.*")

FUNERAL CERTIFICATE OF SIR JOHN MERVYN, KNT.

(*Ms. Coll. Arm : " I. 13" p. 75.*)

HIS WORDE "DU DIEU TOUT."

Thorder of thentyrement & funerall of John Merbyn Knight

Who dep'ted tuesday 19 June 1566 in the theighth yere of the queenes Reigne at his howsse of Founteyne Gyfford in the Countye of Wiltshere abowt v. of the Clocke at nyght.

It'm the sayd knight had ij wyves fyrst Jone late wyfe to William peuerell of bradford peuerell in the Countye of Dorssett by wth Will'm she had onely ij doughters sine p'le & she was doughter to phyllyppe baskerefild of Sherborne in Dorsettshere & after that of Herefordshere & of Elizabeth his wyfe & had issue 13 childerne vidz ij doughters sine p'le James M'vyn Elianor nowe wyfe to Robert Hill of Taunton in the Countye of Som'sett Edythe sine p'le Edmond M'garet nowe wyfe to John Coke of the Ile of Wight Elizabeth wyf to John Ryves of datnayre court by blandford in the Countye of Dorssett John M'garet phyllyppe a son Anne nowe wyf to Edward Cordrey of sute in hampshere son & heyre to . . . Cordrey of . . . in Wyltshere & Ambrose M'vyn.

Also the sayd Sr John hadde nowe to his iijde wyf Elizabeth late wyf to Rychard p'kyns of Ufton in barkshere & had no Issue wth lyved.

James Mervyn Esquier for the bodye to the queenes ma^tie wedd Amye late wyfe to . . . horne pencyon of Saresen in the countye of oxforde doughter to . . . Clerke . . . & suster to Sr Rowland Clerke & hath Iyssue luce.

Edmond mervyn ij^d Son to Sr John wedd Jane late wyf to Robert Gaynesford of . . . in Sotherey by wth Robert she hadde a son.

She was doughter to Rychard Catysbye of the Countye of warwyke knight & hath Issue John Mervyn Edmond & Richarde.

Robert Hyll & Elianor mervyn had Issue Robert sine p'le James gylbert sine p'le John Hugh Jane Elizabeth sine p'le & m'garet.

John Coke & M'garet mervyn had Issue John sine p'le Vrsula & Elizabeth.

John Ryves & Elizabeth mervyn had Issue John Elizabeth George Charles Amye & Henrye.

Edward Cordrey & Anne M'vyn had Issue Amye sine p'le.

It'm by hys wyll he made his executors his ij youngest sons phyllyppe Mervyn & Ambrose Mervyn and hys son in lawe John Ryves hys ou'sear..

It'm hys bodye was bowelled wrapped in cere clothe & chested & so sett in the myddest of his p'lour there on ij tressles wth a velvet pawle thereon sett wth Scocheons the p'lour hanged wth brode clothe & the halle wth other blaks all garnyshed wth Scocheons where it Remayned tyll the buryall Day beinge thursday the fourthe of Julye next that it was carryed to the churche there & buryed in the northe Ile of the same churche by hys fyrst wyfe as after followeth.

It'm in the bodye of the sayd churche was sett beinge made of q'ters a Inclosure or small hersse in length 3 yards & breadth a yarde and therein a table wth tresles all pu'ed wth black garnyshed wth scocheons & at eche corn' of the hersse the quarter was aboue the Rayle A Elle whereon eche was sett ij scocheons & 9 pencells and w^thowt the sayd Inclosure or hersse was sett a Rayle of 5 yards in length & 4 yards in breade for the morn's to knele in cou'ed wth blacke garnyshed wth scocheons & wth in strawed wth Russhes wth v stoles & cusshons also pu'ed.

Also the Chauncell & all the whole churche was hanged wth one breade of cotton garnysshed wth Scocheons.

Thoder in p'ceading fro the sayd howrse to the Churche there the funerall day thursday the 4 of Julye. Inprimis John Whyte & Henrye Freeman as conducters.

Then 12 poore men in blacke gownes.

Then certen synginge men & prestes.

Then the standerde borne by Edward Cordrey gent.

Then 5 gentlemen in gownes as pytts the Drap' alone Francys p'kyns & M^r powton Wm Hussye & John Coke.

Then the preacher M^r p'ctor Chauncellor of the busshop of Salisbury.

Then the pennon borne by Edward Mompesson gent.

Then thelme & crest by Thom^s Mompesson gent.

Then the cote of Armes borne by yorke heralde.

Then the Corpse borne by 6 of his yeoman John brether & Robert Nycha's John ap hoell & Nycha's broke Richard Andrews & George Knight.

Then the Chief morn' Edward Mervyn ij^d son to the defunct.

Then John & phyllyppe Mervyn his iij^d & iv^th sons.

Then Ambrose Mervyn v^th & yongest son wth John Mervyn son to Sr Edmond.

Then his v doughters & his doughter in lawe in hodes.

Then the yeomen ij & ij.

Then the gentlewomen & the gentlemen & after all others.

In wth order they p'ceaded to the Churche where the corpse and all thother being placed York herald read the thankesgeuynge as he Dyd at other tymes accustomed & as followeth.

Blessed be the Kinge of Eternall glorye who thorowe his devyne power hathe translated the ryght W'shipfull Sr John Mervyn knight fro thys Earthlye vnto his hevenlye kingdom.

And then a Psalme beinge songe Mr Chaunceller aforenamed began the Sermond wherein he dyd comend the defunct for his Juste dealinge & for kepynge p'myses wth Sermond ended begun thofferynge the synginge in the meane ceason the cxix psalme.

Then the chief morner wth thother iiij followinge hym p'ceaded vpp to the offeringe wth york herald before them whereat onelye the chief morn' offerid & returned to there places.

Then the sayd Chief morn' wth york before hym p'ceadid agayne vppe & the said morn' standing besydes the pryste yorke returned downe & at thead of the hersse delyu'ed vnto John & phyllyppe m'vyn the cote of Armes who wth York before them offered vppe the same to the Chief morn' aforesayd & he delyu'ed yt to the clerke who placed yt on the table & york wth the ij morn's.

Then thother ij morners at yorks hands received the swerde who in all poyntes as afore offered the same & returned to theyreplaces.

Then the ij fyrst lykewyse offered the target & then thother ij thelme & crest & returned.

Then the pennon of Armes & alsoe the standerde were lykewyse offered & recevid.

Then the Chief morn' offered for hymselfe & returned to his place wth York before hym.

Then offered thother iiij morn's ij after thother ij were returned wth York before them & toke theyre places.

Then offered his doughters & then the gentlemen & yeomen.

Then the p'ceaded forthe wth the comemorac'on at thend whereof the morn's onelye returned home and then the body was buryed in the north Ile of the Churche aforesayd where in the aforenamed York sawe the hatchements orderlye sett uppe & had for his Droyctes.

All the poore people there had 4[d] the pece.

The Paynters byll Robert Grenewood.

In primis his standerd w[th] his creste the Squyrrell p'per coler holdinge w[t]his clawes a nutt collored or terretted g. his worde [*Du Dieu tout*].

It'm the pennon of Armes.
The Cote of Armes.
Thelme p'cell gylte.
The Creste the squyrrell aforesayd.
The wrethe whyte & black.
The mantels of veluett w[th] tersells & knops gylte.
The Targett of hys Armes.
A Swerde cou'ed w[th] veluet wth pomell chape & pendent gylte.
vi Scocheons of buckram ij of hym alone & thother of hym & his wyfes.
It'm one Dorsser in paper in metall.
It'm ij Doorss in coler at.
It'm a headpeece brase of Iron wth a Rodde for the Cote & a pyn for thelmett.
ij other brazen of Iron for the Standerd & pennon.
ij staves had there.

Robert Ma
Manor of
Kent, diꝫ
See foot no

Robert M
fyn, living
1446. Pr
bably the
Robert M
fyn, of An
worth, co.
Kent, who
sided with
Lan castri
and was d
clared a n
1462-3 l
foot note, p

Robert M
eldest son
obtained t
reversal of
father's a
der, 12 & 1
[V., (14
See foot note
p. 3.

Alice, dau
Admin 1
1558-9 of
Ob. 1593.

The desce
(See V

TABULAR PEDIGREE

OF THE

DURFORD ABBEY BRANCH

OF THE

Mervyn Family.

NOTE.—This Pedigree is based upon one compiled about 1799, by G. F. Beltz, *Lancaster Herald* (*Ms. Coll. Arm. "A. ix," J.P.* 9), being an elaboration of Vincent's Pedigree of the Mervyn family (*Ms. Coll. Arm., "Vin. Sussex* 121," *p.* 392). Corrections in, and additions to, it have been made from original documents and records. It may be noted that Dallaway, in his *History of Sussex* (*vol. i. p.* 212), has printed a pedigree of this branch of the Mervyn family, which is not only meagre and imperfect, but very erroneous.

Elizabeth, 3rd daughter and coheiress of Sʳ Edmund Paken—Sʳ Edmund Mervyn, Kⁿᵗ. 2nd son of Walter Mervyn, of Fountel-Giffard, by his wife—Eleanor, daughter of ham, Kⁿᵗ. of Bramshot, co. Sussex. (*Visit. Sussex,* 1530.) Elizabeth Mompesson. He was one of the Judges of the King's Bench (1540), and —Thomas Welles. She survived her husband, and is mentioned in his will (1550). the grantee from the Crown of the demesnes of Durford Abbey, co. Sussex. Will dated (*Visit. Sussex,* 1530.) 24 July, 1550 ; proved in P. C. C. 16 Nov. 1553.

1st wife.

2nd wife.

Geffery Mervyn. (*Visit.* 1530.)	Jane, sole executrix of her husband's will, which she proved in P. C. C. 20 May, 1614.	2nd wife.—Henry Mervyn, of Durford, mentioned in his father's will (1550). His will, dated 10 March, 1609.	1st wife.—Edith, daughter of Sʳ Anthony Windsor, Kⁿᵗ. by Elizabeth, dau. of Sʳ Henry Lovell, of Harting, co. Sussex, Kⁿᵗ. (*Ms. Coll. Arm., Philipot's Mullet, p.* 174ᵇ.)

William Mervyn, mentioned in his father's will (1550) as being then married, and having a son living. →

Edmund Mervyn, *Clerk.* Appointed by his father one of the executors of his will (1550), in which he is described as "Parson of Bramshot," co. Sussex.

3. Edward.
4. Francis.
5. Nicholas.

(*Visit.* 1530.)

Elizabeth.

Eleanor,—Richard Rous, living 1550. of Rogate, co.

(*Visit. Sussex,* 1530.) Sussex, 2nd son of Roger Rous of Modbury, Devon.

(*See Visit. Sussex* 1570. *Ms. Coll. Arm. "G.* 18," *p.* 73ᵃ.)

Agnes. (*Visit. Sussex,* 1530.)

Sʳ Henry Mervyn, Kⁿᵗ., described in his father's will as son and heir ; bapt. at Rogate, 26 Dec., 1583. M.P. for Wooton Basset 1614. Succeeded on death of Sʳ James Mervyn, his wife's grandfather, in 1611, to the Fountel Giffard estates. Appointed 1617, Admiral and Captain General of the Narrow Seas. Will dated 29 May, 1646, and proved P. C. C. the following month.

—Christian, daughter of George Lord Audley, of Heleigh, by Lucy, sole child and heiress of Sʳ James Mervyn, Kⁿᵗ. of Fountel Giffard, co. Wilts. Living 1631, died before 1646. (*See Pedigree of the Fountel branch of the MERVYN FAMILY.*)

Edmund Mervyn, of Durford, and subsequently of Petersfield, co.—Anna, daughter of William Jephson, of Froyle, co. Hants, and sister of Sʳ John Jephson, Kⁿᵗ. (*Visit. Southampton. Will dated 8 Sep, 1604 ; proved 20 Feb, 1604-5. Died 9 Hants* 1622-34. *Ms. Coll. Arm. "C.* 19," *p.* 82.) She survived her husband, who by his will devised Sep, 1604. (*Inq. p.m., 2 Jas. I. part* 12, *No.* 187, *and* 12 *Jas. I. part* to her a life-estate in his property in Sussex and Hants. She resided at Petersfield, and her will is 4, *No.* 175.) dated 31 May, 1625, and was proved P. C. C. 3 July, 1628.

William, bapt. 16 Feb, buried 9 March, 1586.

Edmund, bapt. 15 Nov., and buried 20 Dec., 1593.

Francis, bapt. and buried 23 May, 1599.

Edmund=Mary, Mervyn ; dauʳ of d. 14 and Sir Alexburied ander 19 Aug, Clifford, 1634, at of LonDublin. don, Kⁿᵗ. (Fun. Cert.)

Clifford Mervyn.

Frances Mervyn.

Philip Mervyn.

Eliza=Peter beth, Bettesbapt. 2 worth, April, named 1582, in his marmother'sried 29 will July, (1625) 1600. as an executor.

Richard Mervyn.

Anne, bapt. 17 Oct, 1585.

Dorothy, bapt. 19 March, 1594, buried 14 Feb, 1598.

Cathe-rine, bapt. 7 Sept. 1600.

Blanche, 2nd wife, mentioned in her mother's will, 1625.

John Evatt, Dean of Elphin in Ireland, ob. 1634. (Fun. Cert.)

James Mervyn, mentioned in the will of Sʳ James Mervyn, his maternal great-grandfather (1610). In 1646 was commanding the King's ship "Sᵗ Claude," in the Narrow Seas, under his father. Buried 12th July, 1641, at Dublin, s. p. (Fun. Cert.)

—Elizabeth, daughter of Sir John Philipot, of Thruxton, co. Soton, d. 13th May, 1640. (Fun. Cert.)

Sʳ Audley Mervyn, Kⁿᵗ. 2nd son, but who, on his brother's death, became heir to his father. He settled in Ireland, where he attained eminence in the Law ; and in 1661, was elected Speaker of the Irish House of Commons. He married and had issue.

Lucy, living at her father's death (1646,) unm.

1stly,

Rory Maguire, son of Bren, Lord Maguire.

=Deborah, living 1646.

2ndly,

—Sʳ Leonard Blenerhasset.

Elizabeth, living at her father's death (1646) unmarried.

Frances, living 1646.

m....... Coach.

Katharine, living 1646. m. William Messar.

See Notes as to the Irish branch of the MERVYN family.

Abstracts OF "Inquisitiones Post Mortem."

By **Inquisition** touching EDMUND MERVINE (co. South^{m}.), taken in the *2nd* year of James I. (1604-5) with respect to a lease held by him from his father, the jurors found that he died 9th September, 1604, when his son Henry was in his 21st year.

2 Jas. I. (1604-5.)
Miscell. Inq., part 12,
No. 187.

Inquisition taken after the death of EDMUND MERVYN, Esquire, son of Henry Mervyn, of co. Southampton.

12 Jas. I. (1614-15),
part 2, No. 175.

The jurors found that he held the site of the late Monastery of Durford in Sussex, with the demesne lands of Durford, in Hartinge and Rogatte (Sussex), and in Petersfield (Southampton). That Henry Mervyn was his son and heir.

Abstracts OF Wills.

Sir EDMUND MERVYN, Knt. My body to be buried in the south aisle of the church of Bramshot, "where Sir Edmund Pakenh'm, Knt., and my lady, late his wief, lye." All my plate, redy money, houseboldry goods and chattels to my welbeloved wief Dame Elizabeth Mervyn, subject to payment of debts and legacies, and to remaining his (Testator's) widow. In default of said Elizabeth entering into bond to pay debts, &c., then the bequest made to her to be held by executors, except such as I give to her "*frely,*" viz. : —" My best basyn and ewer of silver, two stonding cuppes, my silver goblet and xij. silver spones." Also, " I "give frely to my said wief my horse I ride on myself, my gelding I had of Mr. Ford, my dune gelding w^t "blacke *lyst* (flank or side), my cloth sacke horse, my curtall y^t my cooke comenly rydeth on, and two "ambling coltes at Westminster." Also, " I give frely to my said wief my best scarlet robe, with all apparell "belonging to the same. I give to Henry my sonne my Wiltshire gelding and another of my coltes not "bequeathed which he lyketh best at Westland." " I give to my daughter Edith, wief to the said Henry, my "Westminster curtall nage and my other scarlet robe with the apparell of the same. I give to Elenor Rous my "daughter my browne blew Abbet and also money "to discharge my consyens for her agenst Ayling." To "Cosyn Nicholas Tichborne my grene Abbet with apparell of the same," and money. To Thomas Erlesman my violet Abbet and money. The rest of my plate, redie money, householdstuf, goodes and cattalles not bequeathed, (my debtes paide) be devyded by my said wief by her discretion amongest my children. Provided that in the dyvision "my sonne Henry shall have for his parte all the plate that I had with the mariage of his wief "that was Sir Anthony Wyndesores ; and my two best saltes and my standing cuppe." To Sr John Probyn, my chaplyn, my ryding gowne and money. At the daye of my buriall fiftie shillinges to be geven to poore people at Petresfeld, and half a quarter wheate to the poore people at Bramshot. "I will that the parson of Bramshot be allowed tenne poundes for his first frutes at the daies apoynted for payment of the same." I hartely desire my said wief to make a new lease to my sonne Willyam Mervyn and his sonne for terme of her lief, of the ferme he dwellith in. To Cosyn Marie Burlegh twentie markes for her mariage, and I do desire my said wief to give her twentie nobles more to make up twentie poundes. I apoynte as executours of my will, my Cosyn Willyam Mervyn, Edmund Mervyn parson of Bramshot, and Richard Rous, giving vnto euery of them for their paynes fourtie shillinges. I apoynte as sup'visour of my will, my Cosyn Sr John Mervyn, Knight, praying hym to take my bokes of lawe for my Cosyn James Mervyn, in recompens of suche rekenynges as be betwen hym and me.

24 July, 4th
Edw. IV.
(1550.)
Abstract.

Testator rescinds bequests of his "habettes to his wife and doughter Edith," &c., and directs "that all "my habettes be solde to the most advantage, and the money rysinge therof to be employed to the payment "of my debtes." If wife should die, then "my sonne Henry or any other that shalbe the next heire to "her shall have the residue of my goods," &c. By will "I appoynted my nevewe William Mervyn and "my sonne Rowse to be myne executors ;" I now "appoynte and assigne my nevew John Mervyn, my "nevewe Willyam Mervyn, and my sonne Edmund Mervyn to be myn executours, and my said sone Rowse "to be none of them, because they be nerer by bloode vnto me and of myn owne name, giving to every of "them for their paynes and labors taken fourtie shillinges." Proved in London, 16 Nov. 1553. (*Regr.* "20 *Tashe.*")

Codicil.

EDMUND MERVYN, of Petersfield, co. Southampton, Esquire. All my estates in Counties of Sussex and Southampton to my wife Anna, to bring up my children now unmarried, and pay them marriage portions. To my son and heir, Henry Mervyn, all said estates at death of my wife. Residue to wife, to be my executrix. Proved in London, 20 Feb., 1604-5.

8 Sep. 1604.
Abstract.

6 Mar. 1609.
Abstract.

HENRY MERVYN. To be buried "in parishe churche where it shall please God I shall depart
"this life, wthout cither ringe of bells, or any other pompe or shewe, more than one bell to be runge presentlie
"after my departure out of this life, to geue knowledge that the kinge hath loste subject ; noe more ringinge
"to be vsed before at or after my buriall." "Whereas it is covenanted betwixte my late sonne Edmund,
"deceased, and me, upon the demise of my howse and tenment of Dursford, that my said sonne, his
"executors, or administrators, is to paie wthin sixe months after my deathe vnto such parsons or person
"as I shall name or appoint the same by my last will, the some of One hundred twentie poundes twelve
"shillinges and tenn pence for certaine goodes as it doth appeare in a schedule vnto the said Indenture
"annexed, and alsoe that it is in the choice of me the said Henry, whether I will chuse the goodes in
"the said schedule, or the money as they are praised at in the said the wch is One hundred twentie poundes
"twelve shillinges tenn pence, I refuse the goodes and doe make choice of the hundred twentie poundes
"twelve shillinges tenn pence, wch some I doe geue vnto my beloved wife, Jane; she to vse and convert
"vnto her owne proper vse." "I do giue alsoe vnto my said wife all other my goodes and chattels, as
"well reall as p'sonall." "My said wife, Jane, to be sole Executrix." Proved in London, 20 May, 1614,
by Executrix. *(Regr. 48 Lawe.)*

31 May, 1625.
Abstract.

ANNA MERVYN, of Petersfield, co. Southampton, Widow, late wife of Edmund Mervyn, of
same place, Esquire, deceased. My brother Sir John Jephson Kn^{t.} and my son-in-law Peter Bettesworth
Esquire; my son Sr. Henry Mervyn and his Lady; my daughter Blanch, wife of Mr. Evett; my linen to
all my daughters; my nephew William Jephson; my grandson Peter Bettesworth; my niece Ann Holland;
my niece Frances Lucas; to all my sons-in-law, my brother Lucas, my sister Lucas, and my niece Elizabeth
Bettesworth. Residue to my said brother Sr. John Jephson, and my son Peter Bettesworth, and make
them executors. Proved in London, 3 July, 1628.

29 May, 1646.
Abstract.

Sr HENRY MERVYN, of the City of Westminster, Knt. To be decently buried at discretion of
executors. Legacies "to my sonne Awdlie Mervyn, and to my daughters the Lady Blenerhassett, Lucie
"Mervyn, Elizabeth Mervyn, and Frances Coach;" Bequest to "my daughter Katharine Messar, wife of
"William Messar;" to "the right hono^{ble.} Dame Rachell Lady Kea for many her noble favors and respectes
"to me"; Legacies are to be paid "out of the arreares due to me as Lieutenant Generall and Admirall
"of his Maties. Navie in the Narrow Seas." Confirm deed of gift bearing even date with will of £12,000
or thereabouts, "long since due to me from his Ma^{tye}" unto William Poe, of St. Edmund Bury, co. Suffolk,
whom failing, "my loving friend, Ellis Holmes of Kensington, gentleman," to be executor, and entitled,
subject to payment of debts, legacies, and funeral expenses, to residue of my estate. Proved in London, 12
June, 1646. *(Regr. 80 Twisse.)*

Extracts FROM Parochial Registers of Rogate, co. Sussex.

Baptisms.	1562.	May	Jane, daughter of Henry Mervyn, Esquire.
,,	1563.	Novemb. 10.	Henry, sonne of Henry Mervyn, Esquire.
,,	1565.	April 19.	John, sonne of Henry Mervyn, Esquire.
,,	1567.	Novemb. 23.	Catharine, daught^r of Henry Mervin, Esquire.
,,	1582.	April 2.	Elizabeth, daught^r of Edmond Mervin, Esquire.
,,	1583.	December 26.	Henry, sonne of Edmond Mervyn, Esquire.
,,	1585.	October 17.	Anne, daught^r of Edmonde Marvyn, Esquire.
,,	1586.	Feb. 16.	Willm sonne of Edmond Mervin, Esquire.
,,	1593.	November 15.	Edmond, sonne of Edmonde Mervin, Esquire.
,,	1594.	March 19.	Dorothy, daught^r of Edmond Marvin, Esquire.
,,	1599.	May 23.	Francis, sonne of Edmonde Marvin, Esquire.
,,	1600.	September 7.	Catherine, daughter of Edmonde Mervin, Esquire.
Burials.	1563.	Novemb. 27.	George, sonne of Henry Mervyn, Esquire.
,,	1565.	April 19.	John, sonne of Henry Marvyn, Esquire.
,,	1570.	January 9.	Jane Mervin.
,,	,,	,, 16.	Catherine Mervin.
,,	1586.	March 9.	Willm, sonne of Edmond Mervin, gent.
,,	1593.	Dec. 20.	Edmond, sonne of Edmond Mervin, Esquire.
,,	1597.	Octob. 19.	Richard Mervin, gent.
,,	1598.	Feb. 14.	Dorothy, daught^r of Edmonde Mervin, Esquire.
,,	1599.	May 23.	Francis, sonne of Edmonde Marvin, Esquire.

Marriages. 1600. July 29. Peter Betteswort and Elizabeth Marvin.

Extract FROM Visitation of Sussex.

The four Heralds' Visitations of the County of Sussex were :—

1. In 1530; taken by Benolte, *Clarencieux* (*Ms. Coll. Arm.* "D 13.")
2. In 1574; taken by Cooke, *Clarencieux* (*Ms. Coll. Arm.* "D 11.")
3. In 1633; taken by Philipot, *Som'set Her.* & Owen, *York Her.* (*Ms. Coll. Arm.* C 29".)
4. In 1662; taken by S' Edward Bysshe, *Clarencieux* (*Ms. Coll. Arm.* "D 16").

I have, by the courtesy of Sir Albert Woods, *Garter*, examined the above records, and the only entry to be found in them relating to the Mervyn family is in the Visitation of 1530, as follows:—

" Edmonde Marvyne maryede furst Elyano', dowghter vnto Thomas Wellys, and hath
" yssewe Willyam, Edmonde, Edwarde, Fraunceys, Nicholas, Elysabeth, Elyano' and
" Augnes."

" The seconde wyffe Elysabeth, thyrde dowghter vnto Syr Edmonde Pay'nam, Knyght,
" and hath ysshewe Henrye and Jefferey."

Copies OF Funeral Certificates.

JOHN EVATT, Dean of Elphine, born at . . . . took to his 1st wife Joane, daughter of Roger Bager, of Knockviecar, in the county of Roscommon, by whom he had issue one son and one daughter, viz' Edward the son and Edith the daughter, both as yet unmarried. The s' John took to his 2nd wife Blanch, daughter of Edward Mervin, of Pettersfield, in Hampshire, in England, by JOHN EVATT. whom he had issue three sons and two daughters, viz' Thomas eldest son ; Philip 2nd son ; Humphry 1634. 3rd son ; Catherine eldest daughter; and Jane the youngest ; all as yet unmaried. The s' John departed Betham's Irish Fun. this mortal life at Porlitan-caslane in the county of Leitrim, on Friday in Easter week, 1634, and was Cert., Coll. Arm. interred in the parish church of Kiltaghock in the s' county of Leitrim. The truth of the premisses is vol. vi., No. 187. testified by the subscription of Humphry Reynolds, Esq'' who hath returned this certificate into my office to be there recorded. Taken by me, Thomas Preston, Esq' Ulster King of Arms, the 9th of May, 1639.
("W. B." *William Betham.*)

CAPTAIN EDMOND MERVIN, of Founthill, in the county Wilts, Esq., deceased the 14th of August, 1634, he had to wife [Mary] daughter of S' Alexander Clifford, of London, Knt., by whom he had issue Clifford Mervin, and one daughter being in London ; he was buried in S' John's Church, Dublin, ye 19th of August. WM. RYVES. EDMOND MERVIN. 1634.

ELIZABETH, the daughter of S' John Philipott* of Thaxton, [Thruxton,] in Hampshire in the Ms. Coll. Arm. Kingdome of England, Knight, wife of Captaine James Mervin, eldest sonne Fun. Cert. and heire apparent of S' Henry Mervin, Knight, Admirall of the Narrow Seas, Ireland, p. 19. by whome she had noe issue. The said Elizabeth departed this mortall life ELIZABETH MERVYN upon Wednesday the 13th of May, 1640, and was interred in the parish church 1640. of St. Warborowes in Dublin upon the —— day of the same monneth. The truth Funeral entries of the premisses is testified by the subscription of Captaine James Mervin, whoe Ulster's Office, hath returned this certificate into my office to be there recorded. Taken by me, Dublin. Thomas Preston, Esq'' Ulvester King of Armes, the 16th of May, 1640. Vol. ix., p. 42.

CAPTAIN JAMES MERVIN, eldest son and heir apparent of Sir Henry Mervin, Kn'. Admiral of the Narrow Seas. The said James took to wife Elizabeth, the daughter of Sir John Philpott, of Thruxton in Hampshire, in the Kingdom of England, Knt., by whom he hath no issue. The said Elizabeth departed this life upon Wednesday the 13th of May, 1640, and the said Captain James departed this life at JAMES MERVYN, Dublin upon Thursday the 10th of July, 1641, and is to be interred in S' Warborough's church in Dublin 1641. the 12th of the same month. The truth of the premisses is testified by the subscription of Capt'' Audley Betham's Irish Mervin, second brother and heir of the defunct, who hath returned this certificate into my office, there to Fun. Cert. be recorded. Taken by me Thomas Preston, Esq., Ulster King of Arms, the 12th of June, 1641. Coll. Arm.
AU. MERVIN. Vol. ix., p. 59.

---

* A pedigree of the Philipott family will be found in the Visitation of the County of Southampton. *Ms. Coll. Arm.*, "C. 19," *p.* 16.

Christopher
Mervyn; eldest
son; living *Visit.*
1565; died
without issue.
Visit. 1623.

Jol
me
Vi
and
s.p.
16

John Mervyn, of Pert-
wood, son and heir;
bapt. 3 Aug. 1595,
living *Visit.* 1623,
æt. 28. Mentioned
in will of his uncle
Thomas (1632), and
in will of his uncle
Augustine (1634). In
1635 he was of Mot-
combe, co. Dorset.

John Mervyn, =Rebe
bapt. 20 April, of C
1624. Mentioned Dird
in will of Tho- lingh
mas Mervyn 11 A
(1632). Letters befor
of administra- of th
tion granted 12 Gilli
Dec. 1692, to burie
widow and son
Thomas. Bur.
1692.

William Thomas Mer
Mervyn, Purchased Bo
of Pert- House, near
wood, canton, co. Do
living in 1702 ; bur
1685. June 1745.

Henry Mervyn, admitted
of the Manor of Gillin
1 Oct. 1745; and sold the
1752 or 3; bur. 15 June

Lambert Mervyn. b. 12, b
Deverill 24 July 1725
1750 unm.

TABULAR PEDIGREE 𝔄,

Showing the issue of the marriage of ELIZABETH MERVYN with PAGET WALTER, and its present (1873) representatives.

𝔄

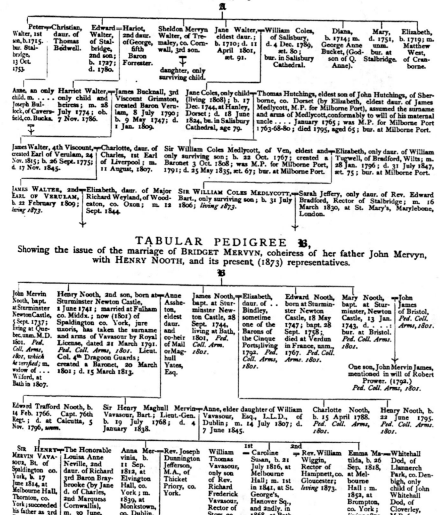

Peter Walter, 1st son, b. 1715. bur. Stalbridge, 13 Oct. 1753. = Christian, daur. of Thomas Bedwell.

Edward Walter, of Stalbridge, 2nd son; b. 1727; d. 1780. = Hariot, 2nd daur. of George, fifth Baron Forrester.

Sheldon Mervyn Walter, of Tremaley, co. Cornwall, 3rd son.
daughter, only surviving child.

Jane Walter, eldest daur.; b. 1710; d. 11 April 1801, æt. 91. = William Coles, of Salisbury, d. 4 Dec. 1789, æt. 80; bur. in Salisbury Cathedral.

Diana, b. 1714; m. George Anne Bucket, (Godson of Q. Anne).

Mary, d. 1751, unm. bur. at Stalbridge.

Elizabeth, b. 1719; m. Matthew West, of Cranborne.

Anne, an only child. m. .... Joseph Bullock, of Caversfield, co. Bucks.

Harriot Walter, only child and heiress; m. 28 July 1774; ob. 7 Nov. 1786. = James Bucknall, 3rd Viscount Grimston, created Baron Verulam, 8 July 1790; b. 9 May 1747; d. 1 Jan. 1809.

Jane Coles, only child (living 1808); b. 17 Dec. 1744, at Hanley, Dorset; d. 18 June 1824, bu. in Salisbury Cathedral, age 79. = Thomas Hutchings, eldest son of John Hutchings, of Sherborne, co. Dorset (by Elizabeth, eldest daur. of James Medlycott, M.P. for Milborne Port), assumed the surname and arms of Medlycott, conformably to will of his maternal uncle .... January 1765; was M.P. for Milborne Port 1763-68-80; died 1795, aged 65; bur. at Milborne Port.

James Walter, 4th Viscount, created Earl of Verulam, 24 Nov. 1815; b. 26 Sept. 1775; d. 17 Nov. 1845. = Charlotte, daur. of Charles, 1st Earl of Liverpool; m. 11 August, 1807.

Sir William Coles Medlycott, of Ven, eldest and only surviving son; b. 22 Oct. 1767; created a Baronet 3 Oct. 1808; was M.P. for Milborne Port 1791; d. 25 May 1835, æt. 67; bur. at Milborne Port. = Elizabeth, only daur. of William Tugwell, of Bradford, Wilts; m. 28 Jan. 1796; d. 31 July 1847, æt. 75; bur. at Milborne Port.

JAMES WALTER, 2nd EARL OF VERULAM, b. 22 February 1809; living 1873. = Elizabeth, daur. of Major Richard Weyland, of Woodeaton, co. Oxon; m. 12 Sept. 1844.

SIR WILLIAM COLES MEDLYCOTT, Bart., only surviving son; b. 31 July 1806; living 1873. = Sarah Jeffery, only daur. of Rev. Edward Bradford, Rector of Stalbridge; m. 16 March 1830, at St. Mary's, Marylebone, London.

TABULAR PEDIGREE 𝔅,

Showing the issue of the marriage of BRIDGET MERVYN, coheiress of her father John Mervyn, with HENRY NOOTH, and its present (1873) representatives.

𝔅

John Mervin Nooth, bapt. at Sturminster Newton Castle, 5 Sept. 1737; living at Quebec, unm. M.D. 1801. Ped. Coll. Arms, 1801, which he verified; m. widow of .... Wilford, at Bath in 1807.

Henry Nooth, 2nd son, born at Sturminster Newton Castle, 1 June 1741; married at Fulham co. Middx.; now (1801) of Spaldington co. York, jure uxoris, has taken the surname and arms of Vavasour by Royal License, dated 21 March 1791. Lieut. 3rd Dragoon Guards; created a Baronet, 20 March 1801; d. 15 March 1813. = Anne Assheton, eldest daur. and co-heir of Mail or Maghull Yates, Esq.

James Nooth, bapt. at Sturminster Newton Castle, 28 Sept. 1744, living at Bath, 1801. Ped. Coll. Arm. 1801. = Elizabeth, daur. of .. Bindley, sometime one of the Barons of the Cinque Ports; living 1792. Ped. Coll. Arms, 1801.

Edward Nooth, born at Sturminster Newton Castle, 18 May 1747; bapt. 28 Sept. 1758; died at Verdun in France, unm. 1767. Ped. Coll. Arms. 1801.

Mary Nooth, bapt. at Sturminster, Newton Castle, 13 Jan. 1743, d. .... : bur. at Bristol. Ped. Coll. Arms. 1801. = John James of Bristol, Ped. Coll. Arms, 1801.

One son, John Mervin James, mentioned in will of Robert Prower. (1792.) Ped. Coll. Arms, 1801.

Edward Trafford Nooth, b. 14 Feb. 1766. Capt. 76th Regt.; d. at Calcutta, 5 Nov. 1796, unm.

Sir Henry Maghull Mervin Vavasour, Bart.; Lieut.-Gen. b. 19 July 1768; d. 4 January 1838. = Anne, elder daughter of William Vavasour, Esq., L.L.D., of Dublin; m. 14 July 1807; d. 7 June 1845.

Charlotte Nooth, b. 15 April 1788. Ped. Coll. Arms, 1801.

Henry Nooth, b. 22 June 1795. Ped. Coll. Arms, 1801.

SIR HENRY MERVIN VAVASOUR, Bt. of Spaldington co. York, b. 17 June 1814, at Melbourne Hall, Thornton, co. York; succeeded his father as 3rd Bart., 4 Jan. 1838. = The Honorable Louisa Anne Neville, 2nd daur. of Richard 3rd Baron Braybrooke (by Jane d. of Charles, 2nd Marquess Cornwallis), m. 30 June, 1853, at St. James's Church, Piccadilly.

Anna Mervinia, b. 11 Sep. 1812, at Elvington Hall, co. York; m. 1839, at Monkstown, co. Dublin. = Rev. Joseph Dunnington Jefferson, M.A., of Thicket Priory, co. York.
3 sons and 3 daurs., living 1873.

William Thomas Vavasour, only son of Rev. Richard Frederick Vavasour, Rector of Stow, co. Gloster.

1st — Caroline Susan, b. 21 July 1816, at Melbourne Hall; m. 1st in 1841, at St. George's, Hanover Sq., and 2ndly in 1868, at Bath.
2nd = Rev. William Wiggin, Rector of Hampnett, co. Gloucester; living 1873.

Emma Matilda, b. 26 Sep. 1818. at Melbourne Hall; m. 1852, at Brompton, co. York; living 1873. = Whitehall Dod, of Llannerch Park, co. Denbigh, only child of John Whitehall Dod, of Cloverley, M.P. for North Shropshire; living 1873.

Blanche, b. 6 June 1854; d. 14 and bur. 19 July in the same year.
Constance, b. at Hatherton Hall, 16 March; bapt. in Eccl. par. of Cannock, co. Stafford, 11 April 1856; living 1873.

TABULAR PEDIGREE C.

Showing the issue of the marriage of FRANCES MERVYN, co-heiress of her father John Mervyn, with ROBERT PROWER, and its present (1873) representatives.

Revd. John Prower, mentioned in his father's will (1792), b. 7 Nov., 1747; collated to the living of Purton, co. Wilts, 22 Dec. 1771; d. 29 Nov. and bur. at Purton, 7 Dec. 1827. — Anne, daughter of Christopher Lippeatt, of Marlborough; m. 1 July 1777, at Great Hallingbury, Essex; d. 25 July 1811, æt. 64; and bur. at Purton.

Fanny, b. 10 Sep. 1746; mentioned in her father's will (1792), survived her husband, and d. 7th and bur. at Cranbourne, 14th March 1827. — Revd. Henry Rigby, Vicar of Hockley, Prebendary of Salisbury, mentioned in will of Robert Prower, (1792).

Biddy, bapt. at Cranbourne, 2 Oct. 1755, mentioned in her father's will (1792); m. at Purley, in the same county; bur. at Cranbourne on 26th May 1837. — Revd. William Storey, M.A., Rector of Hinton Martell, co. Dorset, and subsequently of West Parley, in the same county; mentioned in Hinton Martell, 8 Jan. 1728; Robert Prower (1792), b. 15 July 1734, bapt. at Holywell Church, Oxford; d. 1 Oct. 1797; bur. at Cranbourne.

John Mervyn Prower, b. Purton, 14 January, and bapt. at Purton, 7 March 1784; Colerton Honorary Canon of Bristol. Succeeded his father, (Feb. 1828,) as Vicar of Purton; d. 1 Oct. 1811, aged 25; bur. and bur. at Purton 2nd, and bur. in St. Michael's Church, Gloucester. — Susannah, only child of John Cole, of Codorton House, Neath, co. Glamorgan; m. 20 Sept. 1809, at Purton; d. 7 April 1869.

Anne, bapt. at Purton 18 Jany. 1779; m. at Purton, 30 Oct. 1810; d. 7th and bur. at Purton on 12th April 1834. — Robert Inkerwood of Highgate and Doctor's Commons, about 1781; d. 14th, and bur. at Purton 22 July 1837, æt. 56.

Thomas Prower, b. 1786; d. unm. 27 Oct., and bur. at Purton 1 Nov. 1823.

Harriet, mentioned in will of her grandfather (1792) d. unm. 13 Aug. 1816; d. and bur. at Cranbourne, æt. 40.

Anthony Mervyn Reeve Storey-Maskelyne, of Basset Down House, Salthrop Lodge, and Lydiard Manor, co. Wilts; Horsfield Court, co. Gloucester; and Glenusk, co. Brecon; b. 8 May, 1791, and bapt. at Hinton Martell on 16 July following; educated at Wadham Coll., Oxford; called to the Bar Michaelmas Term 1816; assumed the name of MASKELYNE, 1845; living 1873. — Margaret, only child of the Rev[d] Nevill Maskelyne, of Basset Down House and Purton, D.D., F.R.S., Astronomer Royal, Fellow of Trinity Coll., Cambridge; Rector of North Runcton, co. Norfolk; b. 30 June 1787; bapt. at the Old Church, Greenwich; m. at St. George's, Hanover Square, 22 Nov. 1819; d. 15 Feb. 1858; bur. at Purton.

JOHN ELTON PROWER, of Purton House, co. Wilts, b. 11 Oct., and bapt. at St. Michael's Church, Gloucester, 20 Oct. 1811, was formerly Capt. 67th Regiment, and Major in the Royal Wilts Militia; High Sheriff of Wilts, 1860—3; living 1873. — Harriet, dau. of William Payn, of Kidwelly, Maidenhead, m. at Cookham, Berks, 5 July 1844.

Anna, m. at St. Michael's Church, Highgate, 2 Sept. 1837; bur. 1 January 1855, at St. James's Cemetery, Highgate, æt. 40. — Harry Chester, (son of Sir Robert Chester, M.C. at St. James's), Clerk of the Privy Council, and Chief Secretary of the Educational Department; d. 5 Oct. 1868, æt. 62.

Mervyn Herbert NevilStorey-Maskelyne, M.A., F.R.S., b. 3 Sept. 1823; bapt. at Lydiard Tregoze, Wm. Fellow of Wadham Coll., Oxford; Professor of Mineralogy to the University of Oxford; Keeper of the Mineral Department of the British Museum; Deputy-Lieut. co. Brecon; living 1873. — Theresa Mary, eldest daughter of John Dilwyn Llewellyn, co. Glamorgan, m. at Govelinon Church, Llangyvelach, co. Glamorgan, 29th June 1858.

Edmund Mervin Story-Maskelyne, b. 23 April 1829; bapt. at Lydiard Tregoze; graduated B.A. of Wadham Coll., Oxford, in March 1853; called to the Bar in March 1861; living 1873. — Martha Booth Banger, dau. of Thomas Russell, of Beaminster, co. Dorset; m. 25 Oct. 1860, at St. James's Church Piccadilly.

Anna Maria Antonia, b. 3 April 1827; bapt. at Lydiard Tregoze; d. 9 April 1864, at St. James's Piccadilly; living 1873. — Warrington Wilkinson Smyth, F.R.S., M.A. of Trinity College, Cambridge, of the Italian Order of SS. Maurizio and Lazaro and of the Portuguese Order of Jesus Christ; eldest son of the late Adml. William Henry Smyth, F.R.S. living 1873.

Meryvn Prower, b. 2 May, bapt. at Purton, 6 June 1847, d. 28 Nov. and bur. at Purton, 4 Dec. 1867.

John Elton Prower, b. 11 Oct.; bapt. at Purton, 14 Nov. 1852; living 1873.

Nelson Prower, b. 7 Nov., bapt. at Purton, 14 Dec. 1856; living 1873.

Maude, b. 2 July, bapt. at Purton, 24 April 1854; living 1873.

Marion, b. jany., bapt. at Purton, 24 April 1859; living 1873.

Beatrice, b. 3 Feb., bapt. at Purton, 3 July 1860; living 1873.

Harry, Mervin, Anna, Dulcibella, All died under age and unmarried.

Caroline, living 1873; unm.

Margaret Emma, b. 1 1859; bapt. at St. James's, Paddington; living 1873.

Mary Lucy, b. 8 June 1861, bapt. at St. James's, Paddington; living 1873.

Theresa Charlotte, b. 3 June 1863; bapt. at St. James's, Paddington; living 1873.

Agnes Mary, b. 22 March 1870, bapt. at St. Stephen's, Paddington.

Anthony St. John Storey-Maskelyne b. 31 July 1864, bapt. at Purton, Sept. 1861.

Margaret Mervin, b. 20 Dec. 1824, bapt. at Lydiard Tregoze; living 1873.

Charlotte Sophia, b. 19 March 1821, bapt. at Purton Church; living 1873.

John Story Masterman, b. 14 July, bapt. at St. Leonard's, Wallingford, to Sep. 1849; Exhibitioner of Brasenose College, Oxford, where he graduated B.A., Dec. 1872. — Neville Masterman, b. 13 July, 1851; bapt. at Garsington Church, Oxford, 22 Feb. 1853; Exhibitioner of Corpus College, Oxford.

Margaret Eliza, b. 3 Aug. 1855. — Herbert Warrington Smyth, b. 4 Jun., 1867; bapt. at St. Andrew's Church, Pimlico; living 1873.

Neville Maskelyne Smyth, b. 14 August 1868; bapt. at St. Andrew's Church, Pimlico; 1873. — Agnes Lucy Meta, b. 3 Nov. 1869; bapt. still-diard Tregoze; living 1873.

Visitation OF Wilts, 1565.

(Ms. Coll. Arm. " G. 8." fo. 54.)

Annexed to this pedigree are two shields of Arms in trick, the one being:—"*Argent, a demy-lion rampant, sable, charged on the shoulder with a fleur-de-lis or,*" the other, the same bearing, *charged with a label of 3 points gules for difference.*

WYLLYAM MARVIN of Pertwoode, in com. Wiltes, Gent., nefewe to Walter Marvyn, of Fownteyne, in com. Wiltes Esquire, maried Margarett, doughter to Wyllyam Fletcher, and of Jone his wife, doughter and heire to John Brether of Pertwoode aforsaide and by her had yssue John Marvyn his eldeate sonne and heire, Elizabeth vnmarried.

JOHN MARVYN of Pertwoode aforsaid Gent. eldeste sonne and heire to William Marvyn aforsaide, maried Alyce doughter to John Cockerell of Stoughton in the saide countie and by her had yssue John Marvin his eldest sonne and heire, Phelippe Marvyn seconde sonne, Margarett maried to Aldelme Whitaker of Edington in com. Wilts.

JOHN MARVYN of Pertwoode aforsaide gent. eldest sonne and heire to John Marvin aforesaide, maried Melior, doughter of Robert Gouldesborough of Knoyle in the saide countie, and by her hath yssue Xp'ofer Marvin his eldeste sonne and heire apparante, John Marvin seconde sonne.

Visitation OF Wilts, 1623.

(Ms. Coll. Arm. " C. 22," fo. 23ᵇ)

Arms tricked:—"*Argent, a demy-lyon rampant sable, charged on the shoulder with a fleur-de-lis or.*"

𝔙isitation OF 𝔚ilts, 1677.

(Ms. Coll. Arm. "D. 28," fo. 31.)

Arms tricked :—" *Argent a demy-lyon rampant Sable, charged on the shoulder with a fleur-de-lis or.*"

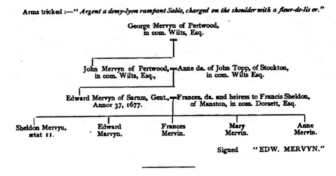

George Mervyn of Pertwood,
in com. Wilts, Esq.

John Mervyn of Pertwood,══Anne da. of John Topp, of Stockton,
in com. Wilts, Esq.,　　　　　in com. Wilts Esq.

Edward Mervyn of Sarum, Gent.,══Frances, da. and heiress to Francis Sheldon,
Annor 37, 1677.　　　　　　　of Manston, in com. Dorsett, Esq.

| Sheldon Mervyn, | Edward | Frances | Mary | Anne |
| ætat 11. | Marvyn. | Mervin. | Mervin. | Mervin. |

Signed　"EDW. MERVYN."

𝔙isitation OF 𝔏ondon, 1664.

(Ms. Coll. Arm. " D. 19," fo. 87ᵇ.)

Arms tricked :—*Argent a demy-lyon rampant Sable, charged on the shoulder with a fleur-de-lis
Argent. A Martlett for difference.*"

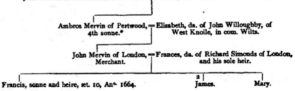

John Mervin of Pertwood in com. Wilts.══Mellior, dauᵗ· of . . . . . . Goldsberry.

Ambros Mervin of Pertwood,══Elizabeth, da. of John Willoughby, of
4th sonne.*　　　　　　　West Knoile, in com. Wilts.

John Mervin of London,══Frances, da. of Richard Simonds of London,
Merchant.　　　　　　and his sole heir.

| Francis, sonne and heire, æt. 10, Anᵒ· 1664. | 2 James. | Mary. |

Signed　"JOHN MERVIN."

---

* In the Visit. 1623 he was described as 6th son, but two of his brothers who were then living, viz.,
Christopher and Thomas, had subsequently died without leaving issue.

Copy of a Modern Pedigree of the Pertwood Branch recorded in the College of Arms, ["8 D 14" p 115] 1801.

John Mervyn, of Pertwood, co. Wilts, Esq. Living 1623,=Anne, daur. of John Toppe, of Stockton, co. Wilts, Esq., and sister of John Toppe, of Lincoln's Inn, Esq., who* aged 28. was 26 years old in 1623.

Edward Mervyn, of Sarum, Gent., was 37 years old in 1677,=Frances, daur. and heir of Francis Sheldon, of Manston, in the county of Dorset, Esq., married to Edward Mervyn died before 1691. about 1662. She remarried in 1691, to John Nicholas, Esq., and was living 1716.

Sheldon Mervyn, eldest son, was 11 years old in 1677. Sold the estate at Manston, to Peter Walter, of Stallbridge, Esq., and afterwards resided at Hanley, co. Dorset. Died unmarried 24 Dec. 1734, and was buried at Pertwood. Will dated 3 Dec. 1725, proved 11 March 1734.

Edward Mervyn, 2 son in 1677, died unmarried before 1725.

John Mervyn, of Sturminster Newton Castle, born after 1677; named in the will of his brother Sheldon Mervyn, buried at Manston, 18 May 1733.=Bridget, daur. of .... Darling; buried at Manston, 29 Jan. 1734.

Frances Mervyn, eldest daur; living unmarried 1725; obiit s.p. Will dated 1716.

Mary, married to Richard Pouldon, of Hanley, co. Dorset, Esq., whom she survived. Died 27 March 1747, buried at Pertwood. Will dated 6 Oct. 1744, proved 5 May 1747, s.p.

Ann, marr⁴ Rev. John Tripsack.

Elizabeth, young⁴ daur. living 1735, wife of Paget Walter, only child of Peter Walter, of Stallbridge, co. Dorset, Esq.

One son and 2 daurs.

2 sons.

Edward Mervyn, clerk, only son, some time Fellow Commoner of Baliol College, Oxford; had a living in Somerset, where he married, but died without issue in the lifetime of his father.

Henry Nooth, of Sturminster Newton Castle,=Bridget, eldest daur. and coheir, gent., marr⁴ there 14 April 1735, called named in the will of her aunt Mary "cousin," by Mary Pouldon, 1744; died 1784, Pouldon, 1744; buried at Manston, buried at Dorchester. 4 October 1769.

Frances, 2⁴ daur. and coheir, married John† Prower, of Cranborne, co. Dorset, surgeon, now M.D., 1792. She buried at Cranborne, 1769.

Henry Nooth, 2⁴ son born at Sturminster=Ann Assheton, Newton Castle, 1 June 1741, married at eldest daur. and Fulham, co. Middlesex; now of Spalding- coheir of Mail ton, co. York, Esq.; jure uxoris has taken Yates, Esquire. the surname and Arms of Vavasour, by Royal License, dated 21 March 1791.

James Nooth, bapt.=Elizabeth, daur. of at Sturminster New- ...... Bradley, of ton Castle, 28 Sept. ...... , some time 1744, now living at one of the Barons of Bath. the Cinque Ports. Living 1792.

Edward Nooth, born at Sturminster Newton Castle, 18 May 1747, bapt. 28 Sept. 1758; died at Verdun, in France, unmarried 1767

Mary, baptized at Sturminster Newton Castle, 13 Jan. 1743, married John James of Bristol, merchant, died buried at Bristol.

One Son.

John Mervin Nooth, bapt. at Sturminster Newton Castle, 5 Sept. 1737, now living at Quebec, unmarried, M.D.

Charlotte, born 15 April 1788.

Henry Nooth, born 23 June 1795.

The above Pedigree is true to the best of my knowledge and belief. Witness my hand this 18th day of April 1801, MERVIN NOOTH.
(Signed) J. MERVIN NOOTH.

Signed in the presence of
RALPH BIGLAND, Richmond.

* It is the age of John Toppe, and not of Anne Toppe, that is here recorded. (See Toppe Pedigree, Ms. Coll. Arm. C. 22, p. 58
† Dr. Prower's Christian name is erroneously given in this Pedigree; it was "Robert." See APPENDIX III. pp. III. & VIII.

Abstracts OF Wills.

8 May 1599.
Abstract.
JOHN MERVIN, of Pertwood, in co. Wilts, gent. To be buried at ditto. All my godchildren, 1 shilling. To my brother Philip, my best apparel, and to his sons, Andrew and Will, 20ˢ. To John Adams who has married my said brother's daughter, and their children, 20ˢ· each. To my son George M., 60ˢ· and every of children £2. 13. 4. To my son William M., 10ˢ· To my son Augustine M., 100 sheep. To my son Ambrose M., 100ˢ· and my house at Hindon for life, and after to my son Thomas M. To my wife Mellior M., all my goods, plate, &ᶜ· All the rest to my said son Thomas M., my executor. My brother-in-law Augustine Gouldesborowe and Mr. John Hale, to be overseers. Proved 13 November 1601, by executor. (Regʳ· 82 *Woodall*.)

22 Feb. 1620.
Abstract.
WILLIAM MARVIN, citizen and brewer of London, sick in body, &c. To be buried in Sᵗ Sepulchre's without Newgate. To my daughters Elizabeth Marvin and Susan Marvyn, both under age, each 100 marks, plate, bedding, &ᶜ· and to the former a gilt cup on which is engraved my name and that of Anne my late wife, and if my said daughters die under age, their shares to be divided between my now wife Ellnor, and the children of my brother Andrew Marvyn, and those of my sister Frisittie Adams wife of John Adams. To my said brother Andrewe Marvyn, £5, and wearing apparel, and to his daughter Katherine Marvyn (under age) £5, and to his son William Marvin (under age), £10. To my apprentice John Adams, 40ˢ. To my sister-in-law Elizabeth Brayman, citizen and clothworker of London, 20ˢ· To Edward Newman and his wife, my wife's father and mother, 40ˢ·, and wearing apparel. To Elizabeth Newman my wife's sister, 40s., at age of 21, or marriage. Francis Baylye citizen and innholder of London, the aforesaid Richard Brayman, Thomas Gresham, citizen and Merchant Taylor of London, and William Shawe, citizen and blacksmith of London, overseers. Residue to my wife Ellnor, sole executrix. Proved in London, 13 April 1621, by Eleanor Marvin, the relict. (Regʳ· 32 *Dale*.)

13 Feb. 1632.
Abstract.
THOMAS MERVIN, of Peartwood, in co. Wilts, Esq. To be buried in Peartwood Church. To the cathedral church of Sarum. To poor of Hindon and of East Knoyle. To Friswide, wife of John Addams, of Hindon, 40ˢ· a year for life out of my lands in East Knoyle, called Roskins. To my wife [not mentioning her name]. To my brother William Mervyn, and to Thomas, said William's son, my godson. To my brother Austin. To my brother Ambrose, 400 sheep. To John, the eldest son of my brother George, estate at Chicklad, co. Wilts, for life; remainder to John, eldest son of said John; remainder to Mathew, one other of the sons of said George my brother; remainder to Richard, one other of the sons of said George; remainder to Thomas, one other of the sons of said George; remainder to my right heirs. To Thomas Mervin, son of my brother George, an annuity of £10, conveyed to me by my said brother George by deed dated 5 May, 20 Jac., and if he dies before the expiration of term named, then Nicholas Mervin, who is mentioned in the deed, to have it, and if he dies, then to go to my brother Ambrose Mervin. My brother George, to be sole Executor and Residuary Legatee. My cousin, Mr. Robert Gouldesborough, late of Meer, the elder, and Mr. William Clone, late of Kinston Deverell, to be overseers. Proved in London, 20 May 1633, by George Mervin. (Regʳ 46 *Russell*.)

20 April 1634.
Abstract.
AUGUSTIN MERVIN, of Knoyle, in co. Wilts, gent. To my daughter Mary 300ˢ· To my daughter Virtue 300ˢ· To my daughter Priscilla 300ˢ· To my daughter Ann 300ˢ·, to be paid at 18. My wife Priscilla to be their guardian, and till my elder son come to 21. To be buried at Knoyle, near my eldest son. The rest of my estate to my said wife and son Christopher Mervin, my Executors. My nephews, John and Matthew Mervin, to be Overseers.

Codicil.
My daughter Katherine Mervin 200ˢ· at 18. Proved 17 November 1637. (Regʳ· 154 *Goare*.)

1 Jan. 1651.
Abstract.
WILLIAM MERVIN, of East Knowell, Wilts, clerk and bachelor. Mr. Thomas Mompesson owes me £104, and Mr. John Bennet and Anthony William owe me £52, and my brother-in-law, Robt. Dominicke, £60. To his wife, my sister Lucy Dominicke, £50. Her sons, William, Nicholas and Francis Waldgrave. My sister, Mellyer Gundery; her son William and daughter Jane Gundery. My sister, Mary Grove. My kinswoman, Mrs. Ellen Mompesson, and Robert Dominicke, to be my assigns or trustees. My kinsman Thomas Mompesson, and his brother Henry Mompesson. Mrs. Rachael Mompesson and her sister Constance. Administration granted by P.C.C., 21 January 1656, to Robert Dominicke, one of the trustees named in the will, the other having renounced. (Regʳ· 22 *Ruthen*.)

11 Dec. 1686.
Abstract.
JOHN MERVIN, of London, merchant. My son, James Mervin, £600, and all my goods in the dyeing-room in his house in St. Clement's Lane, London. My sister, Priscilla Bowles. My niece, Jane Mervin. My godson, Ambrose Mervin, £10, to be paid to my nephew, John Mervin, of Founthill, for his use. Residue to my son, Francis Mervin, sole executor.

Codicil.
My niece, Jane Mervin, £100 more. Proved in London, 25 March 1689, by Francis Mervin.
29 Oct. 1688. (Regʳ·, 34 *Ent*.)

MAGDALEN MERVIN, of Founthill Episcopi. To be buried in the church of Chicklade, co. 20 May 1687. Wilts, near my husband. To my son John Mervin, 10 shillings and sundry household goods. To my son Abstract. Nicholas Mervin, £50. To my son Thomas Mervin, £5, and to his now wife Mary Mervin 5s. and to his son Ambrose Mervin, 40s. To my daughter Mellior Turvill, sundry household goods, and after her death to her son Francis Turvill, and £5 in money. To my goddaughter Mellior Turvill, £5. To my son-in-law Francis Turvill, 5s. To my daughter Jane Mervin, £35. The money I designed for my deceased daughter Elizabeth Hibberd, I give to her children as follows; to my grandson John Hibberd, £10; to my granddaughter Jane Hibberd, £10 and sundry household goods. To my son-in-law Wilks Hibberd, 5s. The residue of my goods, chattels, and effects to my two sons John Mervin and Nicholas Mervin, whom I make joint executors of my will.

NICHOLAS MERVIN, of Fonthill Episcopi, Gent. To my brother Thomas Mervin, 10s., and a 4 July 1689. bond from said Thomas due to me of £4. To Ambrose, son of said Thomas, £5. To Mary, wife of said Abstract. Thomas, 5s. To my brother-in-law Francis Turville, 10s. To my sister Mellior Turville, £10. To Francis Turville, son of Francis Turville, £5, and to his sister Mellior Turville, £5. To my sister-in-law Ann Mervin, a box of linnen. To my sister Jane Mervin, £20. To my brother-in-law Wilks Hibberd, 5s., and to John Hibberd his son, £5. To Jane Hibberd sister of said John Hibberd, £5. To my aunt Boles, 10s. a year. To my cozen Elizabeth Boles, 40s. To my goddaughter Mary Parsons, my little bible. All the residue of my goods and chattels unto my brother John Mervin, whom I make sole executor.

FRANCIS MERVIN, of Eltham, Kent, Gent., sick of body, &c. My brother James Mervin, of 25th April London, citizen and draper, sole executor, to whom all property, bonds, mortgages, &c. Proved 16th May 1702. 1702, by James Mervin, executor. Further administration of goods unadministered granted to Elizabeth, Abstract. widow of said James Mervin, the executor. Dated 22nd January 1704.

FRANCES MERVIN, of Manston, in co. Dorset, spinster. To my mother Mrs. Frances Nicholas, 28 June 1716. one shilling. To my brother Mr. John Mervin, one guinea in gold. To my sister Mrs. Mary Pouldon, Abstract. one hundred pounds. To my sister-in-law Mrs. Anne Trepsack, ten pounds. To my sister Mrs. Elizabeth Walter, Tenne pounds. To my nephew Henry Tripsack, and to my niece Jane Walter, each one broad piece of gold. To Mrs. Francis Vivers, one guinea in gold. All the residue of my personal estate to my brother Sheldon Mervin, Esq., whom I appoint sole executor. *Extracted from the Registry of the Archdeacon of Dorset.*

SHELDON MERVIN, of Hanley, co. Dorset, Esq. To be buried at Pertwood with a black 3 Dec. 1725. marble stone, and an inscription of my name, &c., and my coat of arms fairly cut. My brother John Abstract. Mervin; my sister Frances Mervin; my brother-in-law Revd. John Trepsack; my sister Elizabeth Walter, and her husband Paget Walter, Esq.; my sister Mary Pouldon, widow, and her heirs for ever, all right in advowson of church of Manston and lands, &c., in said parish or elsewhere; she to be sole Executrix. Proved by Executrix 11 March 1734. (Regt. 57 Ducie.)

MARY POULDON, of Ringwood, co. Hants, widow, relict and executrix of Richard Pouldon, 6 Oct. 1744. Esq., and devisee and executrix of Sheldon Mervin, Esq., my late brother, deceased. To be buried in church of Pertwood, near my said brother, under a black marble stone, and arms engraved as my brother's Abstract. is. To my niece Bridget Nooth 4s. To my niece Frances Mervin 5s. To my nephew Henry Trepsack 4s. To my niece Elizabeth Tripsack 4s. To my niece Ann Tripsack 4s. To worthy friends, Thomas Freke of Wyke, co. Dorset, Esq., Henry Windham of New Sarum, Esq., and James Willis of Ringwood, gent., advowson of Manston, co. Dorset, and all lands in said parish, in trust that if my cousin Henry Nooth think fit to educate one of his sons, and such son become capable, to present him thereto, and convey to him said lands. All residue to said Trustees, for my niece Jane Coles, now wife of William Coles, Esq.; but not to use of any husband of hers. Proved 5 May 1747, by James Willis, one of the Executors. (Regt. 133 Potter.)

ROBERT PROWER, of Cranborne, co. Dorset, M.D To my son John Prower, leasehold 31 Aug. 1792. estate at Bishop's-Caundle, co. Dorset. To my daughter Fanny, wife of the Rev. Mr. Rigby, leasehold Abstract. estate at Okeford-Fitzpaine, co. Dorset, for life, remainder to my granddaughter Harriet Rigby. To John Mervin James, son of John James, of Bristol, Wine Merchant. Residue to my two daughters, Fanny Rigby and Biddy, the wife of the Rev. Mr. Storey. All and every child and children of my said daughter Fanny.

Abstract of Inquisition Post Mortem.

43 Elizabeth, 1st part, No. 115.

By **Inquisition** taken at Westbury com. Wilts, 2nd September, 43 Elizabeth (1601), after the death of JOHN MERVYN, Gent. It was found that he died seized in his demesne as of fee of the Manor of Pertwood, and of messuages and lands in Chicklade, Hyndon, Fontel Episcopi, Fountel Gifford, Stopp, and Knoyle Episcopi, com. Wilts. It was also found that said John Mervyn died on 24th June 1601, and that Thomas Mervyn, Gent, then of the age of 34 years and above, was his son and next heir.

Extracts from Parochial Registers.

EAST KNOYLE.

(CERTIFIED BY THE REV. R. N. MILFORD, THE RECTOR, 7TH JANUARY 1873, AND COLLATED BY ME, WITH THE ORIGINAL ENTRIES, 6TH AUGUST 1873.)

Baptisms.

" A.D. 1587. El. R. 29ᵐᵃ
" Henry, sonne of Mr. John Mervine, bapt. Aug. 13th.
" A.D. 1588. E. R. 30ᵃ
" William Marvine, bapt. Novemb. 2ᵃ
" A.D. 1589. E. R. 31ᵃ
" John, sonn of Mr. John Merven, bapt. May 8th.
" A.D. 1592. E. R. 34ᵗʰ
" Mary Marven, daughter of Mr. John Marven, Ap. 2nd.
" A.D. 1593. E. R. 35ᵗʰ
" Luce Marvine, daughter of Mr. John Marvine, bapt. March 10ᵗʰ
" A D. 1594. E. R. 36ᵃ
" Edmond, sonne of John Mervine, Feb. 5th.
" A.D. 1595. E. R. 37ᵗʰ
" John, sonne of Mr. George Marvine, bapt. Aug. 3rd.
" John, sonne of Mr. Edmond Mervine, Nov. 30th.
" A.D. 1596. E. R. 38.
" John, sonne of Edmond Mervine, bapt. Feb. 7th.
" A.D. 1597. E. R. 39.
" Robert, sonne of George Marvine, May 22nd.
" Edward, sonne of Mr. Edmond Marvine, Feb. 28th.
" A.D. 1598. E. R. 40.
" George, sonne of Mr. George Marvine, May 28th.
" Thomas, sonne of John Marvine, bapt. July 28th.
" A.D. 1600. E. R. 42.
" Richard, sonne of Geo. Mervine, gent., Dec. 18th.
" A.D. 1601.
" Mary, daughter of Geo. Mervine, Feb. 12th.
" A.D. 1603. E. R.
" Elizabeth, daughter of Jo. Marvine, bapt. June 10th.
" A.D. 1605. Jacobi 3ᵃ
" Margaret, daughter of Mr. Geo. Marvine, May 16th.
" A.D. 1621.
" Vertuc, daughter of Augustine Marvine, July 22nd.
" A.D. 1623.
" Margaret, daughter of John Marvine, bapt. April 31st.
" Priscilla Mervine, daughter of Austine Mervine, May 17th.
" A.D. 1624. Jaco. 22ᵃ
" John, sonne of John Mervine, bapt. Ap. 20th.
" Ann, daughter of Austine Mervine, gent., March 1st.
" A.D. 1625. Caroli. 1ᵐᵒ
" Mary, daughter of Jo. Mervine, gent., Ap. 25th.
" A.D. 1626.
" Christopher, sonne of Mr. Augustine Marvine, Sept. 26th.
" A.D. 1629.
" Elizabeth, daughter of John Marvine, Nov. 29th.
" A.D. 1631.
" Katherine, daughter of Augustine Marven, Oct. 8th.

Marriages.

"A.D. 1561. John Marvine and Melior Goldisbrough, Sept. 14th.
"A.D. 1605. Wm. Brethers and Ann Marvine, Dec. 16th.
"A.D. 1610. Leonard Snooke and Mary Marvine, April 16th.
"A.D. 1628. Ffrancis Toope and Dorothie Marvin, June 5th.

Burials.

"1580. Richard, son of John Marven, Sept. 19th.
"1597. Edmund, sonne of Mr. Jo. Mervine, July 7th.
"1599. Robt. Mervine, an infant, June 1st.
"1601. Mary, daughter of George Mervine. March 18th.
"1604. Herbstone, sonne of Edmund Mervine, gent., Dec. 10th
"1617. Augustine, son of Mr. Augustine Marvine, Dec. 11th.
"1624. Elizabeth, wife of Mr. George Mervine, Nov. 30th.

KINGSTONE DEVERILL.

Baptisms.

"Lambert Mervin, son of John and Eleanor Marvin, July 24th 1725.
"John, son of John and Eleanor Marvin, July 2nd 1726.
"Mary, daughter of John and Eleanor Marvin, March 6th 1728-9
"William Marvin, May 2nd 1731.
"Jane, daughter of John Marvin and Eleanor his wife, Septr. 1732.

Burials.

"1805. May 20th, John Mervin, aged 78.

St. MARTIN'S, SALISBURY.

Christenings.

"1667. December 26th, John, son of Mr. Edward and
            Mrs. Frances Mervyn.
"1679. May 4th, John, son of Edward and Frances Mervyn.
"1680. December 11th, Eliz., daughter of Edward and
            Frances Mervyn.

Additional Note.

Since the foregoing pages were in print I have found the will of JOAN, the wife of William FLETCHER, and the daughter and heir of John Brether of Pertwood (Vide text, pp. 39 and 41), which corroborates the marriage of MARGARET FLETCHER with WILLIAM MERVYN, but shows that Margaret had a sister AGNES, the wife of John DOWSE. The following is an Abstract of the Will, which is dated 1505, and was proved at Lambeth, 1 March 1506, by John Dowse the Testatrix's son-in-law :—

JOHANE FLEYCHURRE, of Hyndon. To be buried in the chapel of Hyndon, in the parish of   1505.
Est Knoyll. To the mother church of Sarum, my wedding ring & 12^d. To the parish church of Est Abstract.
Knoyll, 12^d. To the chapel of Hyndon, 3^s. 4^d. To each of my godchildren, "an ewen shipp." "I bequeth Will of
to Isabell the dought' of William Mervyn, my son-in-lawe, a hayforde [heifer] of xii months age." To Agnes Joan Fletcher.
Dowse, daughter of John Dowse, "a kow." "I bequith vnto William Mervyn, my son-in-law, and to
Margarete his wif, my dought', a C hede weders [wethers], as they reune owte of the lete and two keen
[kine] the which they haue in their possession." To Robert Stone an ewe and a lamb. To Cristian Longley
an ewe and a lamb. My son-in-law John Dowse and Agnes his wife, my daughter, executors. Witnesses
S^r. John White, par. priest; S^r. W^m. Wade, Chaplain of Hyndon; Tho. Ffrythe; Ric. Payne; Hen. Payne;
John Pynfolde; W^m. Ffletcher & other more. Proved at Lambeth, 1 March 1506, by John Dowse. (*Prerog.
C. Cant. Regr. 20 Adeane.*)

Monumental Inscriptions.

On a gravestone in the North Choir Aisle of EXETER CATHEDRAL is the following inscription :—

EXETER
CATHEDRAL.

Translation.

RICHARDVS MERVIN S.T.P.
E. Pertwood Wilton Antiquo et Generoso stemate ortus.
Cancel : et Canon Resident : huius B. P. Exon :

Here lieth the body of RICHARD MERVIN, S.T.P., of Pertwood, Wilts : descended from an antient and respectable family. Chancellor and Canon Residentiary of St. Peter's, Exeter.

Richard Mervin, D.D., 1669.

Reverendus ut Pater, Humilis ut Filius Eccliæ
Bona et mala temporum perpessus immotus
In omnibus, Deo, Ecclie, regi, sibi constans.

As a father of the Church, revered; as a son, obedient :
During the troubles of the times he was inflexible,
And to his God, his King, his Church, and to himself, steady.

Vir suavissimi, simul et acerrimi ingenii
Libris hand parum, etiam et rebus versatissimus
Sui parcus, in suos largissimus.

His disposition was gentle, and his genius quick,
His knowledge in books, great ; of mankind, extensive :
Parsimonious to himself, to his friends beneficent.

Vixit (Lector) ut tu debes, Piè, justè.
Expiravit ut tu velis, lentè, suaviter.
Suscitandus ut Deus vult, (et nos credimus) Gloriosè.

He lived, (O Reader) as thou oughtest,—religiously and justly ;
He died, as thou would'st, gradually, and with pleasure,
To rise, at the voice of God, (as we hope) with Glory.

Dehinc migravit Oct : 17° An: Dom: 1669;
ætat 69.

He departed hence Oct.r 17th. 1669 ;
aged 69.

On a gravestone in the Chancel of the Church of HEANTON PUNCHARDON, co. Devon :—

HEANTON
PUNCHARDON.

Depositvm VRSVLÆ MERVIN
Fæminæ Lectissimæ
(Vidvæ D.D. Richardi Mervin
Hvjvs Ecclesiæ Rectoris
Nec non Cathedralis Exon
Cancellarii longe Dignissimi)
Sed Virtutes (Quas svmme colvit
Temperantiam Modestiam Urbanitatem
Eleemo»ynas preces Divtinas
Pietatem
Nvilvs capiat Tvmvlvs
Obiit 24° die Octobris
Anno Dom: 1687—ætat 74.

Ursula Mervin,
Widow, 1687.

Juxta sitvs est RICHARDVS MERVIN
Filivs Richardi et Vrsvlæ Mervin
Predict natv minimus in spem
Beatæ Resvrrectionis obiit 20 Apr.
1689.,
Svb Anno. ætatis svæ 37.

Richard Mervin,
1689.

On the stone the following arms are cut, viz. :—[Argent] A demy lyon rampt. [Sable] charged on the shoulder with a fleur de lis, [or] for MERVIN, impaling . . . . . . on a chevron, 3 molets. . . . . . . for TRUST.

APPENDIX IV.

On a second gravestone in the Chancel of the same Church:—

M.S.
GULIELMI MERVIN. A.M.
Aulæ Pembroch: olim socii
Hujus Ecclesiæ deinde Rectoris
per annos. 49
obiit Nov: 2, 1719.
ætatis 77
accubat marito uxor pientissima
CHRISTIANA
Viri vere Reverendi Richardi Newte
de Tiverton, Filia
obiit Aug. 27. 1695.
ætat 46.

The following are the arms engraved on the stone:—[Argent] A demy lyon rampant [Sable] charged on the shoulder with a mullett, for MERVIN, impaling Gules a chevron between 3 hearts argent, pierced by daggers in bend sinister ppr. pomel and hilt or, for NEWTE.—Crest: On a wreath a squirrel sejant.

On a further gravestone in the Chancel of the same church:—

" Hic jacet
SARA, Gulielmi et Christianæ Mervin
Filia natu maxima
Georgii BLAKE de Alwington Rectoris
Conjux Fidelessimæ ;
Obiit May 27. 1722
ætat 45.

The arms on the foregoing gravestone are:—

BLAKE, ... a fess indented . . . . In chief a bow and in base 3 arrows . . . .
Impaling, Argent a demy lyon rampant sable, charged on the shoulder with a mullett, for MERVIN. Crest: A dexter hand, couped at the wrist, grasping a bow.

In the churchyard of Heanton, on a plain flat stone monument encircled by iron rails, are recorded the deaths of,

" WILLIAM MERVIN, A.M., Rector of this Parish, ob: 20 July 1744, aged 67."
" LÆTITIA, his wife, daughter of Dr. Thomas Bouchier, Professor of Law, and Principal of St. Alban Hall, Oxford, ob: 13th May 1730, aged 43."
" THOMAS MERVIN, their son, ob: 1 June 1742, æt: 19."
" CHRISTIAN MERVIN, sister of the above William, and daughter of the Revd William Mervin, sometime Rector of this Parish, ob: 17th August 1748, aged 65."

On the above stone the following arms are engraved:—

MERVIN as above, impaling , ... a chev: . . . . . . between 3 [dogs?] collared, for BOUCHIER.

On a tablet in MARWOOD Church, co. Devon:—

" Here lyeth MARGARET, Wife of Richard MERVIN, Esq., eldest daughter of Robert Burridge, of Tiverton, Merchant—A woman of excellent virtues—she died the 18th of June, 1723, in the 42 year of her age, leaving behind with her husband 5 children, viz., Margaret, Elizabeth, John, Christian, and Samuel."
" In the same Grave lie the remains of JOHN MERVIN, Esq., her eldest son. He died June the 21st 1750, aged 35."

"Here lieth
The body of RICHARD MERVIN, of Marwood Hill, Esq., who died Nov. 15th 1740, in ye 68th year
of his age.
Near this lieth also
The body of SAMUEL MERVIN, Gent., his youngest son, who died January 8th 1743, aged 24."

In the Churchyard :—
"[John Mer]vin, Esq., dyed June 27th , 175[0], aged 35."

"In memory of CHARLES CUTCLIFFE DRAKE, Esq., of Springfield, in this county, who died
18th Oct. 1858, aged 50 years.

"Also of
JOHN ROTHWELL DRAKE, his second son, who died 19th March 1859, aged 16 years."

"Also of
FRANCES DRAKE, mother of the above-named Charles Cutcliffe Drake, widow of Zachary Hammett
Drake, Esq., and daughter of Charles Newell Cutcliffe, Esq., late of Marwood Hill, in this parish. She
died 5th April 1867, aged 86 years."

"Also of
MARY DRAKE, widow of the above-named Charles Cutcliffe Drake. She died 21st Feb. 1870, aged
61 years."

"Here rest the mortal remains of ANNE CUTCLIFFE, second daughter of Charles Newell Cutcliffe,
Esq., and Margaret his wife, late of Marwood Hill, in this parish, who died 2nd May 1859, aged 77 years."

"In memory also of EMMA CUTCLIFFE, fifth and youngest daughter of the above-named Charles
Newell and Margaret Cutcliffe. She died 14th March, 1865, aged 76 years."

"Also in memory of HARRIET ELIZABETH CUTCLIFFE, fourth and last surviving daughter of the
above-named Charles Newell and Margaret Cutcliffe. She died 12th April 1867, aged 80 years."

In the Chapel at LEE, in the parish of Ilfracombe, an edifice erected at his
instance and through his exertions, the following Inscriptions note the death of Zachary
Hammett Drake and of his second son :—

"To the memory of ZACHARY HAMMETT DRAKE, of Springfield, in the parish of Heanton
Punchardon, and of Lee in this parish, Esquire, who put off this mortal for immortality on the 11th day of
March 1847, aged 69. In dutiful affection, this monument is erected by his younger son Charles Cutcliffe,
with the fervent prayer that he may himself emulate the virtues, and follow the bright example, of a
fondly-loved and deeply-lamented father."
"In memory of CHARLES CUTCLIFFE DRAKE, Esqre., the younger son of the late Zachary Hammett
Drake, Esqre., and Frances his wife, daughter of the late Charles Newell Cutcliffe, Esq. He died 18th
October 1858, aged 50."

On a Tablet Monument in the Chancel of the Church at ASHFORD :—

"Sacred to the memory of FRANCES MERVIN GRAHAM, the fondly beloved wife of Captain John
Graham, 55th Regt. B. N. I., and daughter of Z. H. Drake, of Springfield, in the parish of Heanton
Punchardon, Esq., who quitted this transitory life on the 19th of October 1845, at Dacca, in the East
Indies, aged 39 years, beloved and deeply regretted by all who knew her worth. As a tribute of his faithful
and sorrowing affection, this monument is erected by her bereaved and afflicted husband.

It matters little at what hour o' the day
The righteous fall asleep, Death cannot come
To him untimely who is fit to die ;
The less of this cold world, the more of Heaven;
The briefer life—the earlier immortality."

MILLMAN.

MARWOOD— *Continued.*	
Richard Mervin, 1740.	
Samuel Mervin, 1743.	
John Mervin, 1759.	
Charles Cutcliffe Drake, 1858.	
John Rothwell Drake, 1859.	
Frances Drake, 1867.	
Mary Drake, 1870.	
Anne Cutcliffe, 1859.	
Emma Cutcliffe, 1865.	
Harriet Elizabeth Cutcliffe, 1867.	
LEE, ILFRACOMBE.	
Zachary Hammett Drake, 1847.	
Charles Cutcliffe Drake, 1858.	
ASHFORD	
Frances Mervin Graham, 1845.	

ATHERINGTON.

Rev. William Mervin,
1759.

On a gravestone in the Chancel of ATHERINGTON Church, co. Devon :—

M. S.
Reverendi Gulielmi Mervin
Collegii Exonien olim socii
S. T. B.
Tam Clare Portionis in Tiverton
Quam hujus œ Ecclesiæ
Rectoris
Dorotheam Rev⁴ˡ Gawen Hayman
de Southpool
Filiam duxit
Obiit Decem. 17° die A.D. 1759.
æt: 77.

Extracts FROM Parochial Registers.

HEANTON PUNCHARDON, co. Devon :—

Baptisms—

" Birthes 1672. Richard, the son of William Meruin, Rector of this p'ish, & Cristian, his wife, was baptyzed the 11th day of February."

" Date 1676 { he sone of Mr. William Merven."
{ is parish was baptized June 6th."

" 1677. Sarah, daughter of Mr. William Mervin, Rector of this parish, and Christian, his wife, baptized 16th."

" 1723. Thomas, Sⁿ of William and Lætitia Mervin, christened, Nov: 10th 1723."

" 1729. William, son of Jeremiah and Jane Langdon (Mervin) baptized Feb. 22nd."

" 1753. Thomas Mervin, son of the Revd. Mr. John Marshall and Lætitia his wife, christened August 6th."

" 1754. Lætitia, dau. of the Rev. Mr. J. Marshall and Lætitia his wife, christened June 27th."

" 1755. John William, son of the Rev. Mr. John Marshall and Lætitia his wife, christened July 5th, buried July 9th."

" 1756. William, son of the Rev. Mr. John Marshall and Lætitia his wife, born August the fourth, christened August 15th."

" 1758. Frances, dau. of the Rev. Mr. Marshall and Lætitia his wife, christened Nov. 13th."

" 1759. Elizabeth, dau. of the Rev. Mr. Marshall and Lætitia his wife, christened Nov. 26th."

" 1761. Sarah Amy, dau. of the Rev. Mr. Marshall and Lætitia his wife, christened Oct. 10th."

" 1832. Sept. 9th. John Mervin Cutcliffe, son of Zachary Hammett Drake and Eleanor Penrose Drake."

" 1833. Nov. 10th. John Mervin Cutcliffe, son of Zachary Hammett Drake and Eleanor Penrose Drake."

" 1835. July 3rd. Margaret Mary, daughter of Zachary Hammett Drake and Eleanor Penrose Drake."

" 1842. Sept. 12th. John Rothwell, son of Charles Cutcliffe Drake and Mary Drake."

Marriages—

" 1724. Mr. James Gay and Mrs. Elizabeth Mervin, married Feb: 18th."

" The Rev⁴ Mr. Nich: Gay and Mrs. Margaret Mervin, married Jan: 26th, 1742."

" 1838, July 3rd. John Graham, of full age, bachelor, Lieutenant H.E.I.C.S., Pilton, son of Charles Graham, a Captain H.E.I.C.S., married to Frances Mervin Drake, of full age, spinster, of Heanton Punchardon, daughter of Zachary Hammett Drake, Esquire."

Burials—

" 1687. Burials. Mⁿˢ Ursula Mervin, Octᵇ 25th."

" 1689. Mr. Richard Mervin, Aprill 22nd."

" 1693. Mr. Jonas Meruin, Dec. 3rd."

" 1695. Mⁿˢ Christian Mervin, dyed Aug. 27th, and buryed Augᵗ 30th."

" 1719. Reᵛd. Mr. William Mervin, Rector, buryed Nov. 6, 1719."

" Mr. John Mervin, buried 21st May, 1729."

" Mrs. Letitia Mervin, buried May 16th, 1730."
" Mr. Thomas Mervin, buried June 3rd, 1742."
" Mrs. Jane Mervin, buried Oct. 5th, 1742."
" 1744. Revd. Mr. William Mervin, Rector, buried July 22nd."
" 1747. Mary, the wife of the Revd. Mr. Marshall, July 8th."
" 1748. Mrs. Christian Mervin, buried Augt 20th."
" 1765. Mrs. Elizabeth Gay, buried May 4th."
" 1783. Lætitia Marshall, buried Feb. 22nd." .

MARWOOD:—

Baptisms—

"Margaret, the daughter of Richard Mervin, Esq., was born the 8th day of Feb., and baptised 18th, 1711."
" Elizabeth, the daughter of Richard Mervin, Esq., was born the 15th day of March, 1712, and baptized April 8th, 1713."
" John, ye son of Richard Mervin, Esq., was born January 14th, and baptized Feb. 4th, 1714."
" Christian, daur. of Richd Mervin, Esq., was born February 16th, and baptized 27th, 1715."
" Richard & Samuel, sons of Richd Mervin, Esq., were born and baptized Sept. 21st, 1717."
" Samuel, son of Richd Mervin, Esq., was born & baptized Oct. 7th, 1719."
" Dorothy, daughter of John Mervin, Esq., was born and baptized July 1st, 1742."
" Margaret, daughter of Mrs. Dorothy Mervin (relict of Mr. John Mervin, lately deceased), was born and baptized Sept. 6th, 1750."

Burials—

" Richard and Samuel, sons of Richard Mervin, Esq., were buried Sept. 22nd, 1717."
" Margaret, wife of Richard Mervin, Esq., was buried June 19th, 1722."
" Richard Mervin, Esq., was buried Nov. 19th, 1740."
" Mr. Samuel Mervin was buried Jan. 11th, 1743."
" John Mervin, Gent., was buried June 24th, 1750."
" Margaret Cutcliffe, buried May 1st, 1792."
" Mary Cutcliffe, of Ilfracombe, June 21st, 1831, aged 47."
" Dorothy Mervyn, of Ashford, May 16th, 1835, aged 93."
" Zachary Hammett Drake, of Heanton Punchardon, March 17th, 1847, aged 69."
" Charles Cutcliffe Drake, of Heanton Punchardon, buried at Marwood Oct. 23rd, 1858, aged 50."
" John Rothwell Drake, son of the above, March 24th, 1859, aged 16."
" Ann Cutcliffe, of Ashford, buried at Marwood May 7th, 1859, aged 78."
" Emma Cutcliffe, Ilfracombe, buried at Marwood March 20th, 1865, aged 78."
" Frances Drake, Ashford, buried at Marwood April 11th, 1867, aged 86."
" Harriet Elizabeth Cutcliffe, buried at Marwood April 17th, 1867, aged 82."
" Mary Drake, Pilton, buried at Marwood Feb. 24th, 1870, aged 63."

ASHFORD:—

Baptisms—

" 1837. March 27th. Dorothy Mervin, daughter of Charles Cutcliffe Drake and Mary Drake."
" 1839. January 14th. Anne Frances, daughter of Charles Cutcliffe Drake and Mary Drake."
" 1840. July 7th. Charles Henry, son of Charles Cutcliffe Drake and Mary Drake."

Burial—

" 1869. Dorothy Mervin Landon, Ashford, April 5th, [age] 32."

BARNSTAPLE :—

Baptisms—

" 1709. William, s. of Mr. Rd Mervin and Mt his wife, 18th day January."
" 1710. Richard, s. of Mr. Rd Mervin, Minister, and Margritt his wife, bapt 28th day Aprill."
" 1716. Mary, d. of Mr. Richard Mervin and Margaret his wife, bapt 1st day of November."
" 1735. July 3. John, son of Mr. Charles and Mary Marshall."
" 1737. March 30. Dorothy, daughter of Mr. Charles and Mary Marshall."
" 1739. June 17. Margaret, daughter of Mr. Charles and Mary Marshall."
" 1741. August 6. Charles, son of Mr. Charles Marshall and Mary his wife."
" 1783. May 5. Letitia, d. of Revd Mr. Thos. Marshall by Sarah his wife."
" 1784. January 21. Sarah, daug..te: of Mr. Charles Marshall by Sarah his wife."

Burials—
"1710. November 10. William, son of Richard Mervin, Esq."
"1732. November 12. Rich⁴. s. of ye Rev⁴. Mr. Mervin, Vicar of Buckland Brewer."
"1735. October 19. John, son of Mr. Charles Marshall."
"1741. April 1. Mr. Richard Mervin, Clerk.

BRAUNTON :—

Baptisms—
"John, son of John Mervin, gent., and Jane, was born July 1st, baptized July 1st, 1691."
"Ursula, daughter of John Mervin and Jane, was born May 16th, and baptized May 26th, 1695."
"Jane, daughter of John Mervin, yeoman, was born October 18th, and baptized November 7th, 1699."

Marriages—
"Chichester Incledon and Mrs. Christian Mervin, married November 7th, 1741."
"1868. October 6th. Charles Henry Drake Cutcliffe, bachelor, of Ilfracombe, son of Charles C. Drake, Esquire, was married to Henrietta Maria Landon, spinster, of Braunton, daughter of John W. R. Landon, clergyman."

Burial—
"Mr. Jonas Mervin, dyed December 1st, and was buryed at Heanton, December 3rd, 1693."

KENTON :—

Marriage—
"Charles Newell Cutcliffe, gent., of the Parish of Barnstaple, and Margaret Mervin, spinster, of this Parish, were married in this Church by License, this twenty-first day of November, in the year One thousand seven hundred and seventy-six, by me, John Wright, Curate. In the presence of John Bond, Sarah Sydenham."

LEE (Ilfracombe Parish):—

Baptism—
"1869. 5th August. Charles Bernard Mervyn, son of Charles Henry Drake Cutcliffe and Henrietta Maria Drake Cutcliffe."

MORWENSTOW (co. Cornwall):—

Baptisms—
"1805. February the 15th. Zachary Hammett, son of Zachary Hammett and Frances Drake."
"1806. Sept. 29. Frances Mervin, daughter of Zachary Hammett and Frances Drake."

PILTON :—

Baptisms—
"1780. Frances, daughter of Mr. Charles Newell Cutcliffe and Mrs. Margaret his wife, June 6."
"1781. Ann, daughter of Mr. Charles Newell Cutcliffe and Mrs. Margaret his wife, November 4th.
"1808. Charles Cutcliffe, son of Zachary Hammett Drake, Esq., and Frances his wife, September 29th."

Marriage—
"1862. 30th April. Charles Whittington Landon, Bachelor, and Dorothy Mervin Drake, Spinster, by J. W. R. Landon, Off⁸· Min⁸·"

TIVERTON :—

Marriage—
"1707. May 16th. Richard Mervin, Esq., and Mrs. Margaret Burridge."

WESTLEIGH :—

Baptism—
"1746. Feby. ye 25th. Charles Newell, son of Mr. Charles Cutcliffe and Elizabeth his wife."

Burials—
"1813. Charles Newell Cutcliffe, Esq., Marwood Hill, Dec. 22, aged 67."
"1822. John Mervin Cutcliffe, Esq., Webbery House, Alverdiscott, July 16, aged 43."

Abstracts OF Wills.

RICHARD MERVIN, "Professor in Divinity and Chancellor of the Cathedral Church of "St. Peter's in Exeter." He gave to the poor people of the Close of St. Peter's in Exeter £5; to the poor of the parish of Bratton Clovelly £5, and to the poor of the parish of Heanton Punchardon, where he then was Rector, £5. He gave unto his dear wife (*not naming her*) "in lewe of a joynture which was at "first settled in writing and committed to the custody of her father, he being dead many yeares since, and "y⁴ writing not to be found," his Mansion house, gardens, and orchards in Upton and East Knoyle, in Wiltshire, and an annuity for life of £40 a year out of his Barton and Manor there; "wch I purchased of "my eldest bro^r John Mervin of Peartwood, Esqre and was the place of my birth." He also gave to his wife an annuity of £40 out of his "sheaffe and gleebe lands of Stoake Gabrill." To his son, Barnard Mervin, he gave a pecuniary legacy. He bequeathed to his two sons, William and Jonas, the "sheafe of "Stoake Gabrill," in trust to be divided between them, chargeable with the payment of the annuity to their mother. And he provided that if either of his said sons, William and Jonas, or both of them, should happen to die before marriage, then that his sons, John and Richard, should have the part of him or them so dying. He bequeathed to his said sons, William and Jonas, an annuity issuing out of his tenement called "Blackgrave" and Kittleknowle. He bequeathed to Richard Mervin his son his messuage, land, and tenement situate in the parish of Bratton Clovelly, in the county of Devon, commonly called Black-grave; and also his tenement in Curriton, known by the name of Kittleknowle, chargeable with the said yearly annuity to William and Jonas as aforesaid, to hold the said two tenements to Richard Mervin and his heirs, with power to grant the same for the term of the life of such woman as should be his last wife charge-able as aforesaid; and in default of issue, then the two tenements to go unto all his sons that should be then living after the death of his said son Richard Mervin and such woman as should be his last wife, and to their heirs and assigns for ever. He bequeathed to his said son Richard Mervin his tenement in Bratton, commonly called Isaack's tenement, with the appurtenances. He bequeathed to his son John Mervin his Barton and Manor of Upton in East Knoyle aforesaid, to hold to his said son John Mervin and the heirs of his body, chargeable with a yearly rentcharge of three score pounds (as by a conveyance made by him unto his cousin William Hayter upon the marriage of his (Testator's) eldest son George Mervin), and the before-mentioned annuity to his wife; and for default of issue of John Mervin, then Testator gave the same to Barnard Mervin his son after the decease of his (Testator's) wife, chargeable with payment of aforesaid £60 a-year, and subject to his (Barnard's) paying to his three younger brothers £50 apiece; and in default of issue of Barnard, Testator gave and bequeathed said Barton and Manor to his son William Mervin and to the heirs of his body, chargeable as aforesaid, he paying to his two younger brothers £50 apiece; and for default of issue Testator bequeathed same to Jonas Mervin his son and to his heirs, chargeable as aforesaid, he paying to his younger brother Richard Mervin £50; and for default of issue of Jonas Mervin, then to Testator's son Richard Mervin, his heirs and assigns for ever, chargeable as aforesaid; and in case his son Richard should die unmarried, then that his son John Mervin should have Isaack's tenement. And Testator declared his will and mind to be that none of his youngest sons should have their estates until they should attain the age of 23 years, unless their mother should happen to die in the meanwhile; but that their mother should have the disposition of the profits thereof until they should accomplish the said age of 23 years. All the rest of his goods and chattels, subject to the payment of debts, legacies, and funeral expenses, he left to his wife and son William, to be bestowed upon his children according to the discretion of his wife, "as she shall see them dutiful unto her and thinks have been most dutiful unto me." The Testator appointed his wife and son William executors, and that all might be done with the less trouble to his wife and son, he humbly desired his "good relations and ffreinds, my brother Richard Trist, M^r. Oliver Naylor, "Lewes Stevings, and my cossin M^r. Thomas Cox, that they will be my Executors in trust to that purpose, "and in confidence of my dependance vppon them and the affections they haue for mee, my will is that they "shall haue from my executors aforesaid £5 apiece to buy them rings, as the best testimony of my dearest "respects I haue ever from them."—Proved in the Prerogative Court of Canterbury by Ursula Mervin, his widow, and William Mervin, his son, on 29th November, 1670.

10 Sept. 1668.
Abstract.

BERNARD MERVIN, Merchant, resident in the city of Lix. in Portugal. Poor of Bratton £5. Poor of St. Peter's in Exon £5. My mother Ursilla Mervin. My brothers William, John, Jonas, and Richard Mervin. My uncle Richard Trist's five children, viz., Elizabeth, William, Sarah, Elinor, and Mary Trist. Ursilla Mervin, daughter of my brother George Mervin. My cousins, Margaret Bearnes of Mere, and her sisters. My said mother to be Executrix. Proved in London 25 Feb. 1681, by Ursilla Mervin the executrix. (*Regr.* 21 *Cottle.*)

1 January 1675.
Abstract.

GEORGE MERVIN, of East Noyl, in ye county of Wilts, gent. My estate and perpetuall annuity of Sixty pounds p' ann., lying & being in East Noyl, I doe give unto my loving daughter Ursilah Mervin of Devonshire, and to her issue for ever. To my brother John Mervin. To Dorothy Haytor, daughter of George Haytor, Rector of Chagford. Ten pounds per annum to the poor of Branton in Devon. Ten pounds per annum to Katherine's Almshouse in Exon, to enjoy it for ever. Administration granted 22 June, 1680, to Anne Hayter, widow, guardian of Ursula Mervin, a minor, daughter and sole issue of Testator, during minority of said Ursula.

URSULA MERVIN, of Heanton Punchardon, co. Devon, widow. To the poor of each of the parishes of Heanton Punchardon and Bratton Clovelly. My sons William Mervin and Jonas Mervin, Clerks. My son William Mervin, Rector of Heanton Punchardon. My son William to be guardian of my son Richard; in case of the death of said William, my sons Jonas and John shall succeed him in that office. The children of said William and Jonas. To each of my grandchildren [not naming them]. Residue between my four sons before named. My sons William and Jonas and Lewis Stevings Executors. Proved in London 10 March, 1688.

ROBERT BURRIDGE, of Tiverton, co. Devon, Esquire. To my sons-in-law Richard Mervin and Richard Evans. To my brother-in-law Robert Smith and my kinsman Robert Dunsford. To my sister Alice James. To my daughter Martha Burridge. To my cozen Elizabeth Dyer. To my daughter Margaret. To my daughters Mary, Thomazine, Elizabeth and Frances. To my son William Burridge. To said Richard Mervin and Margaret his wife, my daughter. To said Richard Evans and Mary his wife, my daughter. To my son Samuell Burridge, sole executor.

RICHARD MERVIN, of Marwood, in the county of Devon, Esquire. I give unto each of my three daughters [not naming them]. I give unto John Pine, Esquire, and my dear brother William Mervin of Heanton. In trust for my son Samuel. In trust for my son John. Residue to John Mervin my son, whom I ordain sole executor. To be buried nigh my late wife. Proved in the Consistory Court of the Bishop of Exeter 27th January, 1740–1, by John Mervin, the son and sole executor.

JOHN MERVIN, of the parish of Marwood in Devon, A.M. If a son shall be born by my wife within six months (she being quick), ye marriage settlement will show his right, without the trouble of transcribing it. My daughter Dorothy.
Letters of Administration with the above Will annexed were granted by the Bishop's Consistory Court at Exeter, to Dorothy Mervin the widow, 11 August 1750.

CHARLES NEWELL CUTCLIFFE of Marwood Hill, co. Devon, Esquire. I devise unto kinsman John Dene, Clerk, and nephew Charles Cutcliffe, my messuages and hereditaments in parishes of Alverdiscott, Westleigh, Bishops Tawton, and Comb Martin, co. Devon. Upon trust to raise sums for my daughters Anne, Mary, Harriett Elizabeth, and Emma, and to pay debts. Subject thereto upon trust for son John Mervin Cutcliffe, his heirs and assigns for ever. I give to my daughter Drake. John Mervin Cutcliffe, Residuary Legatee. Proved by John Mervin Cutcliffe, Esquire, son and sole executor, P.C.C., 8 June 1814.

JOHN MERVIN CUTCLIFFE, of Webbery, in the parish of Alverdiscott, in the county of Devon. To my beloved wife; my relation and friend John Lord Rolle. My dear wife Residuary Legatee and sole Executrix. Proved in London 28 November 1822, by Charlotte Cutcliffe the widow and sole Executrix.

ZACHARY HAMMETT DRAKE, of Springfield, within the parish of Heanton Punchardon, co. Devon, Esquire. To my dear wife Frances Drake, and my brother Henry Drake. Lands and tenements in Moorwinstow, Heanton Punchardon, and Marwood to my friend John Marshall of Barnstaple, and my said brother Henry Drake, upon trust, &c. To my son Zachary Hammett Drake. To Ellen Penrose Drake the present wife of my said son Zachary Hammett Drake. To my grandson John Mervin Cutcliffe Drake the eldest son of my said son Zachary Hammett Drake. To my son Charles Cutcliffe Drake. To my daughter Frances Mervin Drake. The manors of Warcombe and Lyncombe, and other the property in Ilfracombe parish settled by Mrs. Charlotte Cutcliffe on myself and my said wife and our children. Miss Federetta Cutcliffe. Proved in London 27 August 1847, by Frances Drake the widow.

CHARLES CUTCLIFFE DRAKE, of Springfield, in the county of Devon, Esquire. I appoint my wife Mary Drake, and William Richard Drake, guardians of my children. I appoint the said William Richard Drake trustee and executor. My daughters Ann Frances Drake and Dorothy Mervin Drake; my son John Rothwell Drake; my son Charles Henry Drake. Administration with the will annexed granted by the Prin. Reg. of H.M. Court of Probate on the 23rd September 1859, to Mary Drake, widow, the relict and residuary legatee. Testator died 18th October 1858.

11 July 1854. Abstract.

HARRIET CUTCLIFFE, of the parish of Marwood, in the county of Devon. My friends Mervin Marshall of Barnstaple, Esquire, and John Curzon Moore Stevens of Winscott, Esquire, trustees. My sister Emma Cutcliffe. My two great-nieces Frances Ann Drake and Dorothy the wife of the Rev. Mr. Landon (the two daughters of my nephew the late Charles Drake, Esquire, deceased). My said sister Emma Cutcliffe sole executrix. [Signed, H. E. Cutcliffe.]

31 August 1863. Abstract.

Codicil to the last will and testament of me HARRIET ELIZABETH CUTCLIFFE of Marwood, spinster, in my said will called Harriet Cutcliffe. Whereas by my will bearing date 31 August 1863, I have bequeathed to my trustees Mervin Marshall and John Curzon Moore Stevens, upon trust for my two great-nieces Anne Frances Bridges (therein called Frances Ann Drake) and Dorothy Mervin Landon (in the said will called Dorothy Landon): And whereas my sister Emma Cutcliffe has recently departed this life. To my "grandson" [*clerical mistake for great-nephew*] John Mervin Cutcliffe Drake my share in rent charge of £60 out of farm at East Knoyle, part of the ancient estate of the Mervin family. John Mervin Cutcliffe Drake as the heir-at-law of his aunt Frances Mervin Graham, deceased. My great-nephew Charles Henry Drake.

Codicil. 9 June 1865. Abstract.

FRANCES DRAKE, of Ashford, county of Devon, widow. I appoint William Richard Drake, of Oatlands Lodge, co. Surrey, Esquire, and my grandson Charles Henry Drake, trustees and executors. To my daughter-in-law Mary, widow of my late son Charles Cutcliffe Drake. To my grand-daughter Dorothy Mervin, the wife of the Rev. Charles Landon. To my granddaughter Anne Frances Bridges, widow. To my grandson John Mervin Cutcliffe Drake, Captain in the Royal Engineers. To my sister Harriett Elizabeth Cutcliffe. I devise all my estate and interest at the time of my decease in a certain rentcharge of £60 per annum, issuing and payable out of a farm at East Knoyle, co. Wilts (and which rentcharge was part of the ancient estate of the Mervin family), to my said grandson John Mervin Cutcliffe Drake. The said John Mervin Cutcliffe Drake as the heir-at-law of his aunt Frances Mervin Graham, deceased. To my said grandson John Mervin Cutcliffe Drake such of my plate as formerly belonged to my sister Anne Cutcliffe. Proved in the Prin. Reg. of H.M. Court of Probate, by William Richard Drake, 6th May 1867. Testatrix died 5th April 1867, at Ashford, Devon.

2 June 1865. Abstract.

Mandate FROM KING CHARLES I. TO THE DEAN AND CHAPTER OF EXETER FOR THE ELECTION OF RICHARD MERVIN, D.D., AS CANON RESIDENTIARY.

" Charles R.

" Trusty and welbeloved. We greete you well. Whereas Wee are giuen to vnderstand there is now voyd in our Cathedrall Church of Exeter a Canon's place by the death of Archdeacon Helliar, lately one of yor. Residentiaries; These are therefore to Will and Require you forthwith upon yor. first opportunitie of meeting. to elect and choose into the sayd voyd place our trusty and welbeloved Richard Mervine, Batchelour in Divinity, and one of yor. Prebends. And Whereas all or most of the houses belonging to the simple Residentiaries have been long agoe leased out by you or yor. Predecessors the Deanes and Chapters of that church, Our Will and pleasure is in case the sayd Richard Mervine doe att or before the tyme of his residence, provide himself of a convenient house wherein to keep hospitality and reside, that then no scruple may be made in that point that may be any prejudice to his election aforesayd. Soe expecting yor. ready obedience herein, Wee bid you heartily Farewell.

" Given att our Court att Matson the 18th day of August 1643."

Superscription—" To our trusty and welbeloved the Deane and
Chapter of our Cathedrall Church of
Exeter, 1643."

T A

fe.
Martha, daughter of Sir Hugh Clotworthy of Antrim, Knt. ; d. 24 and bur.
7 August 1685, in St. Werburgh's church, Dublin.

SUSANNA, the youngest daughter ter of Sir Walter BALFOUR, Knt., of Pitcullo, Fife o. Kildare, Bt., and widow of Hugh Hamilton, Baron s, son of Henry co. Fermanagh, Ireland ; d. 1 ; Mar. Art. dat. 23 December 1687, in St. Werb in fun. cert. of Dublin, without issue by her s 685). Henry Mervyn.	Christian, mentioned in her mother's fun. cert. (1685).	Captain Robert Cecil of Tewin, co. Herts, son of William Cecil of Tewin, and grandson of William Cecil, 3rd Earl of Salisbury, K.G.; mentioned in fun. cert. of Martha, Lady Mervyn (1685), ob. January 1705.		

Audley Mervyn of Trelich, co. Tyrone, and also of the Naul, co. Meath, only son ; mentioned in fun. cert. of Richard Coote, Baron Colooney (1683). Party to settlement on his son's marriage (1711) ; bur. in Christ Church, Dublin, 18 June 1717 ; Will dat. 15, and pr. 27 June 1717.	tha, ed Will and to of	Thomas Bamfield Russell of Curragh, co. Dublin ; party to deed 8 Ap. 1731.	Frances, mentioned in her father's Will (1723).	Audley Mervyn	Eleanor	William Cecil	Robert Cecil
			both mentioned in fun. cert. of Martha, Lady Mervyn (1685).			both mentioned in fun. cert. of Martha, Lady Mervyn (1685).

Henry Mervyn of Trelich, mentioned in his father's Will (1717) ; b. before 18 Dec. 1684. Will dat. 7 January 1747 ; admon. 5 April 1765 ; s.p.	Mary, borne ; 23 Dec k the name in dec y Mervyn o deed 1	rdson of yrone. On entioned in Jane, mentioned in father's Will (1717);d. in 1725, s.p. living, died 17	Eu- phalia, bur. 15 Jan. 1714. unm.	Frances, mentioned in her mother's Will (1767), and in her father's Will (1776).	Loetitia, mentioned in her mother's Will (1767) and (1776), where she is cut off with " a shilling." Hogan.

Wesley Harman, mentioned in Will of uncle Henry Mervyn (1747) ; party to of 7 May 1752 ; d. 6 April 1758.	au. ; ny.	Olivia.	Loetitia, mentioned in Will of her uncle Henry Mervyn (1747). m. 1764.	1764 Richard Rochfort, son of Robert Rochfort, Earl of Belvedere and Lieut.-Col. 39th Regt., assumed the name of Mervyn; d. in 1776 in- testate, s.p.

Wentworth Harman, only son.	Lucy Aug

Funeral Certificates.

LUCY MERVYN, 1671.

LUCIA, daur. of Sir Audley Mervin, Kn⁺ departed this life the 1st of Jan⁷· 1671, and was buried in St. Werburgh's Church, Dublin.

Fun. Ent. Ulster's Office, Vol. xiv. p. 123.

SIR AUDLEY MERVIN departed this mortall life the 24 of October, and was buried the 26 of the same month in St. Warbourgh's Church, Dublin, 1675.

SIR AUDLEY MERVYN, 1675. Fun. Ent. Ulster, vol. xi., p. 73.

RICH⁰· COOTE, Lord Baron Cooloney, and one of His Majesty's Most Honble. Privy Council departed this life the 10th of July, and was buried the 12th of the same month, in Christ Church, Dublin, 1683; he mar⁺ Mary, daur. of Sir George S⁺ George, of Drumroosk in the coy. of Leitrim, Kn⁺· by whom he had issue 5 sons and 5 daurs., Cha⁺ the eldest son died in his infancy, and Rich⁺ now Lord of Cooloney who mar⁺ Cath⁺· sole daur. and heir of Bridges Nanfan of Brickmorton, in the Coy. of Worcester, Esq⁺⁼· by whom he had issue Nanfan, and Rich⁺· the 1ˢᵗ about 3 years old, the other about 2; the 1ˢᵗ ment⁺ Rich⁺ Lord of Cooloney had likewise issue Chidley, Tho⁺ and Geo., Tho⁺ was 1ˢᵗ mar⁺ to Eliz⁺ʰ· daur. of Sir Tho⁺ S⁺· George, Kn⁺· by whom he had issue Rich⁺ and Mary, his 2ⁿᵈ· wife was Ann daur. of Christ⁺· Lovett, Alderm⁺· and Mayor of Dublin, son of Sir . . Lovett, Kn⁺· by whom he had issue Frances; the 5 daurs. are Mary, mar⁺ to Sir W⁺ Stewart Lord Visc⁺ Montjoy; Cath⁺· mar⁺ to Ferdinando Hastings, Esq⁺⁼ꞏ Lettice, mar⁺ to Rob⁺ Molesworth, of Breckdenstown, in coy. Dublin, Esq⁺⁼ꞏ Olivia, mar⁺ to Audley Mervin, Esq⁺⁼ꞏ Elizabeth, who is yet unmar⁺

RICHARD COOTE, BARON COLOONEY, 1683. Irish Fun. Ent., Ulster's Office. Vol. xii., p. 17.

MARTHA, daughter of Sir Hugh CLOTWORTHY of Antrim, Kn⁺ departed this mortal life the 24th day of August, and was interred the 27th of the same month, in St. Werburgh's Church, Dublin, 1685. She was married to Sir Audley MERVYN of Omagh, in the county of Tyrone, Kn⁺ son of Sir Henry Mervyn of Funthill, in the county of Wilts, by whom she had issue Hugh Mervyn, George Mervyn, and Christian Mervyn; George Mervyn, married to Elizabeth, eldest daughter of Sir Walter Burrows, Bar⁺ relict of W⁺ Jones, son to Henry Jones, Lord Bishop of Meath; the said George had issue Elinor and Audley Mervyn; Christiana was married to Captain Robert Cecill, son to the Honorable William Cecill, of the House of Salisbury, by whom she had William and Robert Cecill. The truth of the premises is testified by the subscription of the aforesaid Hugh Mervyn, eldest son of the defunct, who hath returned this certificate into the office of Sir Richard Carney, Kn⁺ Ulster King of Arms. Taken by me Sir Richard Carney, Athlone, to be there recorded, 28th August 1685.

MARTHA LADY MERVYN, 1685. Fun. Ent., Ulster's Office, Vol. xii., p. 58.

THE R⁺· HONBLE. SUSAN, Lady Baroness of Glenawly, daur. of the Honble. Sir W⁺· Balfour, Kn⁺ sometime Lieu⁺ of the Tower of London, was 1ˢᵗ mar⁺ to the R⁺· Honble. Hugh Hamilton Lord Baron of Glenawly, eldest son, by the death of Arch⁺ Hamilton without issue, of His Grace Malcolme Hamilton, Lord Archbishop of Cashell, which Malcome Hamilton was descended from the family of . . . . Hamilton, Earl of Arran in Scotland, and Duke of Chatol'droult, France, by which Hugh Lord Baron of Glenawly the s⁺ Lady had issue the Right Honble. W⁺ Lord Baron of Glenawly, killed accidentally, unmar⁺ ; Arabella Hamilton, eldest daur., mar⁺ to Sir John MacGill, Kn⁺ and Bar⁺ ; and Nichola Sophia Hamilton, mar⁺ to Sir Tristram Beresford, Bar⁺· besides sev⁺ other children that died young. The 1ˢᵗ ment⁺ Lady Glenawly was 2ⁿᵈˡʸ· mar⁺ to HENRY MERVYN, Esq⁺⁼· son and heir of Sir Audley Mervyn, Kn⁺· by whom she had no issue. The s⁺ 1ˢᵗ ment⁺ Lady Glenawly departed this mortall life at Dublin the 11ᵗʰ Dec⁺· 1687, and was inter⁺ 14ᵗʰ of same month, in S⁺· Werburgh's Church. The truth, &⁺· is testified by Cha⁺· Balfour, Esq⁺⁼· brother to the defunct, who hath returned this certificate to be recorded in the office of Sir Richard Carney, Kn⁺· Ulster King of Arms of all Ireland, this 22 Feb⁷· 1687-8.

SUSAN, LADY GLENAWLY, wife of HENRY MERVYN, 1687. Fun. Ent., Ulster's Office, Vol. x. p. 117.

MRS. EUPHALIA MERVIN, daughter of Audley Mervin of the Naal, Esq.; she was interred within 2 miles of the said Naal, the 15th of January 1714, with escutcheons.

EUPHALIA MERVYN, 1714. Betham's Irish Fun. Cert. Coll. Arm. Vol. xii., p. 412.

AUDLEY MERVIN, Esq., of the Naal, married Mrs. . . . . Coote, daughter of . . . . Coote, and was interred in Christchurch vaults, with escutcheons, June the 18th 1717.

   * JAMES MERVYN, 3d son of Audley Mervin of the Naal, Esq., was inter'd in the ch. of Clonmarden, February 11th 1721, with 'schns.

Address to the Lord Lieutenant from the Irish House of Commons.

To His Excellency HENRY LORD CAPEL Lord Deputy General and General Governor of Ireland.
The humble Address of the KNIGHTS CITIZENS and BURGESSES
in Parliament assembled.

May it please your Excellency

We the Knights Citisens and Burgesses in Parliament assembled having unanimously voted on the ninth day of September last to grant unto His Majesty a supply not exceeding one hundred sixty-three thousand three hundred and twenty-five pounds and having by an Act passed in the present session of Parliament entitled an Act for an additional duty of Excise on beer ale and other liquors, granted unto His Majesty part of the said supply, and having presented unto your Excellency heads of a Bill for raising a tax &c. by way of a poll and otherwise, and also heads of a Bill for continuing the former Act for an additional Excise for and until the 25th day of December 1698 which falling short of the sum of £163,325 by us voted to be granted to His Majesty for completing the same we have agreed to heads of a Bill for laying an additional duty on Tobacco and several other commodities, and having taken into our serious consideration the debts due from His Majesty's Army to the Country and likewise a debt of £6,000 due to the children of Sir Audley Mervin Knight, formerly Speaker of the House of Commons in this Kingdom for his long and faithful service to the Protestant interest of this Kingdom, for which notwithstanding application made by the then House of Commons on his behalf, neither he the said Sir Audley Mervin in his lifetime, nor his children nor any other person whatsoever at any time since have received any manner of satisfaction, to the utter ruin of his family unless relieved therein ; which said additional duty on Tobacco and other commodities, we have resolved to be granted to His Majesty from the day of the Royal Assent given to the said Bill for and until the 25th day of December 1699 thereby to enable His Majesty to pay some part of the debt due from the Army and likewise the said £6,000.

And whereas Your Excellency has been pleased to signify to us your pleasure that the House should find out some fund for answering the debts due to the country from the Army ; and we not being able at present to find out any certain fund, we humbly beseech Your Excellency to entreat that His Majesty would be graciously pleased that the sum of £30,000 would be paid to such persons who have stated their accounts due from the Army in such proportion as each person's debts bear to the whole, and that the said payment of £30,000 be made by equal portions, the first payment on the 1st day of May next, and the second on the 1st of August following ; and also that the said sum of six thousand pounds be paid to the several persons hereafter named, that is to say, three thousand pounds of the said six thousand pounds to "*Audley Mervin, Esqr., eldest son of Henry Mervin, Esqr., son and heyr of Sr. Audley Mervin, and the other moyty being three thousand pounds to be equally divided betweene Hugh and George Mervin, younger sons of the said Sr. Audley Mervyn,*" and that the same be paid in four years by fifteen hundred pounds a year, the said yearly sum to be paid by equal payments half yearly, the first payment to be made on the 24th of June next in discharge of a debt which in conscience and justice we think ought to be paid. And we humbly beseech your Excellency that your Excellency will please to recommend after the most effectual manner the case of the said Audley Hugh and George Mervin Esq' to His Majesty's Princely Grace and favour.

And though we are very fully satisfied that the several sums by us granted to His Majesty will raise the said sum of £163,325, and likewise discharge the forementioned £30,000 yet we crave leave to give your Excellency this assurance that if the same fall short of what we have voted and intend, we will in the next Session of Parliament make good the same, by which time a very near estimate may be made of the whole granted by us.

Ext· p· THO. TILSON Cler. Parl. Dom. Com.

---

   * In the legal proceedings in connection with the will of Audley Mervyn (APPENDIX V., p. v.), the date of the death of this James Mervyn is stated as 1726.

Abstracts OF Wills.

Will.
SIR AUDLEY
MERVYN, Knt.,
18 Oct. 1675.
Abstract.

SIR AUDLEY MERVYN, Knt. Revokes all former wills and deeds except the deed dated 3rd August last past [*see note of, below*] between Sir Audley Mervyn first part, Lord Viscount Massareene, Arthur Upton, and John Foster second part, Sir Hercules Langford and Henry Whitfield third part, being Deed of Settlement of his estates ; directs that if any of his sons [whom he does not mention by name in the will] opposed said deed the sum therein left to him shall be reduced by the amount his executrix shall be compelled to expend as costs in upholding said deed. Appoints his wife Martha executrix. Will proved 27 January 1676.

Will.
AUDLEY MERVYN,
15 June 1717.
Abstract.
Registered 29 Jan.
1749.

AUDLEY MERVYN of the Naule. co. Meath. To his dearly beloved wife Olivia his plate, household goods, his coach and six coach horses and their harnesses, and three saddle horses, and makes her sole executrix and residuary legatee. All the rest of his goods to be sold, and the produce, as well as £1,100 due him by Richard, late Earl of Bellamont, and £1,000 due him by his (testator's) son Henry Mervyn, and a debt of £1,200 due him by Hugh Mervyn, and all arrears of rent, &c., to pay debts. Devises to his wife and her heirs lands in the county of Tyrone, and also the town and lands of Naule, &c., in co. Meath. To the intent his said wife may have £100 a-year in addition to her jointure, and, by sale of so much as may be required, to pay off any debts unpaid by the personal estate, and subject thereto, the lands to his son Audley for life, &c., in strict settlement. Remainder to his (testator's) son James. Remainder to his (testator's) son Theophilus for like estate, then to his (testator's) son Henry Mervyn for life; remainder to his daughters; remainder to Mervyn Archdall and Henry Cary, testator's nephews, and their heirs. If his sons Henry and Audley both die without issue male in life of testator's son James, whereby the estate settled on testator's son Henry on his marriage shall come to James, then James shall not take the interest devised, but same to go to Theophilus. £2,500, which by settlement on marriage of Henry he had reserved power to charge, to be applied to his sons James and Theophilus, and to his daughters Ellinor, Ann, and Jane, £500 each.

Appeal Case,
House of Lords
1760,
" Teatt v. Strong."
Evidence.

The above Will gave rise to litigation, which had reference specially to lands forming part of the Manor of Arlestown, co. Tyrone, of which Sir Audley Mervyn was seised in fee, and formed with other estates the subject of a settlement which he made in 1675. The estates descended to Audley Mervyn, the testator, who was the only son of Henry Mervyn, Sir Audley's eldest son. After the death of Audley Mervyn (the grandson), his son Henry entered into possession, and in 1729 he sold a portion of the property to the Rev. John Strong, in whose family it appears to have continued until the year 1756, when an ejectment was brought by the sisters of Henry Mervyn and their representatives for the recovery of the lands sold to Strong, on the ground that on the death of Henry Mervyn without issue the reversion in fee in the estates, limited under the terms of the Settlement of 1711 to Audley Mervyn and his heirs, passed under the general devise in his Will. They, in 1759, obtained a decision in their favour from the Court of King's Bench in Ireland, from which, however, Strong's representatives appealed by Writ of Error to the King's Bench at Westminster, who in 1760 reversed the Irish judgment, and the reversal was upheld on an appeal to the House of Lords in the latter year thereby confirming the validity of the sale to Strong.

The printed Cases of the Appellants and Defendants will be found in a collection of Appeal Cases in the House of Lords " 1757–61," p. 487, in the Library of the Incorporated Law Society, in London, under the title of " Teatt v. Strong." The statements and evidence in the proceedings disclose the following facts and dates:—

    1675, Aug. 2 and 3. SETTLEMENT by Sir Audley Mervyn, Knt., of (inter alia) the Manor of Arlestown, co. Tyrone, on his three sons, viz. Henry the eldest, Hugh the second, and George the third. " for the better settling the said estate in his family name and blood," and by which settlement he made a provision for raising a portion for his daughter Christian [who married Robert Cecil].

    1676. Death of Sir Audley Mervyn, and succession of his eldest son Henry, by virtue of settlement of 1675. That Henry Mervyn had issue one son, Audley.

    1684, Dec. 17 and 18. Indentures of lease and release [being a post-nuptial settlement] of this date between said Henry Mervyn and Audley Mervyn his son, 1st part, certain trustees therein named of 2nd and 3rd parts, in consideration of a marriage then lately had between said Audley Mervyn and Olivia, the sister of Richard Coote, Baron Coloony, and for making a provision for her and the daughters and younger sons of said marriage, and for settling the lands and hereditaments thereinafter set forth in the name, blood, and family of the said Henry Mervyn, the said Henry Mervyn and Audley Mervyn conveyed (inter alia) the said Manor of Arlestown, to trustees to pay jointure to said Olivia for life, with remainder to said Audley Mervyn for life; remainder to said Henry Mervyn for life; remainder to Henry Mervyn the first son of said Audley and Olivia in tail male; remainder to second, third, and other sons in tail male; remainder to the heirs male of Hugh, the second son of said Sir Audley; remainder to George Mervyn, brother of said Hugh in tail male, with ultimate remainder to right heirs of said Audley Mervyn.

1699. Death of Henry Mervyn, and succession to the estates of his son Audley.

1711, Dec. 21-22. Settlement by Audley Mervyn and his eldest son Henry, on the marriage of the latter with Mary Titchburne, widow.

That Audley Mervyn, besides Henry Mervyn his eldest son, had issue Audley Mervyn the younger, his second son; James Mervyn his third son; and Theophilus Mervyn his fourth son; and four daughters, viz. Lucy his eldest, who, in the lifetime of the said Audley the elder, intermarried with Wentworth Harman; Ellinor who married Christopher Irwin, then (1760) several years since dead; Ann who married James Mervyn, otherwise Richardson, then (1760) also many years dead; and Jane Mervyn his fourth daughter.

1717, June 15. Will of Audley Mervyn of the Naule co. Meath. [See Abstract above.]

1717, June 17. Death of Audley Mervyn, and succession of Henry his eldest son, by virtue of the limitations of the settlement of 1711.

1720. Death of Olivia the widow of Audley Mervyn.

1725. Death of Jane Mervyn, one of the daughters of Audley Mervyn and Olivia Coote, without issue.

1726. Death of James Mervyn the third son of Audley Mervyn and Olivia Coote, never having had issue. [See ante Fun. Cert. Appendix v. p. iii.]

1727. Death of Mervyn Archdall, son of Elizabeth Mervyn (granddaughter of Sir Audley Mervyn, Knt.), and William Archdall, of Castle Archdall, co. Fermanagh.

1727. Death of Hugh Mervyn, second son of Sir Audley Mervyn, leaving Arthur Mervyn his eldest son and heir.

1729, Sept. 29 and 30.   Sale and Conveyance by Henry Mervyn of the estate to Revd. John Strong.

1735. Death of Mary [Titchburne], the wife of Henry Mervyn, without any issue by him. [See Abstract Deed, post. p. vi, dated 1737-8.]

1736. Death, without issue and unmarried, of Theophilus Mervyn the fourth son of Audley Mervyn and Olivia Coote.

1737. Death of Lucy the wife of Wentworth Harman, one of the daughters of Audley Mervyn and Olivia Coote, leaving Wesley Harman her eldest son and heir.

1746. Death, without issue and unmarried, of Audley Mervyn the second son of Audley Mervyn and Olivia Coote.

1747, Feb. 1. Death of Henry Mervyn [who married Mary Titchburne] never having had any issue.

1756. Sept. Death of Henry Carey, the son of Martha Mervyn [granddaughter of Sir Audley Mervyn] and Edward Carey, of Dungiven.

HUGH MERVYN of Baldwinstown, late of the Naule, second son of Sir Audley Mervyn, Knt., being about 79 years of age, and infirm in body, &c. To my wife Frances Mervyn alias Talbot. To my son Arthur. My daughter Martha, who is entitled by Deed of 10 Sept. 1723, to an annuity of £63 per annum until she be paid her marriage portion of £1,000. My daughter Frances £300, and to have her keep and maintenance until she is 18 years of age. Proved 1728.

HENRY MERVYN of Trelick, co. Tyrone. His lands to Harry Smith, counseller-at-law, and Andrew Knox of Prehen, and Rev. Caleb Cartwright, D.D., to use of testator's brother-in-law James Richardson of Castle Hill, co. Tyrone, for life, in strict settlement for his issue begotten on testator's sister Ann ; in default of issue to Letitia Richardson, daughter of said James Richardson, in strict settlement; in default to Mervyn Archdall, his kinsman, of Castle Archdall, in strict settlement ; in default, remainder to testator's nephew, Wesley Harman for life, in strict settlement ; in default, to testator's nephew William Irwine, in strict settlement ; remainder to testator's right heirs. To Henry Irwine, second son of testator's brother-in-law Christopher Irwine, £500. Administration with will annexed granted 5 April 1765.

ELIZABETH, wife of Arthur Mervyn, late of Baldwinstown, now of the Naule. My brother Charles Hampson of Nonsuch; my sister Letitia Hampson. Lands purchased under powers given me by deed of separate maintenance and separation. Testatrix lived after the separation first at Nonsuch, then at Mullingar. To my daughter Frances Mervyn, lands for her life. To Charles Hampson of Nonsuch, and James Sheridan. My daughter Letitia, wife of . . . Hogan, having disobliged me by her imprudent marriage, I leave her nothing more than one shilling, with the reversion of the lands to her and her issue on the death without issue of her sister Frances. Proved 15 Sept. 1767.

JANE, wife of Arthur Mervyn of the Naule. Being entitled to certain lands, &c. [described in will] expectant on the death of my brother John Cunningham, and my sister Mary Monsell, bequeath all the same to my husband Arthur Mervyn, charged with £500, for my good friend Joshua Davis; my father Daniel Cunningham of the city of Dublin, Merchant; my first husband the Revd. Caleb Cartwright. Proved 26 April 1771.

ARTHUR MERVYN of the Naule, co. Meath. To be buried in the church of Garristown. His properties in Dublin and Kilkenny for payment of debts, residue to testator's daughter Frances Mervyn, to provide her an annuity of £100 for life, and £50 a year to Mrs. Barbara Mathew, wife of testator's relation Mervyn Mathew, and £30 a year for her son Mervyn Mathew, and £30 a year to Mary Anne Barnwell for life, mother of my natural son Arthur Mervyn; and to suffer the said Arthur Mervyn, known by the name of Arthur Russell, to take £100 a year for life.   Leaves to his (testator's) relation Olivia Irwin, £50. To his friend Joshua Davis, Esq., of Stephen Street counsellor-at-law, £50.   To his friend William Knox £200.   Leaves to his (testator's) daughter Letitia one shilling and no more, and that neither she nor her issue shall ever inherit any of his fortune, real or personal.   Leaves the residue of his real and personal estate to William Pollard (of Castle Pollard), his heirs and assigns in tail male; in default to his (testator's) natural son Arthur Mervyn and his heirs for ever.   *Proved* 23 May 1776.

Deeds relating to the MERVYN Family.

The following deeds, evidencing the foregoing pedigree, will be found registered in the Deeds Office, King's Inns, Dublin :—

1677, Sept. 19. Recital (in deed of 22 and 23 June 1711 after-mentioned) of mortgage by way of demise of this date by Hugh, Henry and George Mervyn, sons of Sir Audley Mervyn, Knt., deceased, of the Naule, alias Snowtown, and other lands.

1683, Oct. 20. Recital (also in deed of 22 and 23 June 1711) of conveyance of this date by said Henry and Hugh Mervyn of same lands, and Sir Audley Mervyn's part in lands in co. Dublin.

1710, Aug. 3 and 4. Conveyance by said Hugh Mervyn, described as of the Naule, co. Meath, to Audley Mervyn of Trellick, co. Tyrone, of the Naule alias Snowtown, and other lands in the county of Meath.   The execution of this deed is witnessed by Henry Mervyn and Audley Mervyn, sons of said Audley Mervyn.

1711, Dec. 23. Recital (in a deed of 26 October 1736) of settlement between Audley Mervyn and Henry Mervyn of 1st part, Mary Titchburne, widow, of 2nd part, and trustees of 3rd and 4th parts, being the settlement made on the marriage of said Henry Mervyn and Mary Titchburne then (1736) wife of the said Henry Mervyn.

1729, July 19. Conveyance by Audley Mervyn of the Naule, co. Meath, of lands in Meath and Tyrone to secure an annuity to his brother Theophilus Mervyn, of Trellick.

1731, April 8. Mortgage of lands of Baldwinstown, &c., by Arthur Mervyn of Baldwinstown, co. Dublin, described as only son of Hugh Mervyn of the same place, deceased, and Frances Mervyn, widow and relict of said Hugh Mervyn, and Thomas Bamfield Russell of Curragh, co. Dublin, and Martha Russell alias Mervyn, his wife.

1737-8, March 24. Conveyance from said Henry Mervyn, therein described as of Castle Mervyn, co. Tyrone, to Christopher Irvine of Castle Irvine, co. Fermanagh, of lands in the county Tyrone, subject to life estate of said Henry Mervyn, and the jointure of Mary Mervyn alias Titchburne, his wife.   [*See Statement ante p. v. that she died in* 1735.]

1740, Feb. 11. Settlement on the marriage of Arthur Mervyn of Baldwinstown, co. Dublin, and Elizabeth Magawley.

N.B. This Elizabeth Magawley is party with her husband Arthur Mervyn to a deed of 14 May 1745.

1744, Oct. 26. Renewal of perpetual lease of the lands of the Naul to Arthur Mervyn of Baldwinstown, for the lives of Audley Mervyn of the Naul, and Olivia, daughter of Christopher Irvine of Castle Irvine, &c.

1747, June 10. Deed between Henry Mervyn of Trelick, and others. recites that Audley Mervyn of the Naule, the brother of the said Henry, was party to a deed of 9 Oct. 1744, and that he was then (1747) dead.

1747, Aug. 19. Deed Poll or agreement by Henry Mervyn of the Naul, to make a lease of part of the Naul for the lives of Wesley Harman and Lucy Harman, daughter of said Wesley.

1752, January 7. Deed between William Hamilton of Strabone, co. Tyrone, James Mervyn alias Richardson, and Anne Mervyn alias Edwards, his wife, surviving trustees of the last will and testament of Hugh Edwards of Castlegore, deceased, and Elizabeth Edwards, eldest daughter of said Hugh Edwards, of the first part, and Redmond Kane of the City of Dublin, of the second part, being a grant to said Redmond Kane of £5,150, the incumbrance on the Naul and other lands which descended to Wesley Harman, Ellinor Irvine, and Anne Mervyn, under the limitations in the will of Audley Mervyn.

1752, May 7. Wesley Harman to Christopher Irvine and James Mervyn (i.e. James Richardson) of undivided fourth part of the Naul and other lands.

1752, June 1. Wesley Harman, Christopher Irvine and Ellinor Irvine his wife, James Mervyn alias Richardson, and Anne Mervyn his wife, to Redmond Kane of the city of Dublin.   Deed relating to the same lands as the deed of 7 January 1752.

1752, August 14. Memorial of will of James Mervyn, formerly called James Richardson, of Castle Hill, co. Tyrone.

Inquisition Post Mortem.

ber 13 1687.

Rot: Cancell:
iæ, Vol. I. (16)
foc: II.

By Inquisition of this date, taken at Kilmainham, co. Dublin, it was found that Audley Mervin, Knt., died 24th Oct. 1675, seized of the town and lands of Baldwinstone, &c., co. Dublin, and that Henry Mervin was his son and heir.

INDEX.

Printed by METCHIM & SON, 20, Parliament Street, S.W., and 32, Clement's Lane, E.C.

CPSIA information can be obtained
at www.ICGtesting.com
Printed in the USA
LVOW10*2148290418
575357LV00006B/31/P